Longitudinal Data Infrastructures in Europe

Luciana Taddei • Mario Paolucci
Editors

Longitudinal Data Infrastructures in Europe

Tools for Open Science in Social Science Research

Springer

Editors
Luciana Taddei
Institute for Research on Population and Social Policies
National Research Council
Fisciano (SA), Italy

Mario Paolucci
Institute for Research on Population and Social Policies
National Research Council
Rome, Italy

ISBN 978-3-032-07004-3 ISBN 978-3-032-07005-0 (eBook)
https://doi.org/10.1007/978-3-032-07005-0

This work was supported by Next Generation Foundation (CUP B83C22003950001).

This Springer imprint is published by the registered company Springer Nature Switzerland AG
The registered company address is: Gewerbestrasse 11, 6330 Cham, Switzerland

Acknowledgments This open access book was funded by National Recovery and Resilience Plan (NRRP)—NextGenerationEU, grant number MUR IR0000008 within the FOSSR project "Fostering Open Science in Social Science Research."

We would like to express our sincere gratitude to all those without whose support this work would not have been possible.

We are particularly grateful to *Giuseppe Sindoni* from *ISTAT* for his timely insights and continued engagement. Special thanks also go to the *CONSIP* team, who went above and beyond in assisting us with complex procurement procedures; to the *Direzione Centrale per i Servizi Demografici* of the *Ministero dell'Interno*; and to the staff at the *Autorità Garante per la Protezione dei Dati Personali*, whose collaboration and clarity were crucial throughout.

At the *CNR*, many colleagues have contributed time, expertise, and dedication to this project. While we cannot name everyone, we must acknowledge *Emanuela Reale* for her unwavering commitment, as well as the current leadership team of the *FOSSR* infrastructure—*Giovanni Cerulli* and *Marco Sprocati*—whose support has been central to the realization of this volume, and the *Procurement Office* for practical and legal advice.

To those we have inadvertently overlooked, we ask for understanding—and to the readers of this volume, we ask for the same patience and generosity we have tried to embody in the work presented here.

Introduction

Mario Paolucci and Luciana Taddei

It's not rocket science. This is how we used to introduce the subject of the longitudinal data infrastructures in Europe from the point of view of the National Research Council (CNR) of Italy. Our institution, among other roles, serves as an interface between funders and the broader academic community. For this reason, we often seek to communicate both the benefits and potential risks of building data infrastructures to a variety of audiences.

Building data infrastructures for the social sciences is not necessarily rocket science, but it is certainly a complex undertaking. Establishing a longitudinal panel involves engaging with regulatory agencies and navigating privacy legislation; negotiating the often treacherous waters of national statistical systems; and, last but not least, performing the ongoing care work required to ensure the panel's long-term sustainability.

Compared with our sibling data infrastructures in the hard sciences, those in the social sciences do not typically exhibit large-scale data flow problems—at least not in the same way. While there isn't a need to think about high-throughput data pipelines designed for consistent, automated collection (e.g., sensors, lab instruments, satellites), social sciences data infrastructures must grapple with human variability, privacy concerns, and fragmented regulatory frameworks.

As C.P. Snow (2012) famously observed in The Two Cultures, the divide between the sciences and the humanities is not merely epistemological but also infrastructural. In this sense, infrastructure in the social sciences is not just a technical backbone but also a site of negotiation, trust-building, and long-term stewardship. Social science infrastructures must build for durability, consent, and adaptability—qualities that are often invisible, but essential.

Within the social sciences, a research infrastructure represents a leap in both scale and organizational effort when compared to standard research endeavors. In the European context, local projects may range from individual efforts to small collaborative groups, occasionally extending to EU-funded consortia, usually comprising three to seven institutions. Infrastructures, by contrast, are long-term undertakings that demand not only significantly higher levels of funding but also continuity in that funding—a characteristic that distinguishes them from the more episodic nature of conventional research projects.

What makes social science infrastructures demanding is their hybrid nature: they are at once technical systems, organizational frameworks, and social contracts. Social science infrastructures must deal with and accommodate evolving legal norms, ethical standards, and shifting societal expectations.

This raises the brutal question: do we really need to invest in research infrastructures, particularly in the social sciences? The question is not whether a given infrastructure produces valuable outcomes within its domain—this is generally not in dispute. Rather, the issue is in the opportunity cost: are infrastructures the best use of limited public funds? Could similar resources yield greater impact if directed toward smaller, more agile projects or immediate policy needs? Could we just—be better doing something else? A tricky, self-defeating question.

In this context, we should avoid treating funding as a zero-sum game. Research infrastructures are not only scientific tools—they are political instruments. European infrastructures, by their very design, serve to reinforce transnational cooperation and institutional alignment. As noted in the Council Conclusions on Research Infrastructures (2022), they are seen as "cornerstones of the European Research Area" and as vehicles for "cohesion, resilience, and openness." At a time when European integration faces internal and external challenges, infrastructures represent a long-term investment in unity, interoperability, and shared capacity.

Furthermore, infrastructures support foundational EU values, including the free circulation of knowledge, researchers, services, and capital, as outlined in both the Horizon Europe legal framework and ESFRI Roadmaps. They also help bridge the digital and data divides between member states—especially important for the social sciences, which must contend with fragmented statistical systems and uneven regulatory practices.

Rather than a luxury or a drain, well-designed infrastructures serve as platforms for collective intelligence. Failing to build and sustain them means not only falling behind in scientific capacity but also weakening the institutional scaffolding of the EU itself.

European research infrastructures, by their very nature, reinforce connections among member states. At a time when cohesion within the Union is fragile, these infrastructures help sustain what remains a historically unique experiment in shared sovereignty—a careful balancing act between national priorities and collective European interests. In this light, the promotion of common infrastructures holds strategic value beyond the scientific domain: they support the free movement of people, goods, capital, and services and provide tangible mechanisms for integration and cooperation.

This becomes even more relevant in the wake of geopolitical and structural shocks. The European Union appeared unprepared in the face of a cascading series of crises: the rupture of Brexit, the disruptions of the COVID-19 pandemic, and the rise of new digital oligarchies, fueled by monopolistic practices and by the enshittification (Birch, 2023) of digital platforms. These events have not only challenged Europe's political resilience, but also exposed its vulnerability to technological and infrastructural dependencies. In this context, investing in robust, federated, and publicly accountable infrastructures—especially in the social sciences—is not just a matter of research policy, but of democratic sovereignty.

Attempts to strengthen and integrate European self-awareness through research have long been challenged by a divide that recalls the tension between Snow's "two cultures" of science and the humanities. An illustration of this can be found in the European Commission's only large-scale experiment in catalyzing visionary, "moonshot" research through the FET Flagship program. Among the six finalist proposals, only one—FuturICT (Helbing et al., 2012) —was led by the social sciences, proposing a global observatory to model and simulate (Paolucci et al., 2012) complex socio-technical systems and support evidence-based policymaking. In the end, however, the two selected Flagships focused on hard sciences. The exclusion of a social science-based initiative like FuturICT reflected not just scientific preferences, but deeper structural biases in how transformative research is imagined and funded in Europe.

The missed opportunity also signaled a lack of institutional imagination at a time when anticipatory governance, systemic foresight, and digital democracy were emerging as urgent priorities. As Europe now faces challenges of planetary scale—from algorithmic governance to geopolitical fragmentation—the need for infrastructures that can help integrate human and social dimensions of change is more pressing than ever.

This book, by contrast, has been made possible thanks to an opportunity that was not missed—namely, the decision to channel Recovery and Resilience Facility resources toward a specific and timely objective: the development of infrastructures for high-quality longitudinal data. Here, we bring together experiences, practices, and methodological reflections aimed at building and sustaining one particular kind of infrastructure: probabilistic longitudinal panels. This work has been enabled through the support of the FOSSR infrastructure (*Fostering Open Science in Social Research*), funded under the Italian National Recovery and Resilience Plan (NRRP). FOSSR has provided not only financial support, but also an institutional framework that foregrounds openness, interoperability, and scientific collaboration across disciplines and national borders.

We hope you will find value in the content presented here, and we would like to express our sincere thanks to all the contributors to this volume for their insight, expertise, and commitment.

References

Birch, K. (2023). Data paradoxes. In K. Birch (Ed.), *Data enclaves* (pp. 107–124). Springer Nature Switzerland. https://doi.org/10.1007/978-3-031-46402-7_6

Council of the European Union. (2022). *Council conclusions on research infrastructures*. https://data.consilium.europa.eu/doc/document/ST-15429-2022-INIT/en/pdf

Helbing, D., Bishop, S., Conte, R., Lukowicz, P., & McCarthy, J. B. (2012). FuturICT: Participatory computing to understand and manage our complex world in a more sustainable and resilient way. *European Physical Journal*, *214*(1), 11–39. https://doi.org/10.1140/epjst%252fe2012-01686-y

Paolucci, M., Kossman, D., Conte, R., Lukowicz, P., Argyrakis, P., Blandford, A., Bonelli, G., Anderson, S., Freitas, S., Edmonds, B., Gilbert, N., Gross, M., Kohlhammer, J., Koumoutsakos, P., Krause, A., Linnér, B. O., Slusallek, P., Sorkine, O., Sumner, R. W., & Helbing, D. (2012). Towards a living earth simulator. *The European Physical Journal Special Topics*, *214*(1), 77–108. https://doi.org/10.1140/epjst/e2012-01689-8

Snow, C. P. (2012). *The two cultures*. Cambridge University Press.

Contents

Part I
Open Science and Research Infrastructures for Social Sciences

Chapter 1
Open Science and the Role of Social Sciences Research Infrastructures and Data

Francesca Di Donato

1.1 Open Science Definition

Although Open Science is rooted in an ancient idea, the first widely shared definition is relatively recent and can be found in UNESCO's, 2021 Recommendation on Open Science. The Recommendation was prepared through an inclusive, transparent, and regionally balanced consultation process and guided by the Open Science Advisory Committee. The committee involved stakeholders from 193 countries and gathered input collected over two years of consultation (UNESCO, 2023).

In the Recommendation, Open Science is defined as "an inclusive construct that combines various movements and practices aiming to make multilingual scientific knowledge openly available, accessible and reusable for everyone, to increase scientific collaborations and sharing of information for the benefits of science and society, and to open the processes of scientific knowledge creation, evaluation and communication to societal actors beyond the traditional scientific community. It comprises all scientific disciplines and aspects of scholarly practices, including basic and applied sciences, natural and social sciences and the humanities, and it builds on the following key pillars: open scientific knowledge, open science infrastructures, science communication, open engagement of societal actors and open dialogue with other knowledge systems." (UNESCO, 2021, 7).

The proposed definition is rich, composite and complex, as it encompasses and implies multiple aspects that are worth to be broken down and analysed in order to understand the definition terms.

Firstly, Open Science is defined as an inclusive construct, combining movements and practices. The movements referred to are those that gave rise to the media revolution of the past sixty years—particularly, the Internet and the Web -, and to

F. Di Donato (✉)
Institute of Computational Linguistics "A. Zampolli" (CNR-ILC), Pisa, Italy
e-mail: francesca.didonato@cnr.it

L. Taddei, M. Paolucci (eds.), *Longitudinal Data Infrastructures in Europe*,
https://doi.org/10.1007/978-3-032-07005-0_1

the development of free software; these different communities not only share a way of working, but also the principles and values that underpin their research practices (Leiner et al., 2009), along with a philosophy that defines the network (understood as infrastructure, as architecture, and as a set of communities) as a space for collective intelligence (Lévy, 1994, 1997):

1. the early sharing of ideas, grounded in a paradigm of scientific collaboration based on Requests for Comments (RFCs)—formal standards-track documents developed by working groups within the Internet Engineering Task Force (IETF). RFCs are freely available to download, copy, publish, display and distribute, in a variety of formats under a license granted by the IETF Trust, and constitute forms of open peer reviewing (IETF, 2025);
2. the choice to release the Internet and World Wide Web protocols into the public domain, along with the definition of software licences such as the GNU-GPL (Free Software Foundation, 2022) to encourage maximum sharing;
3. the architectural openness of the network, based on a distributed, scalable and flexible topology (Leiner et al., 2009).

Born in response to the so-called serial price crisis (Guédon, 2001), the Open Access movement is the forerunner par excellence of Open Science. Open Access translated the above mentioned principles into policies and practices aimed at the free circulation of scientific knowledge. As the 2003 Berlin Declaration states:

"The Internet has fundamentally changed the practical and economic realities of distributing scientific knowledge and cultural heritage. For the first time ever, the Internet now offers the chance to constitute a global and interactive representation of human knowledge, including cultural heritage and the guarantee of worldwide access."

From then onwards, new possibilities for knowledge dissemination emerged through the Open Access (OA) paradigm via the Internet. The Berlin declaration defines OA"as a comprehensive source of human knowledge and cultural heritage that has been approved by the scientific community", which includes original scientific research results, raw data and metadata, source materials, digital representations of pictorial and graphical materials, and scholarly multimedia material. To provide full access to scientific knowledge, the movement has equipped itself with tools (trusted repositories and platforms for the creation and management of journals, which share common standards such as the Open Archives Initiative Protocol for Metadata Harvesting (OAI-PMH)[1]) and common practices, endorsed by several funders, including the European Commission, and international coalitions, such as COAlition S.[2] Other important tools are Creative Commons[3] (CC) licenses, which have provided an essential framework, borrowed from the experience of the Free Software Foundation's GNU free licenses.[4] CC licenses make it possible to share

[1] https://www.openarchives.org/pmh/

[2] https://www.coalition-s.org/about/

[3] https://creativecommons.org/

and circulate knowledge through a legal infrastructure that relies on existing laws and bends them to allow the free circulation of texts, with a view to publicising public research (Lessig, 2004).

Significantly, the Open Data movement spread in the years immediately following the Open Access movement, which, beyond its official statements, has focused mainly on opening access to the main outputs of research, namely scientific articles (and, to a lesser extent, monographs). The 2012 Royal Society report *Science as an open enterprise* recognises data openness as an essential element of the scientific method, enabling science to evolve and improve. "Open Science is here defined as open data (available, intelligible, assessable and usable data) combined with open access to scientific publications, and effective communication of their contents" (Royal Society, 2012, 16). In scientific terms, this leads to better, higher-quality science, whose effects also bring important social benefits. The four principles mentioned above—availability, intelligibility, assessability and usability—can be considered precursors to the FAIR data principles published three years later (Wilkinson et al., 2016), which are now among the core pillars of Open Science practices.

FAIR is the acronym of Findable, Accessible, Interoperable and Reusable (Di Donato & Provost, 2025):

1. Findable: Humans and machines must be able to search and discover research data. The automatic discovery of datasets and research products is enabled by complete, accurate, machine-readable metadata following existing standards. Persistent Identifiers (PIDs) must be assigned to data, metadata and research objects for long-term identification. Datasets and metadata must be stored in a trusted, publicly accessible repository for long-term preservation.
2. Accessible: Humans and machines should be able to access data and know who can access it. The data and metadata should be accessible through their PID using a standard communication protocol. Accessible data does not imply openness; it means clear access conditions for humans and machines. The data access protocol should be open, free and universal, with authentication and authorisation when required. Metadata should remain accessible even when the data is unavailable.
3. Interoperable: Humans and machines must be able to understand, interpret and integrate data. The data and metadata should be described following recognised community standards for formats, specifications and vocabularies. Context should be provided through qualified references to relevant datasets and metadata. Data is interoperable when both humans and machines can interpret data exchanged between different systems or organisations, supporting interdisciplinary research.
4. Reusable: To reuse data, humans and machines need to be able to do so for future research. This allows experiments to be reproduced, scientific findings

[4] https://www.gnu.org/licenses/licenses.en.html

to be verified and work to be built on previous analyses. To facilitate this, data and metadata should be described according to community standards and accompanied by rich documentation. This documentation should include contextual information such as data provenance and processing, and a licence that indicates to machines and humans the conditions under which the data can be used.

These principles differ from the concept of Open Data used in the Royal Society report, focusing on the transparency and interoperability of machine-readable data through ontologies, rather than on access and availability for use (Mons et al., 2017; Ramachandran et al., 2021). For this purpose, as we will see later, research infrastructures that support open science and serve the needs of different communities are essential.

1.2 Open Science Concepts: Values and Principles

The UNESCO Recommendation definition contains key concepts which refer to an ancient tradition that is recalled in the Budapest Open Access Initiative (BOAI) declaration (2002), and opens as follows: "an old tradition and a new technology have converged to make possible an unprecedented public good".

The above-mentioned old tradition embodies values and principles rooted in Western philosophical thought since its origins. First, collaboration, which is the foundation of the Socratic-Platonic dialectic. In the Meno dialogue, Socrates contrasts the eristic method, based on a competitive form of refutation, with the dialectic method. Dialectic, unlike the strategy adopted by the Sophists, is based on shared premises and on a collaborative methodology (Plato, 2005). Second, philosophy is understood as a way of life (Hadot, 1995), grounded in the existence of communities of practice, i.e. communities of people who critically discuss the facts of nature in the broadest sense in a collaborative manner, as "friends have all things in common" (Plato, 2002, 279b-c).

Following this tradition, openness, intended as the abandonment of secrecy, is one of the fundamental steps in the birth of modern science. While the idea that essential knowledge was secret prevailed in European culture for many centuries, it was in the modern age that the communication and dissemination of knowledge, including the public discussion of ideas, became values, alongside the emergence of linguistic rigor and the non-allusive nature of terminology. (Rossi, 2000). In this frame, availability, accessibility and reusability are fundamental to both the ethics and methodology of research. Science is in fact based on the idea of open, publicly verifiable debate grounded in the foundations of knowledge. It also rests on respect for rules: starting from the observation of nature in order to formulate hypotheses and explanatory models. These rules were codified as the Galilean method.

As early as 1610, Galileo Galilei understood the necessity to make everything known to everyone and claimed that his discoveries should be subject to free scrutiny by the majority of people (Galilei, 1610). To do this, Galilei had telescopes built so that others could verify his discoveries with their own eyes (Greco, 2010). The aim of this collective and public endeavour is to establish a scientific community whose goal is to build a rational consensus on the facts of nature in a transparent way. The communication of the results of this work to the entire community ensures that everyone can not only know them, but also verify them, thereby contributing to the construction of scientific consensus. However, there is another important consequence of abandoning the paradigm of secrecy: The awareness that science is a social enterprise whose development is governed by precise rules shared by experts is affirmed, but it is also acknowledged that it has enormous social effects, and that confrontation and dialogue with society as a whole cannot be shied away from. On the contrary, society should encourage it (Greco, 2010).

The English expression 'Open Science' appeared in the second half of the Nineteenth century to refer to modern science, which a century later would be defined as the science of the scientific revolution in that it was open, and opposed to occult or initiatory science. By the end of the century, all this translated into a great effort to disseminate scientific knowledge and into the principle of communism, as defined by Merton in his 1942 essay *The normative structure of science* as one of the four institutional imperatives constituting the ethos of modern science, here understood "in the nontechnical and extended sense of the common ownership of goods" (Merton, 1942, 273).

According to this fundamental principle, foundational discoveries belong to the community and constitute a common heritage in which the rights of the individual producer are severely limited. This principle is linked to the imperative of communicating results. "Secrecy is the antithesis of this norm; full and open communication its enactment" (Merton, 1942, 274). Those who do not embrace it are selfish or anti-social. The well-known remark attributed to Newton, "If I have seen farther, it is by standing on the shoulders of giants," (273–74) expresses both a sense of debt to the pre-existing common heritage and a recognition of the essentially collaborative and cumulative nature of scientific results. The scientific method itself is part of this heritage. Merton also anticipates something that Paul David will later observe, namely, that the communism inherent to the scientific ethos is incompatible with the capitalist conception of technology as private property.

The technical and political meaning of Open Science that we commonly refer to dates back to the late twentieth century. The term was first used by Chubin, who observes how the imperative of openness, made explicit through the principle of communism, is in practice challenged by opposing tendencies that make closure and secrecy the usual behavior (Chubin, 1985).

This distinction and tension was taken up in the early 2000s by Paul David (David, 2000, 2014),[5] who defined the two opposing models, that of Open Science and that of commercial science, which embody and represent the tension between the principles of collaboration and competition. The first model — that of Open Science — is based on the principle of collaboration. According to David, it was in

[5] His work, which is more economic than philosophical in nature, is cited in numerous papers in the literature.

the 1980s and 1990s that international organizations established principles, (OECD, 2015) and developed guidelines to protect easy and broad access to scientific data and high-quality information generated by publicly funded entities, and that recommendations began to circulate through implementations.

In his 2011 work *Reinventing Discovery: The New Era of Networked Science*, Michael Nielsen provides a thorough discussion of how digital technologies and online tools are changing the way scientists work. He gives many examples of the practical applications of collective intelligence, open source, Open Science and citizen science. Referring explicitly to Vannevar Bush (1945), Ted Nelson (1987), Pierre Lévy (1994), Douglas Engelbart (1962), Tim Berners-Lee (1999), Eric Raymond (2001), Yochai Benkler (2006) and Clay Shirky (2010), Nielsen describes the transition to open and collaborative science.

It is from this composite framework that the principles and values of Open Science emerge. The UNESCO recommendation lists four Open Science main values (UNESCO, 2021, 17). These values arise from the various effects of making science available to society and applying the rules of openness to every stage of the scientific research process:

1. *Quality and integrity*. Research must be subject to rigorous scrutiny and support academic freedom and human rights. High-quality research is achieved through collaboration and widespread accessibility of scientific methods and results.
2. *Collective benefit*. Science is a global public good, therefore its benefits must be shared universally, and scientific knowledge must be available to all. To achieve this, science must be inclusive, sustainable and equitable.
3. *Equity and fairness*. Scientific knowledge should be accessible to all, regardless of background. No one should be excluded from science or subjected to differential treatment. Producers and consumers of scientific knowledge should have equal opportunities to participate in research.
4. *Diversity and inclusiveness*. Science must be inclusive of all communities. This means encouraging and supporting a wide variety of knowledge practices, workflows, languages and research outputs.

Values are translated into a methodology through the following six guiding principles (UNESCO, 2021, 18–19), which provide a framework for the conditions and practices necessary to uphold these values and make the Open Science vision a reality:

1. *Transparency, scrutiny, critique and reproducibility*. To enhance the impact of science on society and tackle global challenges, we must maximise openness at all stages of the research lifecycle. Greater transparency in scientific data leads to greater openness, which in turn improves trust.
2. *Equality of opportunities*. All people, irrespective of background, should equally access, contribute to and benefit from scientific knowledge. This principle ensures science is open to all, so that all voices can contribute to progress.
3. *Responsibility, respect and accountability*. Researchers and actors involved in the scientific process must conduct research with integrity and be aware of its

wider impacts. This principle highlights the importance of public accountability, conflict of interest avoidance, research integrity and ethics.
4. *Collaboration, participation and inclusion*. To tackle large, complex, societal problems, scientists must collaborate, overcoming barriers related to geography, language, age, resources. Cross-disciplinary collaboration and the effective involvement of diverse knowledge systems, particularly marginalised communities, is essential.
5. *Flexibility*. Research contexts and capabilities vary worldwide, so there is no one-size-fits-all approach to science. This principle promotes flexibility, allowing for various strategies to achieve Open Science goals while upholding core values.
6. *Sustainability*. Ensuring long-term efficiency and impact of science requires sustainable practices, infrastructures and financial models. These should guarantee that researchers from all organisations and countries can take part in knowledge production. The concept of sustainability shows this is best done through not-for-profit, long-term infrastructures which fund Open Science practices, ensuring access to all.

As shown by Nielsen, digital technologies are instrumental to scientific collaboration and to implement Open Science values and principles. In both Nielsen's and the UNESCO definition, the old tradition and the new technologies mentioned in the BOAI are closely linked.

1.3 Open Science Infrastructures

The UNESCO Recommendation identifies specific areas for action, focusing on the necessary steps for governments and communities to implement it. These include Open Science infrastructures, defined as shared research infrastructures that support Open Science and serve the needs of different communities. Along with Open Science knowledge, open engagement of societal actors and open dialog with other knowledge systems, Open Science infrastructures are one of the four key pillars of Open Science referred to in the definition, and represented in the left part of Fig. 1.1.

They are also mentioned in the sustainability principle, "Open science infrastructures are often the result of community-building efforts, which are crucial for their long-term sustainability and therefore should be not-for-profit and guarantee permanent and unrestricted access to all public to the largest extent possible" (UNESCO, 2021, 12).

Fecher and Friesike identified five Open Science schools of thought, one of which focuses on infrastructure. This school of thought "regards Open Science as a technological challenge" (Fecher & Friesike, 2013, 36), with two specific trends. The first is distributed computing, a concept and practice closely linked to the development of the internet and related technologies. The second is the creation of social and collaboration networks for researchers — tools that enable them to

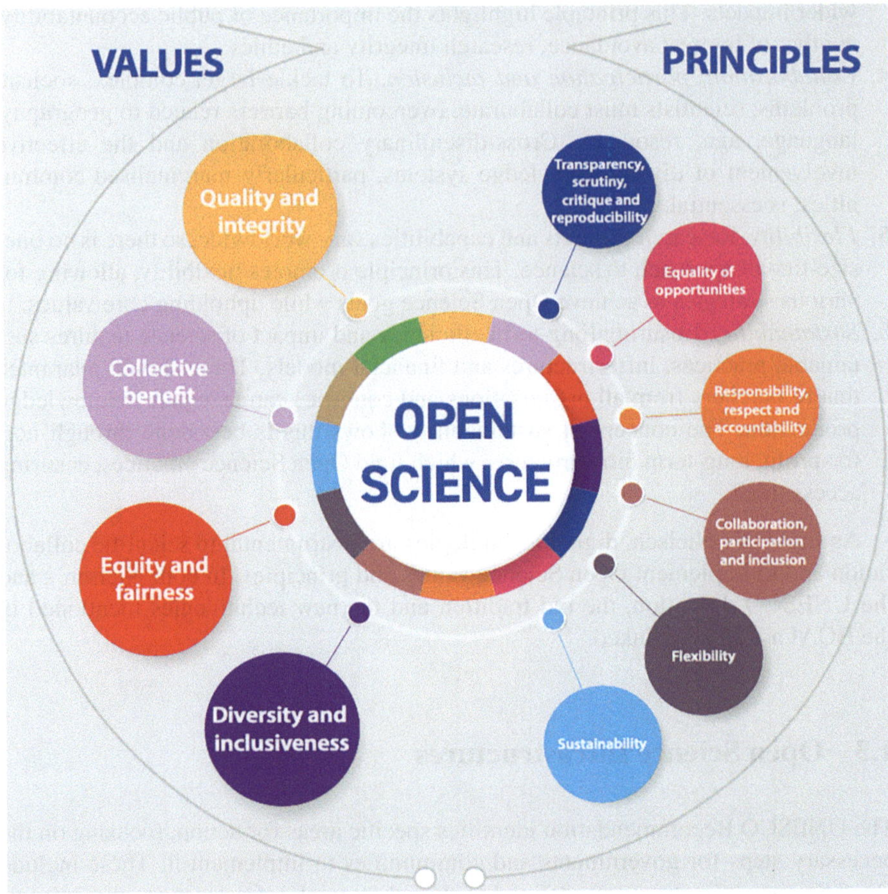

Fig. 1.1 Open Science core values and principles. © UNESCO, 2022. https://doi.org/10.54677/DLYW1405. Attribution-ShareAlike 3.0 IGO (CC-BY-SA 3.0 IGO) license

interact and collaborate. The technological element is thus combined with social aspects of fundamental importance.

Cameron Neylon (2013) recognised the lack of shared infrastructure as a major problem for Open Science uptake. In 2015, the *Principles for Open Scholarly Infrastructure* (POSI) were created to deal with the fact that scientific publications and datasets were becoming more accessible, but the infrastructure for sharing them was not keeping up. The Principles are three (Bilder et al., 2020):

- *Coverage across the scholarly enterprise*—research transcends disciplines, geography, institutions, and stakeholders. Organisations and the infrastructure they run need to reflect this.

- *Stakeholder Governed*—a board-governed organisation drawn from the stakeholder community builds confidence that the organisation will take decisions driven by community consensus and a balance of interests.
- *Non-discriminatory participation or membership*—we see the best option as an "opt-in" approach with principles of non-discrimination and inclusivity where any stakeholder group may express an interest and should be welcome. Representation in governance must reflect the character of the community or membership.
- *Transparent governance*—to achieve trust, the processes and policies for selecting representatives to governance groups should be transparent (within the constraints of privacy laws).
- *Cannot lobby*—infrastructure organisations should not lobby for regulatory change to cement their own positions or narrow self-interest. However, an infrastructure organisation's role is to support its community, and this can include advocating for policy changes.
- *Living will*—a powerful way to create trust is to publicly describe a plan addressing the conditions under which an organisation or service would be wound down. It should include how this would happen and how any assets could be archived and preserved when passed to a successor organisation or service. Any such organisation or service must adopt POSI and honour the POSI principles.
- *Formal incentives to fulfil mission & wind-down*—infrastructures exist for a specific purpose, and that purpose can be radically simplified or even rendered unnecessary by technological or social change. Organisations and services should regularly review community support and the need for their activities. If it is possible, the organisation or service (and staff) should have direct incentives to deliver on the mission and wind down.
- *Time-limited funds are used only for time-limited activities*—operations are supported by sustainable revenue sources—whereas time-limited funds are used only for time-limited activities. Depending on grants to fund ongoing and/or long-term infrastructure operations fully makes them fragile and distracts from building core infrastructure.
- *Goal to generate surplus*—organisations (or services) that define sustainability based merely on recovering costs are brittle and stagnant. It is not enough to merely survive; organisations and services have to be able to adapt and change. To weather economic, social and technological volatility, they need financial resources beyond immediate operating costs.
- *Goal to create financial reserves*—a high priority should be having ring-fenced financial reserves, separate from operating funds, that can support implementing living will plans, including a complete, orderly wind down or transition to a successor organisation, or major unexpected events.
- *Mission-consistent revenue generation*—revenue sources should be evaluated against the infrastructure's mission and not run counter to the aims of the organisation or service.

- *Revenue based on services, not data*—data related to the running of the scholarly infrastructure should be community property. Appropriate revenue sources might include value-added services, consulting, API Service Level Agreements or membership fees.
- *Open source*—all software and assets required to run the infrastructure should be available under an open-source licence. This does not include other software that may be involved with running the organisation.
- *Open data (within constraints of privacy laws)*—for an infrastructure to be forked (reproduced), it will be necessary to replicate all relevant data. The CC0 waiver[6] is the best practice in making data openly and legally available. Privacy and data protection laws will limit the extent to which this is possible.
- *Available data (within constraints of privacy laws)*—it is not enough that the data be "open" if there is no practical way to obtain it. Underlying data should be made easily available via periodic open data dumps.
- *Patent non-assertion*—the organisation should commit to a patent non-assertion policy or covenant. The organisation may obtain patents to protect its own operations but not use them to prevent the community from replicating the infrastructure."

Subsequent to being revised in 2020, 2023 and 2025, respectively, these principles have exerted a considerable influence and continue to serve as a point of reference. Several definitions, including the UNESCO Recommendation, have been developed on this basis.

According to them it is worth underlining that Open Science infrastructures should not be regarded as a mere technical product; rather, they should be considered as a complex system that incorporates a range of tools, institutions and social norms. It is evident that the notion of openness cannot be regarded solely as a technical attribute; rather, it is a fundamental value and a guiding principle that exerts a profound influence on the objectives, governance and management of the infrastructure (Fecher et al., 2021).

More in general, in recent years the development of open scientific infrastructure has become a topic of debate regarding the future of online scientific research. In January 2021, a group of researchers made a call for a Plan Infrastructure (Plan I), aiming at integrating all research outputs on large interoperable infrastructures. In fact, the dependency of research and scholarship on an information infrastructure that treats all scholarly outputs equally, and that is based on open standards and open markets, is paramount. (Brembs et al., 2021, 4).

More recently, the Barcelona Declaration on Open Research Information[7] was launched, whose commitments 2 ('We will work with services and systems that

---

[6] Thanks to which creators are allowed to waive all copyright and related rights in their works, making them freely available for any use without restrictions. Unlike other Creative Commons licenses, CC0 does not require attribution.

[7] https://barcelona-declaration.org/

support and enable open research information') and 3 ('We will support the sustainability of infrastructures for open research information') insist on the need for open, public, sustainable infrastructures, recognising and highlighting their central role as enabling factors in the creation of an open research information space.

It has been observed that the majority of landscape reports on Open Infrastructure have been carried out in Europe—with a lesser number of reports conducted in Latin America (Langlais, 2023).

Of particular note are the efforts made since 2016 to establish the European Open Science Cloud (EOSC),[8] an ecosystem of research infrastructures based on open procedures and standards, which allows data, resources, and knowledge to be shared—thus enabling Open Scholarship to become a reality (European Commission, 2016; Burgelman et al., 2019). This project is being implemented through specific funding programmes (first Horizon 2020 and now Horizon Europe) and its development will continue in the next framework programme, FP10.

Since early 2019, five European Strategy Forum on Research Infrastructures (ESFRI) Cluster projects—including SSHOC, the Social Science and Humanities Open Cloud project—have been initiated with the objective of establishing a connection to the European Open Science Cloud. The projects were invited to contribute to the development and implementation process, with the aim of working together to implement interfaces, integrate computer and data management solutions, create cross-border and open cooperation spaces, and promote clouds via the EOSC portal for a larger user community. (Gotz et al., 2020).

The 2021 ESFRI Roadmap has explicitly embraced Open Science principles: "Most of the Research Infrastructures on the ESFRI Roadmap are at the forefront of the Open Science movement and make important contributions to the digital transformation by transforming the whole research process according to the Open Science paradigm" (ESFRI, 2021, 159).

In Italy, the National Research Programme (PNR 2021–2027) provides strategic guidance for the country's research policies and refers to two strategic documents: the National Plan for Open Science (PNSA) to implement Open Science policies, (MUR, 2022) and the National Research Infrastructure Plan (PNIR) for specific aspects related to research infrastructures. "RIs—as stated in the second document—are crucial to our ability to make scientific progress and promote innovation, and play an enabling role in research and innovation to achieve the most challenging goals set at European and national level" (DM n. 1082, 2021, 3). The document aims to provide more detail on the technical and strategic plan for Research Infrastructures, by defining and updating national priorities. Because of this unique potential, which is inherent to RIs, the document includes both the European and national plans, which are considered closely connected. At the European level, in particular, the document takes its cue from the European framework programme Horizon Europe, which supports the cross-cutting actions

[8] https://research-and-innovation.ec.europa.eu/strategy/strategy-research-and-innovation/our-digital-future/open-science/european-open-science-cloud-eosc_en

of the new European Research Area (ERA), emphasising the fundamental role that RIs can play in this context, especially considering the significant contributions the ESFRI has made to advancing the sector in Europe. At national level, in addition to the PNR, the strategic and forward-looking contribution of the National Recovery and Resilience Plan[9] is fundamental, as it considers RIs as a key factor for the development of the country. Through the infrastructure and projects that build it, including FOSSR—Fostering Open Science in Social Science Research, a space is created to develop tools and services to meet the real needs of researchers.

1.4 Conclusions

In recent years, it has become clear that data on social behaviour and cultural practices (past and present) is essential for addressing key societal issues such as climate change, environmental sustainability, energy transition, migration management, health promotion, and disease prevention. This data must be considered alongside a clear acknowledgement of the importance of ethical, legal, and societal aspects (ESFRI, 2021).

The areas enabled by the FOSSR project are varied and include, among others, the development of research services, which range from data collection, curation, analysis and preservation, online longitudinal panels and survey maker, virtual research and simulation environments, applications for policy evaluation and forecasting, ontogeny-semantics and text analysis, as well as training and documentary and consultancy support. Structuring research as Open Science practices promises to enhance transparency, accountability and inclusiveness.

Social science infrastructures enable the observation and comparison of contemporary societies over time—both synchronically and diachronically. More specifically, panel data—which refers to information collected by the same researchers repeatedly over a period—and longitudinal data—which tracks changes within a sample population over time, regardless of whether the same individuals are observed—are two essential components in the toolkit for social scientists, and are fundamental to research in general. All these efforts underscore a commitment to generate high-quality and robust datasets that can drive insightful social research and inform policy decisions on a national and international scale—and are essential in fostering informed policy-making and active citizenship. SHARE ERIC,[10] CESSDA[11] and its Italian national service DASSI,[12] the GUIDE ESFRI research

[9] https://www.italiadomani.gov.it/content/sogei-ng/it/en/home.html

[10] https://share-eric.eu/

[11] https://www.cessda.eu/

[12] https://www.cessda.eu/About/Consortium-and-Partners/List-of-Service-Providers/Italy-spid1908

infrastructure,[13] and the Generation and Gender survey (GGS),[14] offer a rich environment for both social science and multidisciplinary research. Some of these infrastructures will be detailed in the next chapters of this book.

Despite the central role of Social Sciences data, much remains to be done in the design and development of tools to improve collaboration, data sharing and reuse in Social Sciences, and thus overcome the fragmentation that characterises them, as highlighted in the ESFRI Roadmap 2021. Rafols (2025) examines three well-known models that show the marginalisation of the Social Sciences and Humanities in priority setting in relation to societal challenges, and argues that processes for assessing these challenges should include SSH research to ensure they are sensitive and responsive to society's needs—and that, as a result, certain issues should be prioritised over others. This is an important proposal that deserves further exploration. What is important to emphasise here is that Open Science, and specifically its Social Science infrastructures, data, and tools have a great deal to offer if we are to respond to the global challenges we face today.

References

Budapest Open Access Initiative (BOAI). (2002). https://www.budapestopenaccessinitiative.org/read/

Bilder, G., Lin, J., & Neylon, C. (2020). *The principles of open scholarly infrastructure*. Retrieved June 2025, from https://doi.org/10.24343/C34W2H

Brembs, B., Förstner, K., Goedicke, M., Konrad, U., Wannemacher, K., & Kett, J. (2021). Plan I – Towards a sustainable research information infrastructure. *Zenodo*. https://doi.org/10.5281/zenodo.4454640

Burgelman, J.-C., Pascu, C., Szkuta, K., Von Schomberg, R., Karalopoulos, A., Repanas, K., & Schouppe, M. (2019). Open Science, open data, and open scholarship: European policies to make science fit for the twenty-first century. *Frontiers in Big Data, 2*, 43. https://doi.org/10.3389/fdata.2019.00043

Benkler, I. (2006). *The wealth of networks*. Yale University Press.

Berners-Lee, T. (1999). *Weaving the web: The original design and ultimate destiny of the world wide web*. Harper.

Bush, V. (1945). As we may think. *The Atlantic Monthly Review*, pp. 101–108. https://www.theatlantic.com/magazine/archive/1945/07/as-we-may-think/303881/

Chubin, D. E. (1985). Open Science and closed science: Tradeoff in a democracy. *Science Technology and Human Values, 1985, 10*(2), 73–81.

CIPE. *PNR* 2021–*2027 - Programma Nazionale della Ricerca*. https://www.mur.gov.it/sites/default/files/2021-01/Pnr2021-27.pdf

David, P. (2000). The historical origins of 'open science', an essay on patronage, reputation and common agency contracting in the scientific revolution. *MERIT Working Papers* 2014-082. United Nations University - Maastricht Economic and Social Research Institute on Innovation and Technology (MERIT). https://ideas.repec.org/p/sip/dpaper/06-038.html.

[13] https://roadmap2021.esfri.eu/projects-and-landmarks/browse-the-catalogue/guide/

[14] https://www.ggp-i.org/generations-and-gender-survey/

David, P. (2014). The republic of open science. The institution's historical origins and prospects for continued vitality. *Contributi del Centro Linceo Interdisciplinare 'Beniamino Segre'*.

Decreto Ministeriale n.1082. (2021) del 10-09-2021 - Piano Nazionale Infrastrutture di Ricerca (PNIR) 2021–2027. https://www.mur.gov.it/sites/default/files/2021-10/Decreto%20Ministeriale%20n.1082%20del%2010-09-2021%20-%20PNIR%202021%20-%202027.pdf

Di Donato, F., & Provost, L. (2025). Why isn't FAIR enough? Bringing together methods and values for Open Science uptake. *Umanistica Digitale, 9*(19), 17–46. https://doi.org/10.6092/issn.2532-8816/20976

Engelbart, D. C. (1962), *Augmenting human intellect: A conceptual framework*. Stanford Research Institute Report.

European Commission. (2016). *Open innovation, open science, open to the world - a vision for Europe*. https://ec.europa.eu/digital-single-market/en/news/open-innovation-open-science-open-world-vision-europe

European Strategy Forum on Research Infrastructures (ESFRI) (2021). Roadmap 2021. Strategy Report on Research Infrastructures. https://roadmap2021.esfri.eu/media/1295/esfri-roadmap-2021.pdf

Fecher, B., & Friesike, S. (2013). *Open science: One term, five schools of thought*. Id., Opening science: The evolving guide on how the internet is changing research, collaboration and scholarly publishing. Springer International Publishing.

Fecher, B., Kahn, R., Sokolovska, N., Völker, T., & Nebe, P. (2021). Making a research infrastructure: Conditions and strategies to transform a service into an infrastructure. *Science and Public Policy, 48*(4), 499–507. https://doi.org/10.1093/scipol/scab026. ISSN 0302-3427

Free Software Foundation. (2022). *Licenses*. https://www.gnu.org/licenses/licenses.html.en

Galilei, G. (1610). *Letter to Belisario Vinta*. https://brunelleschi.imss.fi.it/galileopalazzostrozzi/object/GalileoGalileiLetterToBelisarioVinta.html

Gotz, A., Petzold, A., Asmi, A., Blomberg, N., Lamanna, G., & Dekker, R. (2020). ESFRI cluster projects - Position papers on expectations and planned contributions to the EOSC. *Zenodo*. https://doi.org/10.5281/zenodo.3675081.

Greco, P. (2010). Il Sidereus Nuncius e l'origine della comunicazione pubblica della scienza. *S&F_scienzaefilosofia.it*. https://www.scienzaefilosofia.com/2018/03/26/il-sidereus-nuncius-e-lorigine-della-comunicazione-pubblica-della-scienza/

Guédon, J.-C. (2001). *In Oldenburg's long shadow*. Librarians, Research Scientists, Publishers, and the Control of Scientific Publishing, Association of Research Libraries, ISBN 0-918006-81-3.

Hadot, P. (1995). *Qu'est-ce que la philosophie antique?* Gallimard.

IETF. (2025). *About RFCs*. IETF. https://www.ietf.org/process/rfcs/

Langlais, P.-C. (2023). Open science infrastructure. *Petite encyclopédie de la science ouverte*. https://encyclo.ouvrirlascience.fr/articles/open-science-infrastructure/.

Leiner, B. M., Cerf, V. G., Clark, D. D., Kahn, R. E., Kleinrock, L., Lynch, D. C., Postel, J., Roberts, L. G., & Wolff, S. (2009). Brief history of the internet. *ACM SIGCOMM Computer Communication Review, 39*(5), 22–31.

Lessig, L. (2004). The creative commons. *Montana Law Review, 65*(1) https://scholarworks.umt.edu/mlr/vol65/iss1/1

Lévy, P. (1994). *L'intelligence collective*. La Découverte.

Lévy, P. (1997). *Cyberculture*. Rapport au Conseil de l'Europe. Editions Odile Jacob/Editions du Conseil de l'Europe.

Merton, R. K. (1973) [1942]. The normative structure of science, in Merton R. K., *The Sociology of Science: Theoretical and Empirical Investigations*, Chicago: University of Chicago Press, pp. 267–278, ISBN 978-0-226-52091-9, OCLC 755754. Originally published as "Science and Technology in a Democratic Order," Journal of Legal and Political Sociology 1 (1942): 115–26; later published as "Science and Democratic Social Structure," in Robert K. Merton, Social Theory and Social Structure.

Mons, B., Neylon, C., Velterop, J., Dumontier, M., da Silva Santos, L. O. B., & Wilkinson, M. D. (2017). Cloudy, increasingly FAIR; revisiting the FAIR data guiding principles for the European open science cloud. *Information Services and Use, 37*(1), 49–56. https://doi.org/10.3233/ISU-170824

MUR. (2022). *Piano nazionale per la scienza aperta (PNSA) 2021–2027*. https://www.mur.gov.it/it/atti-e-normativa/decreto-ministeriale-n-268-del-28-02-2022

Nelson, T. H. (1987). *Literary machines*. Mindful Press.

Neylon, C. (2013). Architecting the future of research communication: Building the models and analytics for an open access future. *PLoS Biology, 11*(10). https://doi.org/10.1371/journal.pbio.1001691

Nielsen, M. (2011). *Reinventing discovery: The new era of networked science*. Princeton University Press.

OECD. (2015). *Making open science a reality*. OECD Science, Technology and Industry Policy Papers, No. 25. OECD Publishing. https://doi.org/10.1787/5jrs2f963zs1-en

Plato. (2002). *Oxford world's classics* (Phaedrus, R. W. Ed.), Oxford University Press. ISBN: 9780199554027. https://doi.org/10.1093/actrade/9780199554027.book.1.

Plato. (2005). Meno and other dialogues: Charmides, Laches, Lysis, Meno, Robin Waterfield (ed.), Oxford University Press; *Oxford World's Classics*. ISBN: 9780199555666. https://doi.org/10.1093/actrade/9780199555666.book.1.

Rafols, I. (2025). *The relative marginalisation of SSH in research for societal challenges and the need for system level assessment to foster epistemic diversity*. RESSH 2025 book of Abstracts, pp. 66–69. https://vastuullinentiede.fi/sites/default/files/2025-05/RESSH2025_Conference_Book_of_Abstracts.pdf

Ramachandran, R., Bugbee, K., & Murphy, K. (2021). From open data to open science. *Earth and Space Science, 8*, e2020EA001562. https://doi.org/10.1029/2020EA001562

Raymond, E. S. (2001). The cathedral and the bazaar. In *The cathedral and the bazaar: Musings on Linux and open source by an accidental revolutionary*. O'Reilly Media.

Rossi, P. (2000). *La nascita della scienza moderna in Europa, Roma-Bari, Laterza.*

Shirky, C. (2010). *Cognitive surplus: Creativity and generosity in a connected age*. Penguin.

The Royal Society Science Policy Centre. (2012). *Science as an open enterprise*. https://royalsociety.org/-/media/policy/projects/sape/2012-06-20-saoe.pdf

UNESCO. (2021). *Recommendation on open science*. https://doi.org/10.54677/MNMH8546.

UNESCO. (2022). Open science toolkit. Building capacity for open science. https://doi.org/10.54677/DLYW1405

UNESCO. (2023). Development of the UNESCO recommendation on open science. https://www.unesco.org/en/open-science/development?hub=686

Wilkinson, M., Dumontier, M., Aalbersberg, I., et al. (2016). The FAIR guiding principles for scientific data management and stewardship. *Scientific Data, 3*, 160018. https://doi.org/10.1038/sdata.2016.18

Mons, B., Neylon, C., Velterop, J., Dumontier, M., da Silva Santos, L. O. B., & Wilkinson, M. D. (2017). Cloudy, increasingly FAIR; revisiting the FAIR data guiding principles for the European open science cloud. Information Services and Use, 37(1), 49–56. [illegible] 10.3233/ISU-170824
MUR. (2022). [illegible]
Nielsen, M. (2011). [illegible]
Neylon, C. (2017). [illegible]
[illegible]

Chapter 2
Secondary, Longitudinal, and Panel Data in Social Science Research

Ilaria Primerano, Nicolò Marchesini, Francesco Santelli, Luciana Taddei, and Loredana Cerbara

2.1 Introduction

In the field of social science, secondary research plays a pivotal role. It allows for the analysis of existing data to generate new interpretations, deepen the understanding of complex phenomena, and support the development of evidence-based policies (Biolcati-Rinaldi & Vezzoni, 2012). Secondary research differs from primary research, which is based on the collection of new data through the design and implementation of a study related to specific research questions. Primary research can be conducted using various methods, such as surveys, interviews, and focus groups. Unlike primary research, secondary research relies on the analysis of existing data collected from previous studies. Usually, social researchers start from such secondary data to identify potential gaps in the literature on the investigated

I. Primerano (✉)
Institute for Research on Population and Social Policies (CNR-IRPPS), Fisciano, SA, Italy
e-mail: ilaria.primerano@cnr.it

N. Marchesini
Italian National Institute of Statistics (Istat), Rome, Italy
e-mail: nicolo.marchesini@istat.it

F. Santelli
Department of Political and Social Sciences, University of Trieste, Trieste, Italy
e-mail: fsantelli@units.it

L. Taddei
Institute for Research on Population and Social Policies, National Research Council, Fisciano (SA), Italy
e-mail: luciana.taddei@cnr.it

L. Cerbara
Institute for Research on Population and Social Policies (CNR-IRPPS), Rome, Italy
e-mail: loredana.cerbara@cnr.it

L. Taddei, M. Paolucci (eds.), *Longitudinal Data Infrastructures in Europe*,
https://doi.org/10.1007/978-3-032-07005-0_2

topic, and by interpreting, organizing, and analyzing data from prior studies, they are able to generate new knowledge.

Among the many forms of secondary data, longitudinal and panel data are particularly valuable for understanding several aspects of human life, since they capture changes over time. When used in secondary research, longitudinal and panel data offer unique methodological advantages, as they allow the study of changes, causality, and life-course events. Although originally collected as primary data by public institutions, research bodies, or international organizations within the framework of structured surveys and specific objectives, such data take on the nature of secondary data when reused by other researchers for analyses different from those envisaged in the original research design. This shift from primary to secondary data is based on the principle that the nature of data depends not only on how they were collected, but also on the context in which they are used (Vartanian, 2011). Access to these data archives enables the development of new research on emerging topics, making use of the informational potential of existing data, while also promoting the efficient use of scientific resources (Johnston, 2014).

In fact, longitudinal and panel data are especially useful for research aiming to understand the evolution of opinions, behaviors, values, and socio-economic conditions (Ruspini, 2002; Agnoli, 2008). Specifically, these data are indispensable in various domains of social science because of their ability to account for temporal dynamics and individual-level variation. In political science, for instance, they facilitate the tracking of changes in political attitudes and behaviors over electoral cycles (Bartels, 2006; Neundorf & Smets, 2017). In labor economics, they support the analysis of employment transitions, wage trajectories, and job mobility (Arulampalam, 2001). Sociologists use these data to study intergenerational mobility, educational attainment, and demographic life events such as marriage and parenthood (Blossfeld et al., 2005; Bukodi & Goldthorpe, 2013). Furthermore, longitudinal frameworks allow researchers to investigate how macro-level events, such as economic recessions, public health crises, or policy reforms, affect individuals differently over time. For example, the COVID-19 pandemic was studied using longitudinal surveys to assess its impacts on mental health, employment, and inequality (Pierce et al., 2020; Daly et al., 2020). These capabilities enable robust hypothesis testing using fixed-effects models, growth curve modeling, and structural equation modeling. The inclusion of time as a dimension adds analytical depth that cross-sectional designs inherently lack, providing insights into causality and the long-term effects of social processes.

Given the increasing analytical value of longitudinal and panel data, there is a growing and sustained demand among researchers across disciplines for access to such data. As a result, the development and long-term sustainability of high-quality data sources has become a strategic priority for the scientific community. Within this context, the rising importance of FAIR principles (Findable, Accessible, Interoperable, and Reusable) and the broader Open Science movement have fostered the emergence of Research Infrastructures (RIs) specifically dedicated to longitudinal and panel data. This shift reflects a growing recognition of the limitations of traditional data sources in meeting the complex and evolving needs of social research. In fact, unlike traditional data sources such as censuses and official registers, which do not offer the flexibility or frequency required for social research, RIs are designed to meet these demands more effectively. By leveraging the flexible and pre-planned design of longitudinal and panel surveys, RIs enable a regular, more frequent data production and dissemination of high-quality data that capture dynamic social processes over time.

This chapter examines the role of secondary data in Social Science research, the development of social RIs, some methodological challenges, and the main statistical methods associated with the analysis of longitudinal and panel data. Specifically, Sect. 2.2 explores the role of secondary data in social research, clarifying its advantages and limitations, with particular attention given to longitudinal and panel data. Section 2.3 focuses on RIs in the context of social sciences, which serve as the cornerstone for data access, preservation, and sharing, facilitating the implementation of FAIR principles and promoting cross-national comparability. Section 2.4 addresses the methodological issues of longitudinal and panel data. Particular attention is paid to strategies aimed at ensuring the inclusion of marginalized populations and reducing sampling bias. Section 2.5 presents the main statistical approaches for analyzing longitudinal and panel data, highlighting their analytical potential. Section 2.6 concludes the chapter.

2.2 The Role of Secondary Data in Social Science Research

Secondary data are used in both quantitative and qualitative research. Their utility spans multiple disciplines, including sociology, political science, economics, demography, and education. These data represent an essential resource for social scientists seeking to study complex social phenomena, as well as the individual and collective behavior of populations. Over time, their increasing demand, fueled by digitalization process, Open Science principles, and the development of Social RIs, has significantly enhanced their relevance, making them increasingly available and accessible.

Unlike primary data, which are collected based on a specific research design, secondary data refer to datasets previously gathered by other researchers or institutions for purposes different from those of the current investigation. However, they can still address new research questions. This is the reason why secondary data encompass a wide range of sources, including administrative records, sample surveys, censuses, electoral rolls, organizational databases, and publicly available datasets, such as those from the World Bank, Eurostat, or national statistical institutes. The diversity of sources, varying by institution and research topic, makes secondary data multidimensional and therefore suitable for addressing a wide array of research questions.

There are various types of secondary data, each with specific features depending on the research objectives. They differ in origin, structure, content, and purpose. For instance, cross-sectional data provide a snapshot of a phenomenon at a specific point in time, while longitudinal and panel data allow researchers to observe changes over time within the same subjects, thus enabling researchers to monitor changes in behaviors, attitudes, social conditions, or institutional transformations. These data have contributed to reshaping the methodological approaches used to study the evolution of social phenomena over time.

In particular, they allow one to assess both immediate and delayed impacts of social interventions. Thanks to the repeated collection of information on the same statistical units, these datasets allow researchers to reconstruct individuals' life trajectories, following them through different stages of life. This approach enables a deeper understanding of personal transitions such as school-to-work pathways, marriage, retirement, or health decline.

The use of secondary data, in general, and longitudinal and panel data in particular, offers researchers many advantages beyond the wide spectrum of analyzable topics. One of the key advantages often associated with these data sources is the representativeness of the samples, i.e., the extent to which the sample reflects the characteristics of the broader population from which it is drawn. Representativeness is crucial because it allows researchers to generalize findings from the sample to the entire population with greater confidence.

However, not all longitudinal or panel datasets are representative. In fact, while many national longitudinal and panel data, such as those carried out by statistical institutions, seek representativeness through rigorous sampling methods and panel maintenance strategies, others may be designed for different purposes and may not reflect the entire population (see Sect. 2.4).

Another important aspect is related to cost and time savings. By using pre-existing datasets, researchers can avoid the financial and logistical burdens associated with primary data collection, making their research more efficient and less expensive. Furthermore, working with anonymized secondary data can mitigate ethical issues related to direct contact with vulnerable populations, who are often underrepresented or difficult to reach in surveys.

Despite their many advantages, secondary data show some limitations, such as the lack of control researchers have over how the data was collected, how variables were defined, and, particularly in administrative data, the lack of important contextual or theoretical information needed for certain types of analysis. Additionally, secondary data are often unavailable at key levels of territorial aggregation, such as provinces or municipalities in Italy, which limits the scope and granularity of spatial and policy-relevant analysis.

2.3 Research Infrastructures and Social Science

Over the last two decades, large-scale RIs have gained a central role not only in the natural and life sciences, but also within the social sciences, where the complexity of data and the ambition of comparative and longitudinal research have increased substantially. The development of RIs in the social sciences constitutes a critical foundation for advancing scientific knowledge and enabling robust secondary data analysis. These infrastructures are complex, integrated systems that encompass both material resources (such as digital archives, high-performance computing facilities, and laboratories), and immaterial assets, including collaborative networks, standardized methodologies, and open access to curated datasets. In the context of social science research, they facilitate the systematic collection, harmonization, and dissemination of longitudinal, cross-national, and multi-level data, which are essential for comparative and policy-relevant analyses.

European initiatives, particularly through frameworks like Horizon 2020 and the European Research Infrastructure Consortium (ERIC), have played a pivotal role in institutionalizing such infrastructures. By fostering interoperability between national research systems and avoiding unnecessary duplication of efforts, these infrastructures not only enhance data quality and accessibility but also promote cumulative research and theoretical refinement. Consequently, they contribute decisively to the development of evidence-based knowledge capable of informing public policy and addressing complex societal challenges (European Commission, 2019).

Although longitudinal and panel data are essential in social science research to capture dynamic social processes, individual life-course trajectories, and the long-term effects of policy interventions, researchers often find difficulties in finding, collecting, or analyzing these kinds of data. These data are inherently complex and often require substantial effort in cleaning, harmonization, and transformation before they become suitable for analysis. As underlined by Huber et al. (2021), data preparation phase can consume up to 80% of the total research effort (Wickham, 2014; Press, 2016), thereby limiting the time and resources available for substantive analysis. It is not only time-consuming but also technically demanding, particularly when data must be manually retrieved, processed, and integrated into computational environments.

RIs have emerged as crucial facilitators in this context, especially for the hosting, curation, and long-term preservation of high-quality longitudinal datasets. Critically, RIs have the potential to realize effectively the FAIR data principles and to support the seamless integration of data into modern computational workflows (Wilkinson et al., 2025). While progress has been made, further efforts are needed to adopt common web standards and harmonized metadata practices across RIs.

Florio and Sirtori (2016) underline that although RIs can generate significant social value, their impact is highly dependent on the institutional, technical, and economic frameworks within which they operate. In the case of longitudinal and panel data in the social sciences, these challenges are particularly pronounced. First, the long time horizons required for longitudinal data collection often exceed the life cycles of research funding schemes, creating discontinuities in data collection efforts and threatening the sustainability of time-series datasets. Second, while many RIs provide access to large and complex datasets, these are frequently fragmented across national boundaries, lack harmonized documentation, or are governed by heterogeneous legal and ethical standards that complicate cross-country comparability and integration.

Moreover, although the FAIR principles offer a valuable blueprint for data stewardship, their implementation in the social sciences remains uneven (Kalinin & Skvortsov, 2023). There is a great effort to adhere to metadata standards and apply persistent identifiers, making them available and not only linked to landing pages that require manual navigation, rather than enabling machine-readable and automated data discovery (Huber et al., 2021). This could hinder not only reproducibility but also the potential for innovative computational methods such as automated secondary analysis, federated learning, or dynamic modeling across distributed datasets.

Another pressing challenge is the gap between data repositories and computational environments (FAIR-IMPACT, 2025). As current infrastructures rarely provide integrated environments for in-situ analysis, researchers are often forced to export large datasets and replicate complex pre-processing routines in isolated local systems; raising barriers to both efficiency and transparency. Without modular, reusable software interfaces and harmonized APIs, it remains difficult to scale the use of high-quality panel data in large-scale comparative studies or to fully exploit them for policy simulation models. Recent FAIR-IMPACT case studies confirm that many RIs still lack seamless computational integration, and emphasize the need for interoperable tools that enable FAIR data to be used directly within analysis platforms.

Furthermore, ethical and legal constraints, such as those related to privacy, informed consent, and data sovereignty, add an additional layer of complexity, especially when dealing with sensitive individual-level data over extended periods. These constraints, while necessary, can obstruct data linkage or reuse, particularly when infrastructures lack clear and interoperable access protocols that balance data protection with research needs.

Addressing these challenges requires not only continued investment in the technical components of RIs but also coordinated policy action to align legal frameworks, develop sustainable funding models, and promote the co-creation of standards with user communities. Only through such an integrated approach can RIs in the social sciences fulfill their transformative potential, enabling robust, timely, and policy-relevant research grounded in rich, longitudinal data.

Enhanced interoperability would enable the automated transformation of archived longitudinal data into analysis-ready formats, fostering not only reproducible and efficient research but also facilitating advanced machine-assisted data discovery and computational analysis within the social sciences.

2.3.1 European Research Infrastructures

Among the most consolidated and strategically significant RIs in the European social science landscape is CESSDA ERIC (Consortium of European Social Science Data Archives). As a distributed infrastructure involving more than 20 member states, CESSDA serves as the primary archival backbone for social science data across Europe. It provides not only secure and sustainable long-term preservation of datasets, but also access to a vast collection of curated data via the CESSDA Data Catalogue, which includes thousands of studies in multiple languages. Critically, CESSDA promotes metadata harmonization, persistent identifiers, and interoperability standards, thereby supporting the operationalization of FAIR principles across national borders. Through specifical tools, CESSDA actively enables researchers to discover, compare, and reuse longitudinal and cross-sectional datasets, fostering cumulative and comparative research in the social sciences.

Another emblematic example of an ERIC-compliant infrastructure that provides FAIR data is the European Social Survey (ESS), which has become a flagship resource for comparative and longitudinal research in the social sciences across Europe. Conducted biennially in over 30 countries, the ESS gathers repeated cross-sectional data using rigorous methodological standards in sampling design, questionnaire translation, and data quality control. Although not a panel survey in the strict sense, the ESS produces a harmonized time series that enables robust analysis of social change over time (European Social Survey ERIC, 2024).

In addition to these pan-European initiatives, a number of national probability-based online panels have emerged as important infrastructures for longitudinal and panel social research (e.g., LISS Panel in the Netherlands, the ELIPSS Panel in France, the GESIS Panel and GIP in Germany, the Swedish and the Norwegian Probability Panels and so on). These panels provide true longitudinal designs with high-frequency data collection thanks to the online administration, and rich contextual variables, enabling robust within-subject analyses over time. Many of these panels adopt open science practices, facilitate data linkage, and make extensive use of experimental and adaptive survey designs through open calls to the scientific community. Despite being nationally anchored, they are highly relevant to European integration efforts, especially when developed within broader consortia or comparative research programs.

A significant step toward cross-national harmonization in longitudinal infrastructure is represented by the CRONOS panel (CROss-National Online Survey Panel), a transnational project built upon the ESS. CRONOS demonstrated the feasibility of developing harmonized online panels across different national contexts, using probability-based recruitment and shared survey content. It has contributed substantially to methodological knowledge on panel retention, cross-cultural equivalence, and digital survey deployment.

In the domain of demographic and life-course research, the Generations and Gender Programme (GGP), through its Generations and Gender Survey (GGS), provides cross-national panel data on family formation, fertility, partnership dynamics, and intergenerational support. GGP is currently undergoing consolidation as a European RI, building a central hub for harmonized longitudinal data on demographic behaviors across more than 20 countries. In parallel, the GUIDE project (Growing Up In Digital Europe) aspires to become a European RI focused on children's lives. Designed as a cross-national birth cohort study, GUIDE will track children's well-being, digital engagement, and social mobility from early childhood through adolescence. Both initiatives address major policy priorities related to population ageing, education, family change, and social inequality.

Consolidated is the SHARE ERIC (Survey of Health, Ageing and Retirement in Europe), which constitutes the most comprehensive pan-European panel dataset on individuals aged 50 and over. Conducted across more than 25 countries, SHARE combines economic, health, and social data, and includes life histories, biomarkers, and cognitive tests. Its multidisciplinary design and long-standing panel structure make it an indispensable resource for studying ageing, pension systems, health disparities, and intergenerational transfers.

Taken together, these infrastructures illustrate the maturing architecture of European social science RIs. Their growing institutionalization within the ESFRI framework and their convergence around FAIR and Open Science principles signify an ambitious effort to build an integrated European data space for the social sciences. Yet, their further success will depend on sustained political and financial support, as well as on the ability to harmonize legal, ethical, and technological systems across countries. Only through such integration can the transformative potential of longitudinal and panel data be fully harnessed to inform science, policy, and public understanding in the face of Europe's most pressing societal challenges.

2.4 Methodological Features of Longitudinal and Panel Data

Longitudinal and panel studies face a variety of interconnected challenges that impact their long-term sustainability. Addressing these issues requires continuous methodological innovation, effective engagement of the respondents, and adaptable survey designs to ensure the continuity and reliability of the data over time. On the methodological side, one of the main challenges is preserving the representativeness of the sample over time. Representativeness is crucial in socio-demographic research, as it ensures that findings can be generalised to broader populations. In longitudinal and panel designs, representativeness is not only a function of initial probabilistic sampling procedures but also of long-term participation patterns. Even a perfectly representative baseline sample can drift away from the target population if follow-up waves systematically exclude or lose specific subgroups Lynn (2021).

Socio-demographic shifts (e.g., increased mobility, migration, digital divides) make it particularly difficult to retain the representativeness of younger cohorts, non-citizens, ethnic minorities, or precariously employed individuals (Groves & Couper, 1998; Calderwood & Lessof, 2009). Adjusting weights post hoc may correct some biases, but only if the attrition is fully captured by observed variables (Little & Rubin, 2002; Lynn, 2003; Kreuter et al., 2010). This makes pro-active design strategies—such as oversampling vulnerable populations or employing flexible contact modes—essential from the outset.

Jointly with change in population structure, attrition, i.e., participants dropping out of the study over time due to refusal to continue participation, inability to locate respondents, institutionalisation or health-related nonparticipation, emigration or relocation, or mortality, is one of the most critical threats to the validity of longitudinal and panel research. Attrition is rarely random: it is often correlated with factors such as low socioeconomic status, poor health, unstable housing, or lower trust in institutions (Fitzgerald et al., 1998; Watson & Wooden, 2009). This can introduce selection bias, undermining causal inference and generalizability. Therefore, addressing attrition is not solely a statistical problem, but also a design and ethical challenge. Retention requires regular communication, respondent incentives, and attention to participants' burden; particularly in long-term studies such as the British Household Panel Survey (BHPS)/Understanding Society or the Panel Study of Income Dynamics (PSID).

To mitigate the effects of attrition and demographic change, many longitudinal and panel studies implement refreshment samples, the deliberate introduction of new sampled respondents into an existing panel. This strategy aims to restore and maintain the representativeness of the sample, particularly as older cohorts age, populations evolve, or new societal dynamics emerge (Lynn, 2009). Refreshment sampling is a common feature in rotating panel designs such as the European Union Statistics on Income and Living Conditions (EU-SILC), where individuals are typically followed for four years before being replaced by a new cohort, ensuring that both longitudinal and cross-sectional objectives are met. Similarly, Understanding Society, in the UK, incorporated a large refreshment sample of approximately 8000 households in Wave 6 (2014–2015) (Carpenter & Deepchand, 2016), with the explicit aim of enhancing representation of ethnic minorities, while 5800 households in Wave 14 (2022–2024) aiming to incorporate new household in Great Britain (Mitchell et al., 2025). In the United States, the Panel Study of Income Dynamics (PSID) added a new immigrant sample in 1997–1999, in response to major demographic shifts and changes in immigration patterns (PSID Staff, 2000). These additions enabled researchers to maintain the national representativeness of the study despite changing population structures.

While effective in countering sample size reduction, this approach introduces methodological complexities. The incorporation of new sample members often necessitates the recalibration of survey weights to ensure consistency with population benchmarks (Sand et al., 2025; Deng et al., 2013). Furthermore, differences in exposure time between original and refreshed respondents can result in asymmetries in response conditioning, longitudinal measurement error, and panel conditioning effects, all of which require careful statistical treatment to avoid analytical bias (Das et al., 2011; Warren & Halpern-Manners, 2012). Eventually, the addition of new participants may also disrupt the continuity of life-course models or within-individual trajectories, particularly when examining long-term outcomes or cumulative exposures. However, when properly designed and integrated, refreshment samples contribute significantly to the sustainability of long-term panels and enhance the inclusion of newly relevant subpopulations, such as recent migrants, digitally engaged youth, or socially mobile individuals—groups that are otherwise difficult to track through legacy samples alone (Das et al., 2011; Warren & Halpern-Manners, 2012).

Moreover, the spacing between waves is a critical design element in longitudinal research, with significant implications for measurement quality, respondent burden, and analytical validity. Short intervals, typically defined as 6–12 months between waves, are effective in reducing recall error and capturing rapid transitions in employment, health, or household composition (Jäckle, 2006; Warren & Halpern-

Manners, 2012). However, frequent data collection can introduce respondent fatigue and increase operational costs. In contrast, long intervals of 2 years or more are standard in large-scale studies, but they raise concerns about retrospective misreporting and missed life events (Lugtig, 2014; Jäckle, 2006).

To address these challenges, many longitudinal studies employ dependent interviewing, a method that incorporates information from previous waves into current interviews. This approach has been shown to reduce reporting inconsistencies and improve data accuracy, particularly when longer intervals increase the cognitive burden on respondents (Jäckle, 2006). Furthermore, recent experimental evidence from a high-frequency German panel shows that increasing survey frequency does not necessarily lead to greater measurement error or panel conditioning. Cornesse et al. (2023) found minimal conditioning effects when surveying was increased to quarterly intervals, mainly when the questionnaire content remained consistent.

Several studies have adopted hybrid wave strategies, combining annual 'core' waves with periodic rotating modules to balance the respondent burden and the depth of information. In cases where longitudinal designs incorporate refreshment samples, these additions help counteract both attrition and the limitations of longer inter-wave gaps. Deng et al. (2013) emphasise that refreshment samples composed of newly recruited, randomly sampled participants, can provide valuable diagnostic leverage and reduce bias by offering benchmarks unexposed to panel conditioning. Together, these design innovations enhance the validity and sustainability of long-term panels, supporting the robust collection of life-course and socio-demographic data over time.

Longitudinal and panel studies have long struggled to adequately include and retain marginalised populations, including migrants, racial and ethnic minorities, homeless individuals, and low-income or digitally excluded groups. These difficulties stem not only from practical obstacles but also from deeper structural inequalities that shape research participation. Individuals in precarious housing or employment situations often experience higher geographic mobility and instability, which makes them harder to track across waves (Duvoisin et al., 2023; Watson & Wooden, 2009). Others face linguistic or cultural barriers, or may lack trust in academic or governmental institutions due to histories of discrimination or surveillance, particularly among undocumented migrants, or racialised minorities (King-Shier et al., 2017; McMichael et al., 2014). Digital divides further complicate participation in increasingly web-based longitudinal panels. People with low digital literacy or limited internet access–disproportionately older, rural, or socioeconomically disadvantaged–are less likely to respond to online surveys or remain engaged in longitudinal panels that rely on digital follow-up modes (Callegaro et al., 2015; Cornesse & Schaurer, 2021).

Gender significantly influences participation and retention in longitudinal and panel studies, with ample evidence indicating that male respondents exhibit higher attrition rates than female respondents. Systematic reviews of cohort studies show that samples with more men often suffer from reduced retention over time (Teague et al., 2018). Data from a Swiss mixed-mode youth panel support this, revealing that women are more likely to stay engaged–especially in web-based modes–due to differences in perceived benefits, digital confidence, or time availability (Becker, 2022). Furthermore, gender intersects with other socio-demographic factors such as migration background and parental education, resulting in complex attrition patterns among younger respondents (Malschinger et al., 2023). These findings suggest the importance of incorporating gender-sensitive survey design—using flexible scheduling, multimode contacts, and gender-matching of interviewers—to mitigate biases and maintain panel representativeness.

Moreover, standard sampling frames such as population registers or household-based address lists systematically exclude certain groups—such as homeless individuals, institutionalised populations, and undocumented migrants—leading to initial undercoverage (Tourangeau, 2014). These methodological limitations intersect with structural disadvantage, reinforcing a cycle in which the most precarious individuals are both least represented in longitudinal data and most affected by the social phenomena such data aim to study.

Ensuring representativeness in longitudinal and panel studies is an ongoing methodological and ethical challenge, particularly in the context of socio-demographic change and structural inequalities. Attrition, digital exclusion, and the undercoverage of marginalised populations undermine the validity and generalizability of long-term data. While refreshment sampling, hybrid wave designs, and dependent interviewing offer partial solutions, their implementation requires careful calibration to avoid introducing new biases. Ultimately, inclusive and adaptive research strategies are essential for maintaining the analytical integrity and social relevance of longitudinal socio-demographic research.

2.5 Statistical Methods for Longitudinal and Panel Data

While in many applied scientific fields the terms longitudinal data and panel data are often used interchangeably, in the statistical literature, they have distinct meanings. As discussed by Diggle et al. (2002) and Hsiao (2014), longitudinal data broadly refer to data collected over time with the aim of capturing change and temporal dynamics. This category includes both individual-level and aggregate-level data, where time is the key analytical dimension, leading to several formal implications that require specific modeling strategies; some of which have been introduced in previous chapters.

Longitudinal data can thus be seen as an umbrella term encompassing a range of designs. Among them, panel data represent a specific case in which the same statistical units (which can also be higher-level entities such as Countries, schools, or firms) are observed repeatedly over time. In contrast, repeated cross-sectional surveys apply the same data collection instrument (e.g., a questionnaire) across multiple waves, but on different–yet comparable–samples. This design leads to a different sampling error at each wave, and is typically suited for analysing population-level trends rather than individual trajectories.

Time series data can also be framed as a subtype of longitudinal data (Singer & Willett, 2003), in which one or more macro-level variables (e.g., GDP, unemployment rate, oil price) are measured over time for an entity, such as a Country. The analytical focus in time series is generally on trend, seasonality, and autocorrelation, rather than on between- or within-unit variability and heterogeneity.

Overall, from a formal point of view, longitudinal data pose specific statistical challenges and opportunities due to their core structure. The presence, by itself, of repeated observations for each statistical unit over time, as the first argument, implies that observations should be considered non-independent. This is a clear violation of one of the assumptions of the classic statistical regression modeling, that is, the independence among observations (Flatt & Jacobs, 2019).

Often, with longitudinal data, other classes of models are proposed, such as Fixed Effects Models (FE) (Mundlak, 1978; Hedges, 1994). This class aims to control for unobserved time-invariant heterogeneity across units (e.g., individuals, households) by using only within-unit variation (Allison, 2005). It introduces indeed several elements to the classical statistical modeling, in order to account for the temporal dimension: unit-specific intercepts, or removing the temporal variable-mean for each unit (this process is called *demeaning*). This class of models has found great success in the econometric field (Wooldridge, 2010), with a wide range of applications in such contexts given the opportunity to address potential time-varying effects, but not necessarily solving problems related to missing data due to attrition, nor controlling for time-varying unobservables predictors. Moreover, non-random missingness can still bias estimates (Fitzmaurice et al., 2012).

In some cases, there are elements that suggest that covariates are not linked, in terms of statistical correlation, to the individual variability of the units. This property is called *exogeneity* (Engle et al., 1983), often tested through the Hausman test (Amini et al., 2012). In addition, if such a condition holds and part of the interest of the analysis is also set on the between-entities variation, and usually this is the case of panel data, an approach encompassing Random Effect (RE) is suitable. It also allows for proper modeling of a nested structure between individuals (e.g., units nested in a city nested in Countries).

Another class of models, i.e. multilevel models, also known as hierarchical linear models, is specifically designed to handle data with clearly defined nested structures, such as repeated observations nested within individuals, or individuals nested within higher-level units (e.g., families, classrooms, or regions) (Snijders & Bosker, 2011). While dealing with longitudinal data, this class of models is particularly useful for clearly and formally decomposing within-unit and between-unit variation, and for modeling random intercepts and slopes (Goldstein, 2011), dealing with specific covariates effects according to groups.

On the other hand, Growth Curve Models (GCM) estimate proper individual trajectories over time, modeling simultaneously the common trend and the variation in growth parameters (e.g., slope, intercept) across units (Bollen & Curran, 2006). Interestingly, those models are often linked to a Structural Equation Model (SEM) approach, dealing with indicators and latent dimensions (Preacher et al., 2018), allowing for a hierarchical structure in the predictors.

Lastly, Longitudinal Linear Mixed Models (LLMM) are an extension of linear mixed models, exhaustively suited to describe repeated measures over time, incorporating both fixed and random effects to account for correlation at two levels: within individuals and heterogeneity across them (Verbeke & Molenberghs, 2000). LLMMs are considered pretty flexible, allowing for time-varying covariates and fixed covariates such as biological sex, irregular measurement intervals, and missing data under Missing at Randoms (MAR) assumptions. Recent applications include longitudinal analyses during the COVID-19 pandemic, for example a Norwegian cohort study of 4936 adults that modeled trajectories of anxiety and depression using linear mixed-effects models with both fixed and random effects (Ebrahimi et al., 2023), and the use of an ad-hoc survey to examine the sustainable effects of chatbot-based formative feedback on learning performance (Yin et al., 2024).

While this review presents quite a few models that are cornerstones in the statistical and econometric literature for longitudinal and panel data, it is necessary to note that for such class of data recent developments open space for hybrid approaches between statistics, machine learning, and data sciences (Babii et al., 2023), and those new methodologies should not be neglected in a longer and comprehensive review. Furthermore, a broad area of statistical approaches embraces the Bayesian framework, both in parametric (Daniels & Pourahmadi, 2002) as well as non-parametric (Quintana et al., 2016) formalization, implementing also extension such as Latent Growth Curve (Zhang et al., 2007). Fundamentally, these approaches utilize the same techniques as described before, but with a Bayesian specification.

2.6 Conclusions

Social research has undergone a profound transformation in recent decades due to the increasing use of longitudinal and panel secondary data. This chapter has explored the epistemological and methodological value of such data, examining their opportunities and challenges, as well as the infrastructural and analytical context that supports their use.

Longitudinal and panel, data allowing for the analysis of individual and collective changes over time, provide valuable tools for understanding life trajectories, the effects of public policies, and long-term social processes. Their methodological strength lies in the ability to disentangle causal relationships, control for unobserved heterogeneity, and capture dynamic processes that would remain invisible in purely cross-sectional designs. By facilitating the observation of within-subject and between-subject variability across multiple waves, these data structures allow researchers to investigate life-course transitions, policy impacts, and social transformations with a level of precision that other data sources cannot offer.

The establishment of solid research infrastructures, particularly at the European level, has acted as a catalyst for the dissemination and improvement of the use of these data, promoting a culture of sharing, interoperability, and methodological quality. In this framework, the evolution of solid RIs, particularly at the European level, supported by entities like ESFRI and driven by principles of Open Science and FAIR data, has acted as a catalyst for the dissemination and improvement of the use of these data, promoting a culture of sharing, interoperability, and methodological quality. They combine the statistical reliability of probability sampling with the operational advantages of online data collection, ensuring both timeliness and cost-effectiveness. Their growing diffusion is not only a response to logistical and financial constraints but also a reflection of a broader epistemological shift toward more agile, scalable, and responsive research tools. Their expansion marks a methodological turning point, particularly within Europe, where they benefit from strong institutional support.

Looking ahead, the future of empirical social research will increasingly depend on the sustained development of these RIs. It will be essential to invest in initiatives that ensure the sustainability and accessibility of data, as well as the adoption of flexible, inclusive, and interdisciplinary methodological approaches. Projects like FOSSR, developed in the Italian context, represent concrete examples of how the convergence of methodological rigor, technological innovation, and data governance, in order to provide high-quality data useful for a better and empirically-based understanding of social changes.

Disclaimer The opinions expressed in this article by Nicolò Marchesini are his own and do not reflect the view of ISTAT.

References

Agnoli, M. S. (2008). *Il disegno della ricerca sociale*. Carocci.

Allison, P. (2005). *Fixed effects regression methods for longitudinal data using SAS*. Cary: SAS Institute.

Amini, S., Delgado, M. S., Henderson, D. J., & Parmeter, C. F. (2012). Fixed vs random: The Hausman test four decades later. In *Essays in honor of Jerry Hausman* (pp. 479–513). Emerald Group Publishing Limited.

Arulampalam, W. (2001). Is unemployment really scarring? Effects of unemployment experiences on wages. *The Economic Journal, 111*(475), F585–F606.

Babii, A., Ball, R. T., Ghysels, E., & Striaukas, J. (2023, Jul). Panel data nowcasting: The case of price-earnings ratios. arXiv preprint.

Bartels, L. M. (2006). Three virtues of panel data for the analysis of campaign effects. In P. E. Sniderman (Ed.), *The logic of comparative social inquiry* (pp. 134–156). Wiley.

Becker, R. (2022). Gender and survey participation: An event history analysis of the gender effects of survey participation in a probability-based multi-wave panel study with a sequential mixed-mode design. *Methods, Data, Analyses, 16*(1), 3–32.

Biolcati-Rinaldi, F., & Vezzoni, C. (2012). *L'analisi secondaria nella ricerca sociale*. Il Mulino.

Blossfeld, H.-P., Klijzing, E., Mills, M., & Kurz, K. (Eds.). (2005). *Globalization, uncertainty and youth in society: The losers in a globalizing world*. Routledge.

Bollen, K. A., & Curran, P. J. (2006). *Latent curve models: A structural equation perspective*. Wiley.

Bukodi, E., & Goldthorpe, J. H. (2013). Decomposing 'social origins': The effects of parents' class, status, and education on the educational attainment of their children. *European Sociological Review*, *29*(5), 1024–1039.

Calderwood, L., & Lessof, C. (2009). Enhancing longitudinal surveys by linking to administrative data. In P. Lynn (Ed.), *Methodology of longitudinal surveys*. Wiley.

Callegaro, M., Lozar Manfreda, K., & Vehovar, V. (2015). *Web survey methodology*. Sage Publications.

Carpenter, H., & Deepchand, K. (2016). *UK household longitudinal study: Immigrant and ethnic minority boost (IEMB) technical report* (Understanding Society Technical Report No. 2017-11). Institute for Social and Economic Research, University of Essex.

Cornesse, C., Blom, A. G., Sohnius, M.-L., González Ocanto, M., Rettig, T., & Ungefucht, M. (2023). Experimental evidence on panel conditioning effects when increasing the surveying frequency in a probability-based online panel. *Survey Research Methods*, *17*(3), 323–339.

Cornesse, C., & Schaurer, I. (2021). The long-term impact of different offline recruitment strategies on participation in a probability-based online panel. *Journal of Survey Statistics and Methodology*, *9*(3), 402–427.

Daly, M., Sutin, A. R., Robinson, E., & Daly, P. J. (2020). Longitudinal changes in mental health during the covid-19 pandemic in the UK. *Nature Communications*, *11*, 5356.

Daniels, M. J., & Pourahmadi, M. (2002). Bayesian analysis of covariance matrices and dynamic models for longitudinal data. *Biometrika*, *89*(3), 553–566.

Das, M., Toepoel, V., & van Soest, A. (2011). Nonparametric tests of panel conditioning and attrition bias in panel surveys. *Sociological Methods & Research*, *40*(1), 52–95.

Deng, Y., Hillygus, D. S., Reiter, J. P., Si, Y., & Zheng, S. (2013). Handling attrition in longitudinal studies: The case for refreshment samples. *Statistical Science*, *28*(2), 238–256.

Diggle, P., Heagerty, P., Liang, K.-Y., & Zeger, S. L. (2002). *Analysis of longitudinal data* (2nd ed.). Oxford University Press.

Duvoisin, A., Refle, J.-E., Burton-Jeangros, C., Consoli, L., Fakhoury, J., & Jackson, Y. (2023). Recruitment and attrition for panel surveys of hard-to-reach populations: Some lessons from a longitudinal study on undocumented migrants. *Field Methods*, *36*(4), 294–310.

Ebrahimi, O. V., Hoffart, A., & Johnson, S. U. (2023). Mechanisms associated with the trajectory of depressive and anxiety symptoms: A linear mixed-effects model during the covid-19 pandemic. *Current Psychology*, *42*(34), 30696–30713.

Engle, R. F., Hendry, D. F., & Richard, J.-F. (1983). Exogeneity. *Econometrica: Journal of the Econometric Society*, *51*, 277–304.

European Commission. (2019). *Research infrastructures make science happen*. Publications Office of the European Union. https://doi.org/10.2777/446084 (Catalogue number KI-03-19-636-EN-N).

European Social Survey ERIC. (2024). *ESS annual activity report 2023–24*. https://www.europeansocialsurvey.org/sites/default/files/2024-12/ESS-annual-activity-report-2023-24.pdf

FAIR-IMPACT. (2025). *Fair-impact use cases & stories: Real-world fair-enabling practices across scientific domains*. European Commission. https://fair-impact.eu/sites/default/files/2025-02/UseCases_Stories_A4_February2025.pdf

Fitzgerald, J., Gottschalk, P., & Moffitt, R. (1998). An analysis of sample attrition in panel data: The Michigan panel study of income dynamics. *Journal of Human Resources*, *33*(2), 251–299.

Fitzmaurice, G. M., Laird, N. M., & Ware, J. H. (2012). *Applied longitudinal analysis*. John Wiley & Sons.

Flatt, C., & Jacobs, R. L. (2019). Principle assumptions of regression analysis: Testing, techniques, and statistical reporting of imperfect data sets. *Advances in Developing Human Resources*, *21*(4), 484–502.

Florio, M., & Sirtori, E. (2016). Social benefits and costs of large scale research infrastructures. *Technological Forecasting and Social Change*, *112*, 65–78.

Goldstein, H. (2011). *Multilevel statistical models* (4th ed.). Wiley.

Groves, R. M., & Couper, M. P. (1998). *Nonresponse in household interview surveys*. Wiley.

Hedges, L. V. (1994). Fixed effects models. *The handbook of research synthesis*, *285*, 299.

Hsiao, C. (2014). *Analysis of panel data* (3rd ed.). Cambridge University Press.

Huber, R., Schäffer, B., Weigel, T., Ludwig, J., Vancauwenberghe, G., & Wubbe, M. (2021). Integrating data and analysis technologies within leading environmental research infrastructures: Challenges and approaches. *Ecological Informatics, 61*, 101245.

Jäckle, A. (2006). *Dependent interviewing: A framework and application to current research* (ISER Working Paper No. 2006-32). University of Essex, Institute for Social and Economic Research.

Johnston, M. P. (2014). Secondary data analysis: A method of which the time has come. *Qualitative and Quantitative Methods in Libraries (QQML), 3*(3), 619–626.

Kalinin, N. A., & Skvortsov, N. A. (2023). Difficulties of fair principles implementation in cross-domain research infrastructures. *Lobachevskii Journal of Mathematics, 44*, 147–156.

King-Shier, K., Lau, A., Fung, S., & LeBlanc, P. (2017). Retention of ethnic participants in longitudinal studies: A systematic review addressing challenges and effective strategies. *Journal of Immigrant and Minority Health, 19*(6), 1530–1541.

Kreuter, F., Müller, G., & Trappmann, M. (2010). Nonresponse and measurement error in employment research: Making use of administrative data. *Public Opinion Quarterly, 74*(5), 880–906.

Little, R. J. A., & Rubin, D. B. (2002). *Statistical analysis with missing data* (2nd ed.). Wiley.

Lugtig, P. (2014). Panel attrition: Separating stayers, fast attriters, gradual attriters, and lurkers. *Sociological Methods & Research, 43*(4), 699–723.

Lynn, P. (2003). Developing quality standards for cross-national survey research: Five approaches. *International Journal of Social Research Methodology, 6*(4), 323–336.

Lynn, P. (2009). *Sample design for understanding society* (Understanding Society Working Paper No. 2009-01). University of Essex.

Lynn, P. (Ed.). (2021). *Advances in longitudinal survey methodology*. John Wiley & Sons.

Malschinger, P., Vogl, S., & Schels, B. (2023). Drop in, drop out, or stay on: Patterns and predictors of panel attrition among young people. *Österreichische Zeitschrift für Soziologie, 48*, 427–450.

McMichael, C., Nunn, C., Gifford, S. M., & Correa-Velez, I. (2014). Studying refugee settlement through longitudinal research: Methodological and ethical insights from the good starts study. *Journal of Refugee Studies, 28*(2), 238–257.

Mitchell, J., Cabrera Álvarez, P., & Lynn, P. (2025, June 19). *Wave 14 boost sample representativeness* (Understanding Society Working Paper Series No. 2025-09). Institute for Social and Economic Research, University of Essex.

Mundlak, Y. (1978). On the pooling of time series and cross section data. *Econometrica: Journal of the Econometric Society, 46*, 69–85.

Neundorf, A. & Smets, K. (2017). Political socialization and the making of citizens. In *The Oxford handbook of political behavior*. Oxford University Press.

Pierce, M., Hope, H., Ford, T., Hatch, S., Hotopf, M., John, A., Kontopantelis, E., Webb, R., Wessely, S., McManus, S., & Abel, K. M. (2020). Mental health before and during the covid-19 pandemic: A longitudinal probability sample survey of the UK population. *The Lancet Psychiatry, 7*(10), 883–892.

Preacher, K. J., Zhang, Z., & Zyphur, M. J. (2018). Multilevel structural equation modeling. In R. H. Hoyle (Ed.), *Handbook of structural equation modeling* (pp. 497–517). Guilford Press.

Press, G. (2016). *Cleaning big data: Most time-consuming, least enjoyable data science task, survey says.* https://www.forbes.com/sites/gilpress/2016/03/23/data-preparation-most-time-consuming-least-enjoyable-data-science-task-survey-says (Forbes)

PSID Staff. (2000). *Information on the PSID immigrant sample addition of 1997/1999* (Technical Series Paper No. 00-04). Survey Research Center, University of Michigan, Panel Study of Income Dynamics.

Quintana, F. A., Johnson, W. O., Waetjen, L. E., & B. Gold, E. (2016). Bayesian nonparametric longitudinal data analysis. *Journal of the American Statistical Association, 111*(515), 1168–1181.

Ruspini, E. (2002). *An introduction to longitudinal research.* Routledge.

Sand, M., Bruch, C., Felderer, B., Schaurer, I., Kolb, J.-P., & Weyandt, K. (2025). Creating design weights for a panel survey with multiple refreshment samples: A general discussion with

an application to a probability-based mixed-mode panel. *Methods, Data, Analyses, 19*, 1–19 (Special issue).
Singer, J. D., & Willett, J. B. (2003). *Applied longitudinal data analysis: Modeling change and event occurrence*. Oxford University Press.
Snijders, T. A. B., & Bosker, R. (2011). *Multilevel analysis: An introduction to basic and advanced multilevel modeling*. Sage.
Teague, S., Youssef, G. J., Macdonald, J. A., Sciberras, E., Shatte, A., Fuller-Tyszkiewicz, M., et al. (2018). Retention strategies in longitudinal cohort studies: A systematic review and meta-analysis. *BMC Medical Research Methodology, 18*, 151.
Tourangeau, R. (2014). Defining hard-to-survey populations. In R. Tourangeau, B. Edwards, T. P. Johnson, K. M. Wolter, & N. Bates (Eds.), *Hard-to-survey populations* (pp. 3–20). Cambridge University Press.
Vartanian, T. P. (2011). *Secondary data analysis*. Oxford University Press.
Verbeke, G., & Molenberghs, G. (2000). *Linear mixed models for longitudinal data*. Springer.
Warren, J. R., & Halpern-Manners, A. (2012). Panel conditioning in longitudinal social science surveys. *Sociological Methods & Research, 41*(4), 491–534.
Watson, N., & Wooden, M. (2009). Identifying factors affecting longitudinal survey response. In P. Lynn (Ed.), *Methodology of longitudinal surveys* (pp. 157–181). Wiley.
Wickham, H. (2014). Tidy data. *Journal of Statistical Software, 59*(10), 1–23.
Wilkinson, S. R., Aloqalaa, M., Belhajjame, K., Crusoe, M. R., de Paula Kinoshita, B., Gadelha, L., Garijo, D., Gustafsson, O. J. R., Juty, N., Kanwal, S., & Khan, F. Z. (2025). Applying the fair principles to computational workflows. *Scientific Data, 12*, 328.
Wooldridge, J. M. (2010). *Econometric analysis of cross section and panel data*. MIT Press.
Yin, J., Goh, T.-T., & Hu, Y. (2024). Using a chatbot to provide formative feedback: A longitudinal study of intrinsic motivation, cognitive load, and learning performance. *IEEE Transactions on Learning Technologies, 17*, 1378–1389. https://doi.org/10.1109/TLT.2024.3364015
Zhang, Z., Hamagami, F., Lijuan Wang, L., Nesselroade, J. R., & Grimm, K. J. (2007). Bayesian analysis of longitudinal data using growth curve models. *International Journal of Behavioral Development, 31*(4), 374–383.

Chapter 3
Open Cloud Platform

Mario Ciampi, Emanuele Damiano, Giovanni Massafra, Pier Giuseppe Meo, and Mario Sicuranza

3.1 Introduction

The methodological frameworks and ethical considerations discussed in the previous chapters lay the groundwork for understanding why longitudinal data infrastructures are essential for social science research. However, the practical realization of these goals requires a technological foundation capable of handling the unique challenges of social science research data and specifically tuned to those.

Social science research presents distinctive infrastructure demands that differ significantly from other scientific domains. Longitudinal studies, by their very nature, generate data over extended periods that must remain accessible and linkable across time. Panel data requires sophisticated data management capabilities that can handle both the volume and the complex relational structures inherent in tracking individuals, households, or communities over years or decades. Moreover, the sensitive nature of much social science data—involving personal information, health records, and socioeconomic details—demands security architectures that can protect privacy while enabling legitimate research access.

As social-science research increasingly relies on large-scale, heterogeneous datasets and advanced analytical tools, a resilient and interoperable computational backbone becomes indispensable. Building directly on the principles laid out in Chap. 1—where the imperatives of Open Science and the role of research infrastructures were established—and on the methodological scaffolding of Chap. 2, which detailed the management of longitudinal and panel data, this chapter presents

M. Ciampi (✉) · E. Damiano · G. Massafra · P. G. Meo · M. Sicuranza
National Research Council of Italy, Institute for High Performance Computing and Networking, Naples, Italy
e-mail: mario.ciampi@icar.cnr.it; emanuele.damiano@icar.cnr.it; giovanni.massafra@icar.cnr.it; piergiuseppe.meo@icar.cnr.it; mario.sicuranza@icar.cnr.it

L. Taddei, M. Paolucci (eds.), *Longitudinal Data Infrastructures in Europe*,
https://doi.org/10.1007/978-3-032-07005-0_3

the FOSSR "Open Cloud Platform" as the technological keystone of the volume's overarching vision.

This chapter addresses and documents the critical question: *"How do we build a technological infrastructure that can support the full lifecycle of longitudinal social science research while adhering to FAIR principles and open science paradigms?"* The FOSSR platform represents an example of a comprehensive answer to this challenge.

Understanding this technological foundation is essential for several reasons. First, it illuminates how abstract principles like FAIR data management translate into concrete technical specifications. Second, it reveals the complexity involved in creating truly interoperable research infrastructures that can serve the diverse needs of the European social science community. Finally, it demonstrates how cloud-based platforms can address the scalability and sustainability challenges that have historically limited the scope and impact of longitudinal social science research.

As we examine the FOSSR platform's architecture, security protocols, and integration capabilities, we will consider how these technical choices enable the research methodologies and ethical frameworks outlined in earlier chapters.

By providing this robust cloud foundation, the chapter bridges conceptual discussions of Open Science with the hands-on capabilities researchers need to **collect, curate, analyze, and share data at scale**. It thus sets the stage for the ethical reflections of Chap. 4—on data governance and privacy—and opens the door to the survey and infrastructure focused case studies in Part II.

3.2 Context and Objectives

In the evolving landscape of social science research, the capacity to work with large-scale, distributed, and longitudinal datasets has become not only a technical requirement, but a strategic enabler of scientific progress. Researchers are increasingly called upon to integrate diverse data sources—ranging from administrative records and surveys to behavioral and geospatial data—into coherent analytical workflows. However, the fragmentation of data repositories, the lack of common access protocols, and the variability in data governance practices present significant barriers to progress. These challenges are further compounded by the ethical and legal obligations associated with handling sensitive information over long time spans and across national jurisdictions.

FOSSR emerges as a response to these multifaceted challenges, with the explicit goal of **enabling a new generation of FAIR-compliant, cloud-native, and interoperable research infrastructures** tailored to the needs of longitudinal social science research. Its design is grounded in three key premises:

- **Decentralized data** must be made accessible through a unified interface, enabling researchers to discover, access, and integrate datasets without needing to know their physical location or institutional context.

Table 3.1 FOSSR platform objectives and solutions

Objective	Technological solution
Consistent Data Access	Single Sign-On (SSO) with institutional credentials; standardized REST API interface.
FAIR Data Management	Integrated framework for metadata standards, data archiving, persistent identifiers, and controlled access mechanisms.
Resilience and Scalability	Federated and distributed cloud architecture across multiple secure data centers with built-in fault tolerance and elastic scaling.
Integration with External Infrastructures	Interoperability via standard protocols (SPARQL, REST API) and connectors to platforms such as CESSDA, RISIS, SAHRE, and Open-IT.

- **Data must be curated and analyzed** within secure, scalable, and ethically sound environments, aligning with both the methodological rigor and the normative expectations of Open Science.
- **Interoperability** is not optional: it is a structural necessity for connecting with existing European infrastructures such as CESSDA (Consortium of European Social Science Data Archives), RISIS (Research Infrastructure for Science and Innovation Policy Studies), SHARE, and Open-IT, ensuring that national efforts are synergistic with continental frameworks.

FOSSR's objectives, therefore, go beyond technical efficiency. They seek to transform the culture and practice of data-driven social science research, fostering an ecosystem in which data is treated as a shared public good, accessible, and reusable under clear and transparent conditions. Table 3.1 shows the main FOSSR platform objectives and solutions.

Through these elements, FOSSR aims to lower the technical barriers to longitudinal research, while raising the standard for data stewardship, access control, and methodological transparency. It positions itself not merely as a service layer, but as a research enabler—**supporting the full data lifecycle** from acquisition and annotation to long-term preservation and collaborative analysis.

By aligning technical solutions with the broader objectives of the European Open Science Cloud (EOSC) and related initiatives, FOSSR contributes to a strategic vision of digitally empowered, ethically grounded, and internationally connected social science research.

3.3 Platform Architecture

The FOSSR platform implements a federated cloud architecture interconnecting multiple high-performance data centers, offering resilience, elasticity, and seamless resource orchestration—an approach echoing federated HPC platforms described in similar open science contexts (Grossman et al., 2016).

Specifically, the FOSSR platform is built on a federated cloud architecture that interconnects a **network of five strategically located data centers** managed by the National Research Council of Italy. This architectural model combines the benefits of local control and autonomy with the systemic resilience and scalability of a distributed infrastructure. The overarching objective is to provide a robust technological foundation that enables **seamless access to services and datasets while ensuring operational continuity, security, and interoperability**.

At the core of the FOSSR platform lies a modular and service-oriented design, which allows the dynamic orchestration of computational and storage resources across geographically dispersed nodes. Each data center contributes computational capacity, persistent storage, and specific service capabilities, while collectively acting as a unified research infrastructure accessible via a centralized web portal and APIs.

A modular, service-oriented design supports dynamic orchestration across geographically distributed nodes, consistent with architectural paradigms in federated cloud infrastructures (Rochwerger et al., 2009).

Key architectural features include the main components described below.

- **Federated Data Center Network**

The infrastructure consists of five interlinked data centers, located in CNR Institutes with domain expertise in data-intensive social science research. Each site is equipped with:

- *Virtualized computing environments* (via OpenStack or Kubernetes-based orchestration).
- *Secure and redundant storage systems* for hosting both structured and unstructured datasets.
- *High-speed connectivity* with redundant network paths to ensure low-latency inter-site communication and data replication.

This federated model provides geographic resilience, load balancing, and resource elasticity. If one data center experiences downtime or increased load, computational tasks and services can be rerouted or replicated to another node in the federation, guaranteeing fault tolerance and service continuity.

- **Cloud-Native Infrastructure Services**

The platform supports a broad range of Infrastructure-as-a-Service (IaaS) capabilities. These include:

- *Virtual Machines and Containers*: users can deploy customizable environments for data processing, simulation, or modeling using Docker and Kubernetes technologies.
- *Persistent and Elastic Storage*: data volumes can scale dynamically according to the needs of specific research workflows, with automatic backup and replication policies.

- *Authentication and Authorization Infrastructure (AAI)*: federated identity management via Single Sign-On enables access with institutional credentials, ensuring a seamless yet secure user experience across national and European contexts.

- **Resilience and Resource Optimization**

To guarantee both operational robustness and efficient resource use, the platform integrates:

- *Dynamic Resource Allocation*: based on workload characteristics and priority levels, resources (CPU, RAM, bandwidth) are automatically allocated and optimized across sites.
- *Monitoring and Alerting Systems*: real-time monitoring of services, infrastructure health, and usage statistics ensures proactive maintenance and adaptive scaling.
- *Disaster Recovery and Data Redundancy*: the platform employs distributed backup strategies and redundant storage clusters to preserve data integrity and enable fast recovery in case of hardware failures.

- **Application Services Layer**

- Beyond core infrastructure services, the FOSSR platform hosts a rich layer of cloud-native application services to support the full data lifecycle.
- *Data Ingestion and Harmonization Pipelines*: tools for collecting, standardizing, and integrating data from multiple sources and formats.
- *Metadata Management and FAIR Compliance Tools*: services for generating, validating, and publishing metadata in line with DDI, DCAT, and other relevant standards.
- *Secure Data Enclaves and Controlled Access Environments*: sandboxed environments for working with sensitive or identifiable data under strict governance constraints.
- *Statistical and Analytical Toolkits*: pre-configured environments with R, Python, Jupyter, and other open-source tools, ready for advanced quantitative and qualitative analysis.

- **FOSSR Marketplace and Web Portal**

The platform includes a dedicated web portal that functions as both a user interface and a discovery tool. Key features include:

- *Marketplace of Services and Datasets*: a catalog of reusable software components, datasets, virtual lab environments, and workflows, accessible via intuitive user dashboards.
- *Federated Search and Data Catalog*: users can browse and query metadata records from multiple distributed repositories using a unified interface powered by SPARQL and REST APIs.

- *Workflow Management Interface*: researchers can compose, execute, and monitor data workflows directly from the portal, fostering reproducibility and collaboration.
- *Role-Based Access Control*: fine-grained access control mechanisms support differentiated user roles (e.g., data providers, analysts, principal investigators), aligned with ethical and legal requirements.

3.3.1 Key Functionalities

The FOSSR platform is designed to support a comprehensive range of functionalities tailored to the specific needs of the social science research community. These functionalities are not only technologically robust, but also strategically aligned with the principles of Open Science, FAIR data stewardship, and secure, ethical data use.

At the core of the platform are two primary interfaces that mediate access to resources and services:

- *Multilingual Web Portal*: a user-friendly, browser-based interface offering centralized access to the platform's services and resources. It is designed for human users, including researchers, data stewards, and institutional administrators, supporting a wide range of roles and research workflows.
- *REST APIs and SPARQL Endpoints*: a machine-actionable layer that allows external applications and infrastructures to query, retrieve, and integrate FOSSR resources in automated workflows. These interfaces are critical for ensuring interoperability, scalability, and alignment with European research infrastructure standards.

The platform integrates a rich set of functionalities that span the entire data lifecycle—from ingestion and curation to analysis and reuse. Table 3.2 provides an overview of key features and their associated benefits.

3.3.2 Integration with Existing Infrastructures

FOSSR does not operate in isolation: its design and implementation explicitly embrace **interoperability and alignment with major European and national research infrastructures**. This strategic integration expands both the availability of high-quality data and the range of analytical and methodological tools accessible to social science researchers. The goal is to enable seamless, standards-based collaboration across institutional and national boundaries, fostering a truly transnational research ecosystem.

The platform leverages open protocols (e.g., REST, SPARQL, and OAuth) and widely adopted metadata standards (such as DDI and DCAT-AP) to ensure that services and datasets hosted within FOSSR are findable, accessible, interoperable,

Table 3.2 FOSSR platform functionalities and benefits

Functionality	Benefit
Resource Marketplace	Facilitates the discovery and reuse of datasets, software tools, workflows, and documentation through a unified, searchable catalog. Supports keyword search with multilingual support.
Support for Virtual Machines and Containers	Enables researchers to instantiate fully customizable analysis environments using pre-configured or user-defined images. Facilitates reproducibility and portability of computational workflows.
REST API Interface	Allows programmatic access to data and services. Ideal for automated ingestion, transformation, and retrieval of large datasets or metadata records across platforms.
SPARQL Endpoint	Enables semantic querying of metadata and structured data using standard vocabularies (e.g., DCAT, DDI). Enhances discoverability and supports complex data integration scenarios.
Role-Based Access Control	Provides differentiated access levels for users based on roles and permissions, ensuring secure access to sensitive datasets and compliance with governance frameworks.
Workflow Execution Engine	Allows researchers to design, schedule, and monitor end-to-end data workflows directly from the platform interface. Supports graphical editors and Jupyter-based execution environments.
Metadata Management Toolkit	Facilitates the authoring, validation, and publication of rich metadata descriptions compliant with FAIR principles. Supports persistent identifiers (DOIs, Handles) and crosswalks with external standards.
Data Upload and Harmonization Services	Provides web-based and API-based services for data upload, format validation, harmonization, and versioning. Ensures consistency and traceability of longitudinal datasets.
Secure Data Enclaves	Offers virtual environments with restricted access for handling sensitive or personally identifiable information (PII), ensuring compliance with GDPR and national data protection laws.
Visualization and Analysis Tools	Integrates with analytical platforms (e.g., RStudio, JupyterLab, KNIME) and supports interactive data visualization, exploratory data analysis, and modeling workflows.
Multilingual Support and Accessibility	Ensures inclusivity through full localization of the user interface and support for non-English data and metadata, with attention to accessibility standards.
User and Project Dashboard	Allows users to manage active projects, access computational usage statistics, monitor job execution, and receive notifications and alerts.

and reusable (FAIR) in a broader European context. Integration efforts focus on both technical interoperability—the ability to exchange data and services across infrastructures—and semantic interoperability—ensuring that the meaning and context of the data are preserved and correctly interpreted.

Three key integration domains are prioritized:

- *Data federation and catalog synchronization*: metadata records from external infrastructures such as CESSDA, RISIS, and SHARE can be harvested, indexed,

Table 3.3 FOSSR platform strategic collaborations

Functionality	Benefit
CESSDA	Access to standardized European social science datasets; metadata harvesting and cross-infrastructure search; alignment with DDI and controlled vocabularies.
RISIS	Exchange of structured data for studies on research, innovation, and socio-economic systems; collaboration on data linking and policy analysis.
SHARE	Integration of harmonized longitudinal microdata on health, aging, and socio-economic status across European populations; support for sensitive data governance.
Open-IT	Interconnection with Italian and European public administration datasets; promotion of open data reuse and transparency.
EOSC Core Services	Alignment with EOSC authentication, monitoring, and interoperability services; compliance with EOSC Rules of Participation.

and made discoverable through the FOSSR marketplace and SPARQL endpoints. Conversely, datasets curated within FOSSR can be registered and shared back with these platforms through persistent identifiers and metadata crosswalks.

- *Workflow portability and service composition*: thanks to the use of containerized environments and standard workflow description languages, users can import analysis workflows developed in other ecosystems (e.g., CESSDA Data Processing Toolbox) and execute them within the FOSSR infrastructure without modification. This enhances reusability and fosters cross-platform collaboration.
- *Authentication and authorization federation*: FOSSR supports federated access via SSO, enabling researchers affiliated with European institutions to access resources using their home institution credentials. This aligns with AAI mechanisms already in use in EOSC and infrastructures like CLARIN and ECRIN, promoting a frictionless user experience.

Through these integration efforts, **FOSSR becomes part of a distributed research infrastructure landscape**, complementing and extending existing services rather than duplicating them. It acts as both a consumer and provider of data and applications within the EOSC architecture.

Table 3.3 summarizes some of the strategic collaborations established or planned by the FOSSR initiative.

3.3.3 FOSSR HPC Data Center Network

A cornerstone of the FOSSR platform is its **high-performance, distributed cloud infrastructure**, designed to support scalable, secure, and efficient services for social science research. This infrastructure is built on a federated network of national data centers equipped with cutting-edge hardware and a flexible, cloud-native software stack. Its primary aim is to provide robust computational and storage resources

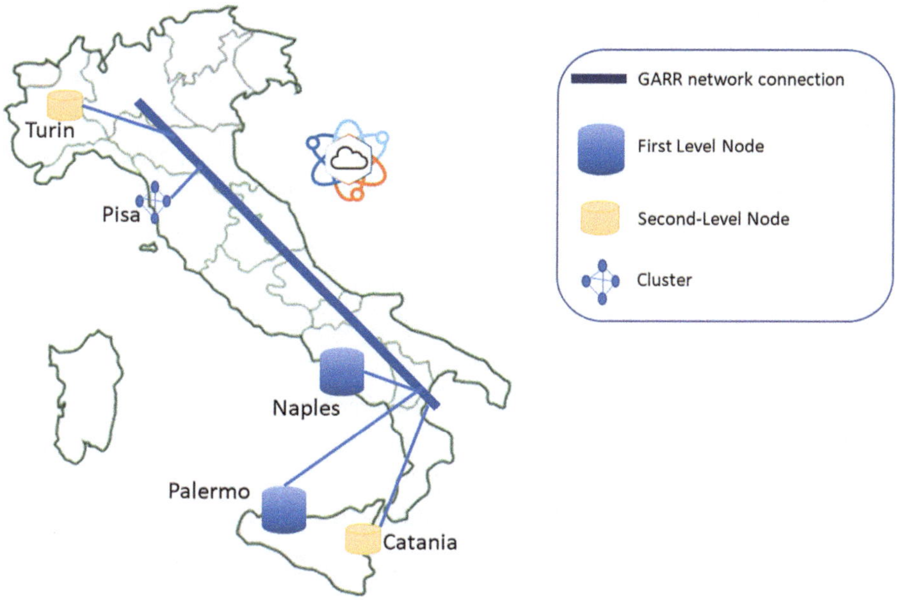

Fig. 3.1 FOSSR network data center

that underpin the advanced services and applications described in previous sections, while ensuring fault tolerance and elastic scalability.

- **Distributed Infrastructure and Hardware Resources**

As shown in Fig. 3.1, the current deployment of the FOSSR infrastructure includes 247 high-performance computing servers, 52 GPU units, and a combined storage capacity of over 8.5 petabytes. These resources are strategically distributed across a network of four operational nodes, with a fifth aimed at hosting a virtual research environment:

- *Two First-Level Nodes (1LNs)*: located at the CNR-ICAR sites in Naples and Palermo, these nodes serve as the backbone of the infrastructure, offering high availability, significant computational throughput, and large-scale storage capabilities.
- *Two Second-Level Nodes (2LNs)*: hosted at CNR-IRCrES in Turin and CNR-ISTC in Catania, these nodes provide additional capacity and geographic redundancy, supporting load balancing and distributed service provisioning.
- A further node is established at CNR-ISTI in Pisa, which is specialized in hosting *Virtual Research Environments* (VREs) and facilitating container-based, on-demand research services.

Table 3.4 Core OpenStack components in FOSSR

Component	Function
NOVA	Management of virtual machines instances.
NEUTRON	Provision of virtual networking services.
GLANCE	Image repository for VM templates and snapshots.
HORIZON	Web-based dashboard for graphical cloud management.
(Optional components)	
HEAT	Infrastructure orchestration (*“infrastructure as code”*).
CEILOMETER	Monitoring and telemetry collection.
SAHARA	Big Data provisioning and Hadoop-based analytics.

This hierarchical structure ensures both geographic resilience and operational flexibility, allowing services to be reallocated dynamically across sites in response to workload, availability, or failure scenarios.

- **Software Architecture and Cloud Enablement**

The FOSSR platform implements a two-tiered software architecture designed to deliver IaaS capabilities. These layers provide a foundation for the deployment, orchestration, and management of virtualized and containerized research services.

- **Infrastructure Layer: OpenStack-Based Cloud Environment**

At the core of the infrastructure layer is OpenStack, the open-source cloud operating system that enables virtualization, resource allocation, and storage management across the federated network. The platform’s OpenStack configuration emphasizes redundancy, high availability, and failover to support mission-critical research applications.

Key OpenStack components are illustrated in Table 3.4.

This layer ensures that infrastructure services are provisioned in a scalable, programmable, and resilient manner, supporting both interactive and batch workloads typical of social science data analysis.

- **Application Layer: Container Orchestration and Microservices**

To address the need for flexible deployment of data services and applications, the application layer integrates a container orchestration environment based on Kubernetes. This enables the FOSSR platform to manage containerized workloads across nodes, facilitating high-density resource use, rapid service deployment, and fine-grained scaling.

Key container management technologies are illustrated in Table 3.5.

This layered approach supports both traditional VMs and lightweight containers, giving researchers the flexibility to choose the optimal execution environment for their workflows.

Table 3.5 Key container management technologies

Technology	Function	Implementation detail
Kubernetes	Orchestration of containerized applications	Cluster architecture with replicated master and worker nodes across multiple availability zones.
Rancher	Kubernetes cluster management platform	Provides intuitive graphical interfaces for cluster management.
Docker	Creation, management, and distribution of containers	Enables containerization of applications and services.

- **Toward a Scalable and Future-Proof Infrastructure**

The current configuration of the FOSSR HPC cloud network is only the first step in a broader vision for a federated, FAIR-aligned research infrastructure. Future development includes:

- Additional nodes for thematic services or regional needs.
- Expansion of GPU resources to support AI-driven analytics.
- Integration of automated provisioning tools and orchestration policies to support hybrid-cloud and edge computing scenarios.

By combining powerful hardware, cloud-native software, and federated governance, the FOSSR HPC infrastructure delivers a resilient backbone for data-driven research in the social sciences—enabling new levels of methodological innovation, computational reproducibility, and collaborative data stewardship by using advanced artificial intelligence-based services (Li et al., 2023).

3.4 FOSSR Security and Services

FOSSR provides the social sciences community with an integrated secure ecosystem of cloud services, accessible through a unified web portal. This ecosystem not only offers advanced computational resources and storage for executing research studies, but also facilitates the discovery, management, and sharing of data, tools, and services, thereby significantly fostering collaboration and Open Science principles.

The encrypted transport, pseudonymization, and federated SSO approach aligns with contemporary frameworks combining security-by-design and privacy-by-default in cloud infrastructures handling sensitive social science data (Rahdari et al., 2025).

3.4.1 Security and Data Protection

Security is a core component of the architectural and operational framework of the FOSSR platform, which includes both the cloud infrastructure and the associated

Table 3.6 Key security principles and implementations

Security aspect	Implementation details
Design Philosophy	Security by Design, Privacy by Design and by Default.
Compliance Standards	GDPR, ISO/IEC 27001/27002:2022, NIST, NIS 2, OWASP.
Data Encryption	TLS 1.3.
Privacy Enhancement	Pseudonymization, Anonymization.
Access Management (IAM)	WSO2 Identity Server, Keystone; RBAC, Least Privilege Principle.
Authentication	Federated access via institutional Identity Providers (SSO).
Monitoring & Detection	Logging system, IDS/ADS, optional SIEM integration.

web portal. The platform adheres to the principles of **Security by Design and Privacy by Design and by Default**, ensuring that protection mechanisms are integrated throughout the system lifecycle. Compliance with the General Data Protection Regulation (GDPR) is rigorously enforced, in conjunction with best practices derived from international standards such as ISO/IEC 27001, ISO/IEC 27002:2022, NIST, NIS 2 Directive, and OWASP.

Data protection is achieved through the application of state-of-the-art cryptographic techniques, including TLS 1.3 for data in transit. Additionally, pseudonymization and anonymization strategies are employed to mitigate re-identification risks. The platform features a robust Identity and Access Management (IAM) system, based on open-source technologies such as WSO2 Identity Server and Keystone, supporting RBAC and the Least Privilege Principle to regulate permissions. Authentication is managed through integration with European institutional Identity Providers, enabling federated access using institutional credentials commonly adopted in the academic and research domains. This federated model enhances both user convenience and access security, while maintaining institutional accountability.

Access control policies are highly configurable and designed to enforce fine-grained restrictions on resource availability. A detailed logging system ensures comprehensive traceability of user and system activities, with audit logs accessible only to authorized personnel. Real-time monitoring supports the identification of anomalous behaviors or potential security threats, with optional integration into Security Information and Event Management (SIEM) platforms for advanced analysis and incident response. Key security principles and implementations are described in Table 3.6.

To ensure data resilience, the platform distinguishes between critical and non-critical data replication strategies. Synchronous replication is adopted for user-generated content, such as interview data, ensuring strong consistency across distributed storage nodes, albeit with increased latency. In contrast, asynchronous replication is applied to less critical services such as data processing workflows, achieving reduced latency with eventual consistency.

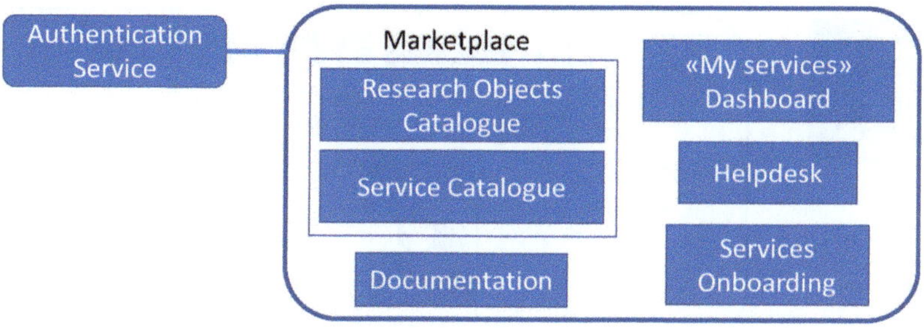

Fig. 3.2 FOSSR web portal components

Energy efficiency and sustainability are also central to the platform's design. Computational resources are dynamically provisioned based on current demand, with energy-aware scheduling policies that deactivate non-essential components during periods of low activity. This contributes to minimizing the platform's environmental impact while preserving system performance in compliance to the Do No Significant Harm (DNSH) principle.

The FOSSR web portal, as the main access point to the infrastructure, is built following modern cybersecurity standards. It incorporates TLS-based encryption, implements secure development practices, and is hardened against common web vulnerabilities. The integrated security model thus ensures that the FOSSR platform provides a secure, compliant, and sustainable environment for digital research infrastructures in the social sciences.

3.4.2 Web Portal and Marketplace

The FOSSR project aims to enhance research in the social sciences through the creation of a unified web portal and a robust distributed cloud infrastructure. The FOSSR portal, whose main components are shown in Fig. 3.2, serves as the unified interface for accessing, managing, and sharing scientific resources and advanced services. It acts as a **single point of access to the services** offered by the cloud platform, supporting researchers and professionals within the scope of Open Science. It is designed with a user-oriented front-office architecture.

The multi-language web portal (supporting at least Italian and English) serves as the exclusive entry point to the FOSSR cloud platform. As mentioned, it features a SSO authentication system, allowing users to leverage credentials provided by their home institutions (research organizations and/or Universities).

It allows dynamic management of the front-end and the marketplace through a Content Management System (CMS), enabling easy insertion or removal of content.

The back-end implements flexible interfaces based on OpenAPI to facilitate the addition or removal of services and functionalities.

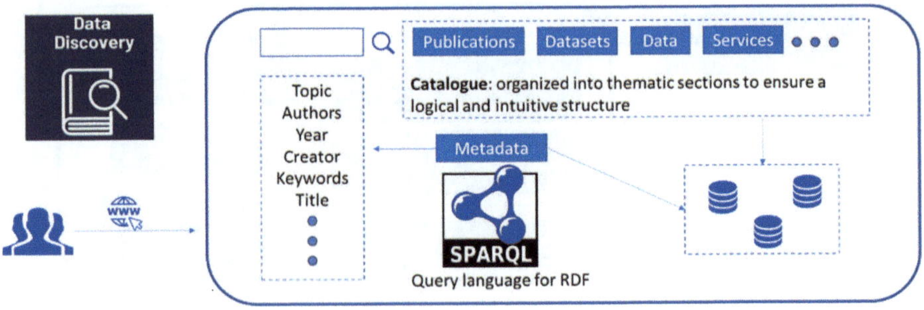

Fig. 3.3 FOSSR marketplace components

Through this intuitive portal, users are empowered to:

- *Request* the provisioning of computational resources (computing capacity via VMs and containers) and storage space.
- *Manage* (upload, add, remove) their own applications and services, allocating them to virtual machines and containers made available by system administrators.
- Ingest new data and datasets into the platform.

The marketplace integrated within the web portal represents the operational core of the portal, centralizing access, discovery, and utilization of digital resources allowing:

- *FOSSR Resource Catalogue*: the centralized infrastructure for the aggregation, cataloguing, and dissemination of digital scientific resources, based on a Data Model that defines entities and relationships (Provider, Resource, Service, Dataset, Research Product, Data Source, Catalogue).
- *Resource Integration*: integrates both FOSSR cloud services (storage, computing, data analysis) and external resources.

The main components of the FOSSR marketplace are shown in Fig. 3.3.

The functionalities embedded within the marketplace are summarized in Table 3.7.

- **Types of Resources Available**
  - *Data*: public and protected datasets, scientific data from various sources, with available metadata and details.
  - *Tools and Services*: tools and services related to the social sciences, both internal and external.
  - *Scientific Publications*: research, articles, technical documents accessible through the platform.
  - *Reports and Exports*: statistics and analyses generated by FOSSR tools.

Table 3.7 FOSSR marketplace key features

Feature	Description
Advanced Resource Search	Comprehensive search capabilities for data (by keyword, topic, data type) and tools/services (internal or external).
Virtual Research Environments (VREs)	Access to virtual workspaces facilitating collaboration and resource sharing among scientific community members.
Metadata Exploration	Detailed metadata exploration for each listed resource, enhancing discoverability and usability.
Interoperability	Seamless search functionality extending beyond FOSSR to integrated European research infrastructures (e.g., CESSDA, RISIS, SHARE).
Data Quality Feedback	Mechanism for users to provide feedback on data quality, promoting continuous improvement.
Research Data Documentation	Tools and guidelines for documenting scientific research data, fostering FAIR principles.
Service Documentation	Access to comprehensive documentation detailing all services offered by FOSSR.
User Support Access	Direct access to user support services.
Platform Monitoring	Visualization of server status and resource utilization statistics.

- **Search**
  - *Advanced Search*: support for full-text search and advanced filters on data and metadata. Filters based on keywords, topic, publication date, resource type, category, accessibility, research methods.
  - *Federated Search*: the marketplace is capable of conducting searches both within the FOSSR infrastructure and externally, connecting to other research infrastructures such as CESSDA, RISIS, and SHARE. Utilization of a meta-search engine to forward queries to external infrastructures and aggregate the results in a single unified view. Federated search results are clearly labeled with the source.
  - *MDC Integration*: integration with a Media Data Center (MDC) that provides a customizable search engine to generate API-accessible feeds of metadata, content, and data.
- **Data Access**
  - SPARQL is a W3C standard query language designed specifically for querying data represented in the Resource Description Framework (RDF). RDF is a graph-based data model that excels at representing interconnected data from diverse sources. This makes SPARQL a powerful tool for tackling the data silo problem. The system allows querying of data and metadata through an interface based on the SPARQL language. This enables accessibility (via HTTP/s), interoperability (machine-to-machine), and data reuse, in line with the FAIR principles.

- Sharing through API: the platform implements RESTful APIs for sharing social science data based on the FAIR interoperability principles and outlines the following best practices:

  REST Architecture: APIs are designed following the RESTful architecture, a software development paradigm that enables the creation of flexible and scalable application interfaces.

  Data and Metadata: data and metadata are consistently represented to enhance their interoperability.

3.4.3 Data Curation

The **implementation of comprehensive and well-structured metadata schemas** plays a central role in ensuring that each resource—whether datasets, services, or tools—is described in accordance with established standards within the social sciences domain. These schemas are designed to promote semantic accuracy, interoperability, and long-term reusability of research outputs. Alignment with internationally recognized conceptual models, as well as full compatibility with FAIR principles, ensures that data and services can be effectively integrated into broader research ecosystems.

In order to facilitate interoperability with external infrastructures and repositories, the system supports the export of standardized metadata in machine-readable formats. This enables seamless integration with European and global platforms such as OpenAIRE and Zenodo, thereby increasing the visibility and impact of research data. The provision of rich, well-documented metadata allows users—both human and machine—to assess the relevance, quality, and potential utility of resources with precision and confidence.

Specific and advanced **data curation techniques** are applied throughout the data lifecycle to guarantee the creation and maintenance of high-quality, FAIR-compliant datasets. These include the adoption of best practice frameworks for metadata enrichment and enhancement, with the objective of improving data discoverability, consistency, and contextualization across diverse disciplinary domains.

Among the key services provided is the implementation of structured workflows for the identification and resolution of licensing issues related to data reuse. This includes the evaluation of legal, ethical, and institutional constraints, ensuring that data can be shared and reused under clear, transparent conditions. Where necessary, licensing recommendations or standardized licenses (e.g., Creative Commons) are proposed to facilitate responsible openness.

Dedicated procedures for the anonymization of sensitive data are also in place, particularly in the context of research conducted in the social sciences and humanities. These procedures follow established methodological and legal guidelines to ensure compliance with data protection regulations (such as GDPR), while preserving the analytical value of the datasets.

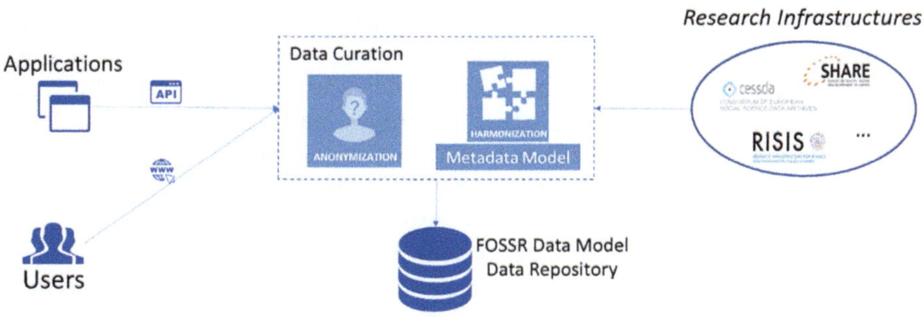

Fig. 3.4 Data curation process

Furthermore, specific techniques support the harmonization of data derived from repeated or longitudinal studies, enabling comparability over time and across research settings. This harmonization process involves both technical and semantic alignment of variables, terminologies, and data structures, thus fostering robust integrative analyses.

To enhance user engagement and support knowledge discovery, the system includes tools for the exploration of data at varying levels of granularity. These tools allow users to navigate datasets from general overviews to detailed variables, and to identify semantically or thematically related datasets, facilitating cross-study comparisons and integrative research perspectives.

Collectively, these services contribute to the establishment of a robust, scalable, and sustainable environment for the management, sharing, and reuse of research data. They support the implementation of open science policies at national and European levels, promote transparency and reproducibility, and enhance the social and scientific value of publicly funded research.

Data curation techniques are applied before and after that data are stored into the FOSSR data repository, as shown in Fig. 3.4.

Metadata enrichment, persistent identifiers, SPARQL endpoints, and export mechanisms underline the platform's alignment with the CloudFAIR architecture, which demonstrates performance gains and scalable reproducibility in open science repositories (Umbach, 2024).

Data harmonization pipelines and machinereadable metadata in distributed contexts draw on principles from data federation surveys emphasizing interoperability, schema alignment, and quality constraints (Hogan et al., 2021).

3.4.4 Application and Integration Services

The platform integrates sophisticated services for container management and orchestration, utilizing technologies such as Kubernetes and Rancher. These services are essential for the **efficient deployment of applications and microservices**. To further enhance the resilience and scalability of containerized applications, the architecture anticipates the utilization of a Service Mesh (e.g., Istio). IAM is based on open-source solutions such as WSO2, ensuring secure and granular control over user permissions. Programmatic consumption of resources and services is facilitated by the exposure of the APIs conforming to OpenAPI specifications.

API management is implemented to create, govern, and distribute the APIs, controlling access and applying security policies.

Users are able to add their own application services by allocating them to VMs and containers. Autonomous management of created resources is assured, with the possibility of making changes to configurations, starting, or stopping resources, and, when appropriate, removing resources that are no longer needed to ensure efficient use of the infrastructure. In closing, the Open Cloud Platform described in this chapter much more than simple processing and storage capabilities: it provides openness, interoperability, and resilience. By leveraging federated identity and SSO, researchers gain frictionless entry to a rich ecosystem of data and tools for social sciences. The platform's adherence to FAIR metadata standards and its modular, container-based services ensure that workflows can be shared, reproduced, and extended long after a project's initial planning.

3.5 Conclusion

For the broader social science community, understanding these technical foundations is crucial for several reasons. It enables more informed decisions about data collection and management strategies, facilitates better collaboration with technical teams, and supports more effective advocacy for the infrastructure investments necessary to sustain longitudinal research programs. Moreover, as artificial intelligence and computational social science methods become increasingly central to the field, researchers who understand their infrastructure will be better positioned to leverage these emerging capabilities responsibly and effectively.

Practically speaking, social scientists can harness the platform to:

- rapidly prototype analyses in reproducible environments (e.g., spun up JupyterLab or RStudio instances);
- integrate new data sources via REST or SPARQL APIs without reinventing ingestion pipelines;
- discover and compose community developed applications through the built in service marketplace.

In more detail, for research infrastructure managers, the distributed architecture and fault-tolerance mechanisms provide a blueprint for building resilient systems that can support decades-long longitudinal studies without single points of failure.

The multi-site approach ensures that valuable panel data remains accessible even as institutional priorities shift or funding cycles change.

For data stewards and archivists, the platform's FAIR-compliant metadata schemas, SPARQL endpoints, and RESTful APIs offer concrete tools for making social science data truly findable and reusable. The integration with established infrastructures like CESSDA, RISIS, and SHARE demonstrates how technical interoperability can break down the silos that have traditionally isolated valuable datasets from broader research communities.

Principal investigators and research teams benefit from the platform's Virtual Research Environments and containerized analysis tools, which lower the technical barriers to conducting sophisticated longitudinal analyses. The single sign-on authentication and federated access mean that researchers can focus on their substantive questions rather than navigating complex access procedures across multiple institutions.

Moreover, by situating this infrastructure within larger European research networks, the chapter lays out a clear pathway for cross border collaboration and data sharing that will be explored in depth in Chap. 4's discussion of governance and privacy. In short, the Open Cloud Platform is both the technological bedrock and the launchpad for all downstream analytical, methodological, and ethical work presented in the rest of this book.

References

Grossman, R. L., Heath, A. P., Murphy, M., Patterson, M., & Wells, W. (2016). A case for data commons: Toward data science as a service. *Computing in Science & Engineering, 18*(5), 10–20.

Hogan, A., Blomqvist, E., Cochez, M., de Melo, G., Gutierrez, C., Kirrane, S., Gayo, L., Emilio, J., Navigli, R., Neumaier, S., Ngomo, A. C., Polleres, A., Rashid, S. M., Rula, A., Schmelzeisen, L., Sequeda, J., Staab, S., Zimmermann, A., & d'Amato, C. (2021). Knowledge graphs. *ACM Computing Surveys, 54*(1), 1–37.

Li, Y., Hwang, K., Shuai, K., Li, Z., & Zomaya, A. (2023). Federated clouds for efficient multitasking in distributed artificial intelligence applications. *IEEE Transactions on Cloud Computing, 11*(2), 2084–2095.

Rahdari, A., Keshavarz, E., Nowroozi, E., Taheri, R., Hajizadeh, M., & Mohammadi, M. (2025). A survey on privacy and security in distributed cloud computing: Exploring federated learning and beyond. *IEEE Open Journal of the Communications Society, 6*, 3710–3744.

Rochwerger, B., Breitgand, D., Levy, E., Galis, A., Nagin, K., Llorente, I. M., Montero, R., Wolfsthal, Y., Elmroth, E., Caceres, J., Ben-Yehuda, M., Emmerich, W., & Galan, F. (2009). The RESERVOIR model and architecture for open federated cloud computing. *IBM Journal of Research and Development, 53*(4), 1–11.

Umbach, G. (2024). Open Science and the impact of Open Access, Open Data, and FAIR publishing principles on data-driven academic research: Towards ever more transparent, accessible, and reproducible academic output? *Statistical Journal of the IAOS, Lecture Notes in Computer Science, 40*(1).

Chapter 4
Ethical Implications in Building Longitudinal Data Infrastructures

Loredana Cerbara, Dario Germani, and Michele Santurro

4.1 Introduction

The transition to open science has been increasingly recognized as a transformative movement in the research landscape. It goes beyond merely providing open access to publications and data, promoting instead new norms of collaboration, inclusivity, and public accountability. The promise of open science lies in its ability to democratize knowledge production, enhance reproducibility, and enhance public engagement with science (Fecher & Friesike, 2014; Haven et al., 2022).

As open science initiatives expand in scale and complexity, they raise important ethical questions. How can openness be balanced with privacy protection? What are the implications of making basic personal data more widely accessible? How can transparency coexist with the need for confidentiality, particularly when working with vulnerable populations? What safeguards are needed to mitigate risks associated with personal data processing? These questions highlight the necessity of embedding ethics at the core of open science practices right from the design stage.

Rather than treating ethics as a checklist of requirements, contemporary approaches advocate for an embedded ethics model that integrates ethical reflection into all stages of the research process (Iphofen, 2017). This framework shapes study design, consent procedures, data sharing strategies, and infrastructure development, ensuring legal compliance alongside genuine respect for participants' autonomy and dignity. In open social science research, this means embedding respect for autonomy, privacy, and fairness throughout the research lifecycle, from design to data dissemination (European Commission, 2023). Key components include transparent consent, strong data protection, and inclusive communication tailored to diverse populations (Sieber, 2012).

L. Cerbara (✉) · D. Germani · M. Santurro
Institute for Research on Population and Social Policies (CNR-IRPPS), Rome, Italy
e-mail: loredana.cerbara@cnr.it; dario.germani@cnr.it; michele.santurro@cnr.it

L. Taddei, M. Paolucci (eds.), *Longitudinal Data Infrastructures in Europe*,
https://doi.org/10.1007/978-3-032-07005-0_4

In this chapter, these overarching ethical challenges are addressed through a comparative analysis of prominent European longitudinal studies—namely, the LISS Panel (Netherlands), the UK Household Longitudinal Study (UKHLS), and the German Socio-Economic Panel (SOEP). These cases offer concrete illustrations of how data protection, informed consent, and trust-building mechanisms are implemented in practice, in accordance with the General Data Protection Regulation (GDPR) and broader ethical standards. The discussion then turns to the Italian experience of the FOSSR project (Fostering Open Science in Social Science Research), which illustrates how open science principles can be embedded in the development of new research infrastructures. Special attention is given to four longitudinal surveys developed within FOSSR—GUIDE, GGS-II, SHARE, and IOPP—each characterized by a specific thematic and demographic focus. The chapter outlines the tools and materials adopted to ensure legal compliance, ethical accountability, and transparent communication across these initiatives. Together, these experiences underscore the importance of designing longitudinal data infrastructures that are not only technically sound and legally compliant, but also ethically proactive and socially responsive.

4.2 Implementing Ethics and Privacy Standards: The Cases of LISS, UKHLS, and SOEP

The ethical and privacy management of longitudinal survey data in Europe requires robust frameworks that protect participant confidentiality while enabling meaningful social science research. A primary challenge is safeguarding sensitive personal information, including health data, against disclosure risks. Over recent decades, considerable attention has been devoted to statistical disclosure limitation techniques, which reduce the possibility that individuals can be re-identified from anonymized datasets (e.g., Lambert, 1993; Fuller, 1993; Jabine, 1993; Rubin, 1993; Fienberg & Willenborg, 1998; Doyle et al., 2001). This concern is especially relevant in longitudinal studies, where repeated measurements may create unique patterns facilitating re-identification. As Couper et al. (2008) highlight, participants' willingness to engage in surveys depends not only on technical and legal protections but also on their perceptions of privacy risks and confidentiality. This highlights the importance of transparent communication and trust-building in ethical and privacy-friendly survey design.

Statistical disclosure risk refers to the potential for linking anonymized records to external databases with overlapping attributes containing identifiable information, thus compromising confidentiality even without direct identifiers like names or addresses. Documented re-identification cases (Winkler, 1997; Malin & Sweeney, 2000) demonstrate the need for ongoing vigilance. However, empirical evidence quantifying disclosure risks in public-use datasets remains limited.

Beyond technical safeguards, ethical frameworks in European longitudinal surveys must also address participants' perceptions and concerns about privacy and confidentiality, as these significantly affect willingness to participate and sustain panel integrity over time. However, evidence from large-scale U.S. surveys such as the decennial censuses of 1980, 1990, and 2000 suggests that increased privacy concerns correlate with substantial reductions in response rates, with up to a 23-percentage point drop during the 1990 census depending on respondents expressed concerns (Singer et al., 1993, 2003; Hillygus et al., 2006). Comparable data are needed to fully understand the impact of privacy concerns on European longitudinal studies. Nonetheless, these findings underscore the importance of not only implementing technical protections but also effectively communicating these safeguards to participants to build trust and encourage engagement.

Although similar data are scarce for European surveys, these insights highlight the need for clear communication and transparency alongside robust data protection. In this context, the LISS Panel (Netherlands), the UK Household Longitudinal Study (UKHLS), and Germany's Socio-Economic Panel (SOEP) stand out as key examples of longitudinal studies that successfully combine technical, ethical, and communicative measures to safeguard participant privacy and foster engagement.

The LISS panel, administered by Centerdata and originally established in collaboration with the Netherlands Institute for Social Research (SCP), exemplifies a comprehensive privacy and ethical framework that integrates advanced data protection strategies with transparent governance practices. It employs stringent anonymization procedures, including the suppression, recoding, and generalization of potentially identifying variables, in line with the principles of data minimization and privacy by design. Participation is based on multi-stage informed consent protocols that clearly delineate the scope, purpose, and duration of data collection, as well as participants' rights regarding access, rectification, and erasure of their information, as required under the General Data Protection Regulation (GDPR). Access to sensitive microdata is regulated through a tiered dissemination model: researchers must submit formal applications, sign a legally binding Statement for the Use of Data, and complete a training program before obtaining authorization. These procedures are supported by a secure computing environment and the oversight of dedicated Information Security and Privacy Officers. Furthermore, confidentiality and technical transparency is ensured through the regular publication of documentation, including metadata, privacy impact assessments, and preservation policies. The panel's ethical commitments are also codified in an internal protocol, which includes review of survey instruments prior to fieldwork and ongoing assessment of compliance with national and EU-level legal frameworks (Scherpenzeel, 2018; Centerdata, 2023a, 2023b).

Similarly, the UK Household Longitudinal Study (UKHLS), also known as Understanding Society, operates under rigorous ethical and data governance standards established by the University of Essex in partnership with the Economic and Social Research Council (ESRC). The study employs comprehensive data protection mechanisms, including pseudonymization techniques that replace direct identifiers with codes to protect participant anonymity while maintaining data utility for research purposes. Access to individual data is tightly controlled through the UK Data Service's secure infrastructure, which implements a tiered access model requiring researchers to apply formally, agree to strict data usage conditions, and undergo security training prior to data release (University of Essex, n.d.). Informed consent is obtained through transparent communication protocols that inform participants about the purpose and scope of data collection, their rights to access, rectify, or request deletion of personal data, and the option to withdraw consent at any stage without consequences. This consent framework aligns with the principles set forth by the European General Data Protection Regulation (GDPR) and is supported by independent ethics oversight. The UKHLS also provides detailed documentation and privacy notices to both participants and researchers, fostering transparency and enhancing trust in its data handling processes.

The final case considered is Germany's Socio-Economic Panel (SOEP), coordinated by the German Institute for Economic Research (DIW Berlin), which exemplifies a data governance model aligned with both national legislation and the European General Data Protection Regulation (GDPR). SOEP implements a rigorous data protection strategy that includes a legally binding data distribution contract to regulate microdata access and ensure compliance with legal and ethical standards. Upon approval, researchers can download encrypted datasets via secure links, a process reinforced by multi-factor authentication, including SMS-based password delivery. To safeguard personal information, SOEP adopts a tiered access model: anonymous datasets are publicly available, while detailed or regionally disaggregated data (e.g., geocodes) are accessible only through secure environments, either on-site at the SOEP Research Data Center or remotely via SOEPremote, following submission of a data protection concept approved by DIW Berlin's Data Protection Officer. Informed consent procedures are fully embedded within the longitudinal design, with clear communication to participants regarding how their data will be shared, linked, and protected. Record linkage to administrative sources (e.g., pension data) is subject to explicit consent, reinforcing ethical autonomy (DIW Berlin, 2025a, 2025b). Encryption practices, secure download protocols, and periodic reassessment of disclosure risks, particularly for geographically specific or linked datasets, underscore SOEP's adherence to privacy-by-design principles and a continuous risk management approach (Goebel et al., 2019).

All three panels symbolize adherence to the General Data Protection Regulation (GDPR), which has introduced explicit legal requirements that directly shape data collection, processing, and storage practices in longitudinal surveys. Among its core principles, data minimization mandates that researchers collect only the information strictly necessary for the stated research purposes, avoiding the accumulation of superfluous or intrusive data. Purpose limitation requires that data be used solely for the specific, explicitly stated objectives for which consent has been obtained, preventing repurposing without renewed consent. Additionally, the GDPR strengthens participant rights, ensuring that individuals can access the data collected about them, rectify inaccuracies, and request erasure (the "right to be forgotten") under certain conditions.

For longitudinal surveys, these provisions have profound operational implications. Consent procedures must be granular and specific, often requiring modular or layered formats to allow participants to make informed choices about different aspects of data use. Surveys must implement privacy-by-design approaches, embedding data protection measures (such as pseudonymization and secure storage) from the earliest stages of study planning. Moreover, data protection impact assessments (DPIAs) are required for studies that involve systematic, large-scale tracking of individuals over time, such as household panels, making ethical and legal review processes more central and continuous than before.

These regulatory standards have catalyzed a broader shift toward enhanced data governance protocols, which include not only technical safeguards but also clear documentation, transparent data-sharing agreements, and the establishment of formal oversight structures (e.g., ethics committees or data protection officers). Collectively, these practices ensure that participant autonomy, confidentiality, and informed consent are not simply ethical ideals but legally enforceable elements at the core of longitudinal research infrastructures (European Union, 2016).

4.3 Best Practices in FOSSR

It is within this broader reflection on the ethical foundations of open science that the FOSSR project—Fostering Open Science in Social Science Research—finds its relevance and operational scope. Funded under Italy's National Recovery and Resilience Plan (PNRR)—NextGenerationEU, the infrastructure offers the scientific community a comprehensive suite of certified resources, including tools, datasets, and services, to support excellence in social science research. A central component of the project is the development of an Open Science Cloud, designed to serve as a point of access and mediation between data producers and users. This Cloud will also provide access to data and a wide range of methodological resources for data collection and analysis, tailored to the needs of both the scientific community and relevant stakeholders. By bringing together data archives from across Europe, FOSSR enhances the visibility, accessibility, and interoperability of social science data, fostering national and international collaboration and promoting the advancement of knowledge in the field.

Within this project, a team with more than eight researchers and technology experts, under the label "Improving longitudinal and panel data infrastructures in Italy", is responsible for establishing strategic connections between FOSSR and the leading European research infrastructures in the social sciences. This collaboration, which includes partnerships with several Italian Universities, facilitates the integration of large-scale panel surveys and supports the collection of high-quality longitudinal data on the Italian resident population. This integration enables the collection, through panel surveys managed by the respective research infrastructures, of high-quality longitudinal data on the resident population in Italy. These data provide a comprehensive view of the life course of the population across a broad spectrum of topics:

- Growing Up in Digital Europe (GUIDE), Europe's first comparative birth cohort study of children's and young people's wellbeing. The aim of the GUIDE study is to track children's personal wellbeing and psychosocial development, in combination with key indicators of children's homes, neighbourhoods, and schools, across Europe. In Italy, the pilot phase is currently underway, coordinated by the National Research Council (CNR) and University of Bologna. At the European level, the survey is led by University College Dublin (UCD) and Manchester Metropolitan University (MMU). Particular attention is paid to safeguarding minors, requiring enhanced ethical scrutiny and age-appropriate consent mechanisms.
- Generations and Gender Survey—Round II (GGS-II), coordinated by the Gender & Generations Programme (GGP), focuses on family trajectories, gender relations, and reproductive behavior among individuals aged 18–79. The survey explores intergenerational and gender dynamics as expressed through care arrangements and the organization of both paid and unpaid work. These features substantially enrich the knowledge base for social science and policy-making in Europe and other high-income countries. Ethical challenges in this context involve safeguarding privacy when reporting sensitive life events and ensuring confidentiality in the longitudinal tracking of intimate life-course decisions. In Italy, the National Research Council (CNR) is currently preparing the second round of GGS in collaboration with Bocconi University.
- Survey of Health, Ageing and Retirement in Europe (SHARE-ERIC), which collects data on the population aged 50 and above across multiple European countries. The international SHARE-ERIC infrastructure is centrally coordinated by the SHARE Berlin Institute. Currently, the University of Padua serves as the national coordinator for the project "Survey of Health, Ageing and Retirement in Europe" (SHARE) in Italy, in collaboration with the National Research Council (CNR). SHARE is a reference for GDPR-compliant informed consent procedures, especially in contexts involving cognitive decline, health data, and cross-country harmonization of ethical approvals.
- Italian Online Probability Panel (IOPP), the first national probability-based online panel in Italy designed by CNR-IRPPS in collaboration with the University of Milan, covering the resident population aged 18–74. IOPP aims to integrate cutting-edge data protection standards and to serve as a model for responsible digital data collection, balancing inclusiveness, autonomy, and secure access.

All four strands have been developed in accordance with the ethical and scientific standards outlined in the CNR's Guidelines for Research Integrity (2019). These guidelines articulate fundamental principles such as intellectual honesty, transparency, scientific diligence, and accountability toward society. They emphasise the responsibility of researchers not only to uphold rigorous scientific standards, but also to protect the dignity, rights, and privacy of individuals and groups involved in research activities. The document specifically calls for clarity in the communication of research objectives, explicit and revocable informed consent procedures, and a proactive commitment to the protection of personal data in line with European legal frameworks. Moreover, it stresses the importance of appropriate supervision mechanisms and the identification of potential conflicts of interest, as well as the need to ensure that research outputs contribute meaningfully to the public interest.

While each survey targets a specific age group and thematic focus, all four surveys share a common commitment to ethical integrity. For each of them, general and line-specific materials have been prepared to address ethical and legal obligations under the GDPR (EU Regulation 2016/679) and to support informed, transparent communication with participants. These materials include:

1. privacy notice, developed in compliance with Article 13 of the GDPR, which clearly outlines the purpose and legal basis of data processing, data retention periods, contact points, participants' rights, as well as information on the data controller and the entities responsible for the implementation of the survey. This material also includes a comprehensive overview of the questionnaire's main sections to ensure that respondents are fully informed about the nature of the questions posed in each part of the survey;
2. invitation letters, written in accessible language to ensure comprehensibility across the general population, explaining the objectives of the survey, the voluntary nature of participation, and the safeguards in place to ensure data confidentiality;
3. informed consent forms, through which participants confirm that they have read the privacy notice and provide their consent to the processing of their personal data, thereby formally agreeing to take part in the survey.

The harmonized but differentiated approach adopted within WP4 reflects FOSSR's commitment to maintaining high ethical standards across a variety of research designs and target populations. Rather than applying a uniform model, the infrastructure promotes responsible practices that are both population-sensitive and legally robust.

4.4 Conclusions

As a first logical conclusion, we must stress the importance of integrating ethical and privacy considerations at the core of longitudinal data infrastructures, with a particular focus on probabilistic panels. Looking at the cases of LISS, UKHLS and SOEP, as well as the FOSSR initiative in Italy, it is clear that ethical frameworks are not static checklists, but dynamic processes that require continuous adaptation and vigilance. Central to this goal is the establishment of transparent consent procedures, robust data protection measures and clear communication strategies aimed at maintaining participant trust and safeguarding research autonomy.

At the same time, the evolution of open science and the growing reliance on longitudinal data infrastructures invite us to look to the future. The integration of advanced data linkages, increased data granularity and real-time updates, while offering unprecedented research opportunities, also raise complex ethical and privacy issues. In particular, the possibility of re-identification through the combination of multiple data sources poses significant challenges for privacy protection (Fienberg & Willenborg, 1998). The tension between data openness and individual privacy will require renewed efforts to strengthen privacy-preserving methodologies, such as differential privacy techniques and advanced anonymization frameworks (Narayanan & Felten, 2014).

Furthermore, future developments call for a more participatory approach in longitudinal survey design, emphasizing co-responsibility and active involvement of participants in data use decisions. Ethical guidelines will need to constantly evolve to address emerging issues such as algorithmic bias and the potential impact of longitudinal tracking on individuals (European Commission, 2023).

Within this perspective, promoting a culture of ethics and integrity becomes a collective commitment that transcends legal compliance, with the aim of protecting the social value of research and sustaining public trust. Longitudinal data infrastructures, especially those based on probabilistic panels, will therefore serve as a crucial testbed for balancing the ideals of open science with the imperative of respecting privacy and individual rights. Future research should continue to explore innovative governance models and technical safeguards that can support this delicate balance.

References

Centerdata. (2023a). *Privacy statement – LISS panel*. https://www.lissdata.nl/privacy.

Centerdata. (2023b). *Ethics – LISS panel*. https://www.lissdata.nl/about-panel/ethics.

Consiglio Nazionale delle Ricerche, Commissione per l'Etica e l'Integrità nella Ricerca. (2019). *Linee guida per l'integrità nella ricerca (Revisione dell'11 aprile 2019, Prot. n. 0067798/2019)*.

Couper, M. P., Singer, E., Conrad, F. G., & Groves, R. M. (2008). Risk of disclosure, perceptions of risk, and concerns about privacy and confidentiality as factors in survey participation. *Journal of Official Statistics, 24*(2), 255–275.

DIW Berlin. (2025a). *Data access – Conditions for downloading SOEP microdata*. https://www.diw.de/en/diw_01.c.601584.en/data_access.html.

DIW Berlin. (2025b). *SOEP Research Data Center – Access to sensitive & regional data*. https://www.diw.de/en/diw_01.c.739961.en/edition/data_access.html.

Doyle, P., Lane, J., Theeuwes, J. J. M., & Zayatz, L. V. (2001). *Confidentiality, disclosure, and data access*. Elsevier–North Holland.

European Union. (2016). Regulation (EU) 2016/679 of the European Parliament and of the Council of 27 April 2016 on the protection of natural persons with regard to the processing of personal data and on the free movement of such data, and repealing Directive 95/46/EC (General Data Protection Regulation). *Official Journal of the European Union, L 119*, 1–88.

European Commission. (2023). *Ethics and integrity in research*. Publications Office of the European Union. https://op.europa.eu/en/publication-detail/-/publication/8a4e03c7-279a-11ef-a195-01aa75ed71a1

Fecher, B., & Friesike, S. (2014). Open science: One term, five schools of thought. In S. Bartling & S. Friesike (Eds.), *Opening science* (pp. 17–47). Springer.

Fienberg, S. E., & Willenborg, L. C. R. J. (1998). Disclosure limitation methods for protecting the confidentiality of statistical data (Special issue). *Journal of Official Statistics, 14*, 337–345.

Fuller, W. A. (1993). Masking procedures for microdata disclosure limitation. *Journal of Official Statistics, 9*(3), 383–406.

Goebel, J., Grabka, M. M., Liebig, S., Kroh, M., Richter, D., Schröder, C., & Schupp, J. (2019). The German Socio-Economic Panel (SOEP). *Jahrbücher für Nationalökonomie und Statistik, 239*(2), 345–360.

Haven, T., Gopalakrishna, G., Tijdink, J., van der Schot, D., & Bouter, L. (2022). Promoting trust in research and researchers: How open science and research integrity are intertwined. *BMC Research Notes, 15*(1), 302.

Hillygus, D. S., Nie, N. H., Prewitt, K., & Pals, H. (2006). *The hard count.* Russell Sage Foundation.

Iphofen, R. (2017). *Ethical decision making in social research: A practical guide.* Palgrave Macmillan.

Jabine, T. B. (1993). Statistical disclosure limitation practices of United States statistical agencies. *Journal of Official Statistics, 9*(3), 427–454.

Lambert, D. (1993). Measures of disclosure risk and harm. *Journal of Official Statistics, 9*(3), 313–331.

Malin, B., & Sweeney, L. (2000). Determining the identifiability of DNA database entries. In *Proceedings of the AMIA Symposium* (pp. 537–541). American Medical Informatics Association (AMIA).

Narayanan, A., & Felten, E. W. (2014). *No silver bullet: De-identification still doesn't work.* Princeton University.

Rubin, D. J. (1993). Discussion: Statistical disclosure limitation. *Journal of Official Statistics, 9*(3), 461–468.

Scherpenzeel, A. C. (2018). "True" longitudinal and probability-based internet panels: Evidence from the Netherlands. In *Social and behavioral research and the internet* (pp. 77–104). Routledge.

Sieber, J. E. (Ed.). (2012). *The ethics of social research: Surveys and experiments.* Springer Science & Business Media.

Singer, E., Mathiowetz, N., & Couper, M. P. (1993). The impact of privacy and confidentiality concerns on census participation. *Public Opinion Quarterly, 57*(4), 465–482.

Singer, E., Van Hoewyk, J., & Neugebauer, R. (2003). Attitudes and behavior: The impact of privacy and confidentiality concerns on participation in the 2000 Census. *Public Opinion Quarterly, 65*(3), 368–384.

University of Essex. (n.d.). *Understanding Society: Ethics and data security. Understanding Society.* https://www.understandingsociety.ac.uk/about/ethics.

Winkler, W. E. (1997). *Views on the production and use of confidential microdata* (Research Report No. RR97/01). U.S. Census Bureau.

Goebel, J., Grabka, M. M., Liebig, S., Kroh, M., Richter, D., Schröder, C., & Schupp, J. (2019). The German Socio-Economic Panel (SOEP). *Jahrbücher für Nationalökonomie und Statistik, 239*(2), 345–360.

[illegible]

Part II
European Infrastructures and Surveys

Chapter 5
The Rise of Social Science Infrastructures in Europe and Italy

Luciana Taddei and Mario Paolucci

5.1 Introduction: The European Context

In recent years, the European Commission has consolidated its strategic role in shaping a coherent and sustainable ecosystem of Research Infrastructures (RIs) in the social sciences, acting not merely as a funding agency but as an orchestrator of alignment and interoperability across national systems.

Central to this effort is the goal to reduce fragmentation within the European Research Area by fostering distributed, open, and FAIR-aligned (Findable, Accessible, Interoperable, Reusable) infrastructures that support long-term longitudinal studies and large-scale data sharing. Through instruments such as the European Strategy Forum on Research Infrastructures (ESFRI) Roadmap[1]—which articulates investment priorities for the next two decades—and the legal framework provided by the European Research Infrastructure Consortium (ERIC),[2] the Commission promotes governance models that cross national boundaries while ensuring inclusivity and scientific excellence (European Commission, 2024d). Notably, the European Open Science Cloud (EOSC)[3] represents a key digital infrastructure that integrates

[1] www.esfri.eu

[2] https://research-and-innovation.ec.europa.eu/strategy/strategy-research-and-innovation/our-digital-future/european-research-infrastructures/eric_en

[3] https://eosc.eu/

L. Taddei (✉)
Institute for Research on Population and Social Policies, National Research Council, Fisciano (SA), Italy
e-mail: luciana.taddei@cnr.it

M. Paolucci
Institute for Research on Population and Social Policies, National Research Council, Rome, Italy
e-mail: mario.paolucci@cnr.it

L. Taddei, M. Paolucci (eds.), *Longitudinal Data Infrastructures in Europe*,
https://doi.org/10.1007/978-3-032-07005-0_5

social science datasets within a broader cloud-based environment, enhancing cross-domain interoperability.

At a practical level, the Commission actively opens up national infrastructures to international researchers, encourages joint planning to avoid duplication, and provides EU-level funding through Horizon 2020 and Horizon Europe programmes. The impact is not only systemic but also tangible, generating substantial investments with over €6.6 billion in EU funds, €10 billion in national investments, and €2.4 billion in regional development funds supporting RIs between 2014 and 2020 (European Commission, 2019). Through this framework, 20 consortia have now achieved ERIC status, covering domains from marine biology to social sciences (ESFRI Roadmap, 2018). These infrastructures enable access to state-of-the-art laboratories, digital platforms, and shared datasets, making collaborative science not just possible, but structurally embedded within the European Research Area. Within this architecture, social science RIs such as SHARE-ERIC[4] and CESSDA-ERIC[5] exemplify the movement toward a coordinated European approach, both in terms of data governance and methodological innovation.

5.2 Building the European Research Infrastructure Ecosystem: ESFRI, ERIC, and EOSC

The European Strategy Forum on Research Infrastructures (ESFRI) plays a pivotal role in shaping the long-term vision of the European Research Area (ERA)[6] by providing strategic guidance, coordination, and foresight in the field of Research Infrastructures (RIs).

Established by the EU Council to support a strategy-led approach to infrastructure policy-making, ESFRI acts as both a policy incubator and strategic hub for funders, developing a pan-European Roadmap that identifies priority projects and updates them regularly to reflect evolving scientific and technological needs (European Commission, 2024b; ESFRI, 2017). The ESFRI Roadmap 2021, for instance, includes 22 Projects in their development phase and 41 Landmarks that represent mature, world-class infrastructures across all scientific domains—together representing a combined investment of nearly €20 billion in capital value (ESFRI, 2021).

A key feature of the ESFRI Roadmap 2021 is its enhanced Strategic Landscape Analysis, which offers an advanced and service-oriented assessment of Europe's research infrastructure (RI) system. This analysis maps existing RIs across thematic

[4] https://share-eric.eu/

[5] https://www.cessda.eu/

[6] https://research-and-innovation.ec.europa.eu/strategy/strategy-research-and-innovation/our-digital-future/european-research-area_en

domains, identifies capacity gaps, and informs future strategic investments to maintain European leadership in global science (ESFRI, 2021, p. 16). The 2021 edition underscores the role of RIs in addressing pressing societal challenges—including sustainability, digital transformation, and health emergencies—through a more impact-driven approach. Notably, the Landscape Analysis is structured into three sections: (1) a domain-specific overview of current RIs and their evolution; (2) an analysis of interconnections across disciplines; (3) and an assessment of the societal impact of RIs in areas such as the Sustainable Development Goals (SDG),[7] crisis response, and EOSC integration (ESFRI, 2021, pp. 16–17). The 2021 Roadmap also expands the ESFRI portfolio with new Projects that fill strategic gaps—including Growing Up in Digital Europe (GUIDE)[8] and Generations and Gender Programme (GGP)[9] for social sciences—and strengthens the European RI ecosystem by advancing Projects to Landmark status (ESFRI, 2021). Social science infrastructures like the Survey of Health, Ageing and Retirement in Europe (SHARE-ERIC) and the Consortium of European Social Science Data Archives (CESSDA-ERIC), recognized as ESFRI Landmarks, exemplify how long-term, internationally coordinated investments contribute to both scientific excellence and policy-relevant data ecosystems (ESFRI, 2021, p. 19).

Complementing ESFRI's strategic planning function, the European Research Infrastructure Consortium (ERIC) represents a pivotal legal instrument in the governance of pan-European research infrastructures, designed to facilitate their establishment and long-term operation beyond national boundaries. Introduced by the European Commission to accelerate the creation of transnational research facilities, the ERIC model combines the legal status of an international organisation with operational flexibility, offering a simplified pathway to cooperation for EU Member States and associated countries (European Commission, 2024c). As a legal entity recognized across all EU countries, an ERIC enjoys privileges such as VAT and excise duty exemptions, customized procurement rules, and freedom to conduct limited economic activities directly related to its research mission. This framework has proved essential for infrastructures operating in fields where data harmonization, shared governance, and open access are foundational, such as the social sciences.

To qualify, an ERIC must demonstrate significant added value to the European Research Area (ERA), ensure effective access to the research community, and promote the mobility of knowledge and researchers across Europe. Importantly, the model accommodates both new and existing infrastructures, including those hosted by non-EU countries, thereby supporting a more globally integrated European research ecosystem (European Commission, 2024c). The Commission's commitment to this model is evident in the growing number of ERICs—now numbering over 20—including major social science infrastructures like SHARE-ERIC and

[7] https://sdgs.un.org/

[8] https://www.guidecohort.eu/

[9] Generations and Gender Programme (GGP).

CESSDA-ERIC, which illustrate the role of ERICs not only in administrative cohesion, but in epistemic innovation and cross-national data cooperation.

Another key instrument for developing Research Infrastructures is the European Open Science Cloud (EOSC). It represents one of the most ambitious policy instruments for enabling a truly open and data-driven research environment in Europe. Envisioned as a federated "system of systems", EOSC aims to provide European researchers with a secure, interdisciplinary platform where data, tools, and services can be shared, discovered, and reused in accordance with FAIR (Findable, Accessible, Interoperable, Reusable) principles (European Commission, 2024a). By linking national and domain-specific data repositories, research infrastructures, and e-infrastructures, EOSC fosters not only interoperability but also accelerates scientific reproducibility and innovation across disciplines. The launch of the EOSC EU Node in October 2024 marks a significant milestone in the cloud's operationalisation, providing a reference node and facilitating the onboarding of other national and thematic nodes into a broader EOSC Federation (European Commission, 2024a).

EOSC is embedded in a tripartite governance model, involving the European Commission, Member States (via the EOSC Steering Board), and the research community (via the EOSC Association), which ensures strategic coordination and accountability across national and institutional levels. This structure underpins the EOSC Strategic Research and Innovation Agenda (SRIA) and reflects EOSC's role as a core component of the European Research Area (ERA) and of Europe's common research and innovation data space (European Commission, 2024a). Ultimately, EOSC is not just a technical infrastructure but a political and epistemic project: one that redefines the circulation of knowledge, lowers entry barriers to data-intensive science, and fosters a more integrated European research ecosystem. Table 5.1 illustrates the current status of those European social science infrastructures dealing with panel data and metadata, within this framework.

However, despite the strategic ambition of the European Open Science Cloud to serve all scientific domains, the integration of the social sciences presents

Table 5.1 Main European social science research infrastructures in ESFRI/EOSC (September 2025)

Infrastructure	Included in ESFRI	ERIC status	Contribution to EOSC	Thematic area
SHARE-ERIC	Yes (Landmark)	Yes	Longitudinal data contributions	Ageing & Health
CESSDA-ERIC	Yes (Landmark)	Yes	Interoperable data repository	Social Data Services
GGP	Yes (Project)	Preparing	Planned	Demography & Family
GUIDE	Yes (Project)	Preparing	Planned	Demography & Childhood

specific challenges. EOSC's foundational architecture, terminology, and data management practices have largely been shaped by the needs of the so-called "hard sciences", where data are often structured, standardized, and generated under controlled conditions. In contrast, social science data—such as survey responses, administrative records, and qualitative datasets—are typically more heterogeneous, context-dependent, and subject to stricter ethical and legal constraints related to personal and sensitive information.

One major difficulty is achieving true interoperability: existing metadata standards and ontologies in EOSC are not always easily adaptable to the epistemological and methodological diversity of social research. Furthermore, aligning social science data with FAIR principles, while essential, often requires significant effort in documentation, anonymization, and format harmonization—tasks that are resource-intensive and sometimes incompatible with the iterative, interpretive nature of social inquiry.

The fragmentation of data infrastructures within the social sciences further complicates integration, as does the lower degree of digital maturity in some institutions or countries. Overcoming these barriers requires not only technical adaptation but also a cultural shift within both EOSC governance structures and the social science community itself, fostering greater mutual understanding, co-design of services, and long-term investment in disciplinary-specific tools and standards.

While the development of a coherent and standardised European research infrastructure ecosystem brings clear benefits in terms of interoperability, efficiency, and data accessibility, it also raises several critical issues. First, the push for harmonisation may generate tensions between uniformity and national specificity, potentially disadvantaging countries with less mature digital infrastructures, differing scientific traditions, or limited institutional capacity. Moreover, compliance with shared frameworks—such as FAIR principles or ERIC governance models—may become a prerequisite for accessing funding and collaborative networks, thereby reducing flexibility for locally driven or emerging initiatives that do not fully align with European standards.

Another challenge lies in the complexity of multi-level governance: while it ensures coordination across Member States, it may also slow decision-making processes and dilute national autonomy, particularly in disciplines like the social sciences where methodological and epistemological diversity is essential. In addition, reliance on centralised digital infrastructures raises concerns around digital inclusion and the potential creation of new forms of epistemic inequality—both among countries and among research communities within them.

Addressing these tensions requires a balanced approach that recognises the value of standardisation while preserving the diversity and contextual richness that are vital to robust and inclusive scientific ecosystems.

5.3 The Strategic Engagement of Italy in the European Data Ecosystem

The implementation of European social science infrastructures in Italy reflects Italy's commitment to aligning with the standards and practices promoted by the European Research Area. Among the most significant initiatives is Italy's participation in CESSDA-ERIC (Consortium of European Social Science Data Archives), a pan-European infrastructure providing large-scale, interoperable access to research data in the social sciences. Italy participates in CESSDA through the Consortium of Italian Social Science Data Archives (DASSI), which connects national actors to the broader European ecosystem and contributes to the development of shared metadata standards, training resources, and FAIR-aligned data services. CESSDA plays a key role in supporting open data practices and fostering methodological innovation, ensuring that Italian researchers can both contribute to and benefit from cross-national data harmonization and secondary data use.

A second foundational infrastructure is SHARE-ERIC, a longitudinal and multidisciplinary panel survey that collects harmonized data on health, socio-economic conditions, social and family networks among individuals aged 50 and over across 28 countries. Italy has been a key partner in SHARE since its inception, implementing all survey waves to date. The national coordination, based at the University of Padua and Venice, oversees recruitment, fieldwork, and dissemination activities, ensuring that the Italian dataset adheres to the rigorous methodological and ethical standards set at the European level. Italy's SHARE data are not only widely used by the national research community, but also serve institutional and academic actors in Italy and abroad. The Italian experience with SHARE also reflects growing institutional support: it is recognized as a national research infrastructure and funded through national and European programs, confirming its strategic role in promoting evidence-based policymaking and Open Science.

Unlike SHARE and CESSDA, which are established ERICs, the Generations and Gender Programme (GGP) is currently in a preparatory phase toward acquiring ERIC status. Developed to explore key demographic and social dynamics—including fertility, partnership trajectories, intergenerational exchanges, and gender relations—the Generations and Gender Survey (GGS) is the core data collection instrument of the programme. Italy joined the GGS initiative early on, implementing a first wave in 2003–2004, followed by a second panel wave in 2007, coordinated by a national consortium. This participation reflects Italy's commitment to strengthening longitudinal demographic research capacity. Positioned between SHARE, which focuses on older populations, and GUIDE, which will explore early life stages, GGS helps complete a comprehensive infrastructure for life-course research in the social sciences.

GUIDE—Growing Up In Digital Europe—is the first Europe-wide cohort study specifically designed to follow children and adolescents over time, with the aim of understanding how early life conditions influence later outcomes in education, health, and well-being. As a longitudinal infrastructure, GUIDE addresses critical

Table 5.2 Italy's participation in social science research infrastructures (September 2025)

Infrastructure	Launch year	National coordination	Current status
SHARE-ERIC	2004	CNR, Padua, Venice	Active participation
CESSDA-ERIC	2019	DASSI (CNR, Bicocca)	Active participation
GGP	2003	CNR, Bocconi	Active participation
GUIDE	2024	CNR, Bologna	Pilot study launched
IOPP	2024	CNR, Milano	Under construction

dimensions of childhood development in the context of rapid digital and social transformation. Italy is actively engaged in the preparatory phase of the study and, through the GUIDE Italia initiative, has launched its first national pilot survey in 2025. By joining GUIDE, Italy contributes to shaping one of the most ambitious child cohort studies in Europe. Together with SHARE and GGS, GUIDE reinforces the construction of a harmonized, life-course-oriented research infrastructure spanning early life, adulthood, and ageing. This triad supports the design of cross-generational, evidence-based public policies and offers a robust empirical foundation for understanding long-term social change in Italy and beyond. Table 5.2 summarizes Italy's current involvement in these European infrastructures, with the inclusion of the IOPP initiative that will be detailed in the next section.

5.4 The Italian Online Probability Panel (IOPP) and Its Challenges

European level data assures comparability, and the EU framework guarantees dependability and accuracy. Yet there is sometimes a need to respond more quickly to events, or to a reach a deeper understanding of local phenomena. This is why some countries developed a national panel. In Italy, a probability panel of the national population is currently under development with the support of the FOSSR infrastructure (Fostering Open Science in Social Research), funded under the Italian National Recovery and Resilience Plan (NRRP).

The purpose of these efforts is the development of the first Italian Online Probability Panel (Santurro et al., 2025), that aims to establish a robust, nationally representative infrastructure for online survey data collection based on probability sampling. Inspired by similar panels already operational in several European countries (such as Longitudinal Internet studies for the Social Sciences (LISS) in the Netherlands or Étude Longitudinale par Internet Pour les Sciences Sociales (ELIPSS) in France), the Italian Online Probability Panel is designed to support academic research and policy evaluation with timely and reliable data. It responds to the growing need for agile and methodologically sound data collection mechanisms, particularly in light of rapid social change and digital transformation. The project represents a strategic investment to align Italy with European best practices in longitudinal and probabilistic survey infrastructures.

The development of a structured probability panel is a highly complex and long-term undertaking that requires robust methodological design, sustained institutional coordination, and substantial technological and financial infrastructure. Since the rise of self-administered computerized surveys in the late 1980s, the development of probability panels has unfolded incrementally—often over the span of a decade or more—through phases of pilot testing, infrastructure building, recruitment experimentation, and data harmonization (Callegaro et al., 2014).

Early breakthroughs such as the Dutch telepanel in 1986, which involved 1000 households equipped with internet-connected computers for weekly data collection, highlight the pioneering vision and logistical demands of these initiatives (Saris, 1998). Subsequent developments in the U.S., such as the KnowledgePanel (1999), the American Life Panel (2003), and the Gallup Panel (2004), laid the foundation for scalable, longitudinal online research through probability-based recruitment and digital engagement. In Europe, a second wave of expansion began with the launch of the LISS Panel in 2007, which remains a benchmark example: based on a probability sample from the national population register, it ensures total inclusion by equipping offline households with necessary hardware (Scherpenzeel, 2009, 2011).

What these experiences reveal is that building a successful probability panel requires not only advanced sampling and incentive strategies, but also mechanisms for respondent retention, cross-wave coherence, and data FAIRness. As noted by Blom et al. (2016), the technical and social components of panel maintenance—especially when aiming at representativeness—pose persistent challenges that only long-term planning and institutional stability can resolve. Moreover, cross-national comparisons (Kocar & Kaczmirek, 2023) underscore how national contexts—e.g., population registers, digital infrastructure, statistical tradition—profoundly shape implementation models and timelines.

Against this backdrop, the emergence of the Italian Online Probability Panel (IOPP) must be read as a major, transformative step for the national research ecosystem in social sciences. While Italy has historically relied on international infrastructures or mixed-mode designs, the construction of IOPP—still in progress—is rooted in best practices from mature OPPs, especially the LISS model. The IOPP aims to achieve full population representativeness through a Computer-Assisted Web Interviewing (CAWI) longitudinal survey and probability-based sampling, including provisions for digital inclusion. Its success will depend on harmonizing methodological rigor with technological scalability, ensuring transparency and data accessibility, and embedding the panel in a long-term governance framework. In this light, IOPP is not simply an innovative project, but a structural investment to align Italy with leading European standards in social research infrastructure.

5.5 From Vision to Reality: The IOPP Implementation Experience

The development of Italy's Online Probability Panel (IOPP) provides a revealing case study of how the theoretical benefits of European research infrastructure integration encounter complex practical realities at the national implementation level. While the previous sections have outlined the ambitious framework for harmonized, FAIR-aligned research infrastructures across Europe, the IOPP's practical experience illustrates the considerable gap between policy vision and operational execution. Drawing on European best practices—particularly the Dutch LISS Panel and French ELIPSS models—IOPP was designed to align Italy with leading standards in probabilistic online survey infrastructure. However, the implementation process has revealed how probability panels must navigate local institutional, legal, practical and administrative frameworks that require significant adaptation and learning to accommodate such innovative research approaches. This tension between European integration goals and national implementation realities, despite the inevitable differences between national context, may offer insights into the practical challenges of building a truly integrated European Research Area in the social sciences.

At the heart of the IOPP implementation challenges lies the issue of access to reliable lists. In our case, this was attempted first by a collaboration with National Statistics (ISTAT). But, even if ISTAT was supportive of the IOPP objectives, this attempt encountered obstacles; interpretation of data protection law (GDPR) and a strict reading of institutional mandates revealed a lack of legal basis for such list transfers. This regulatory impasse required a complete procedural redesign.

Following guidance from the Garante per la protezione dei dati personali (the GDPR Italian authority), the only alternative was accessing the Anagrafe Nazionale della Popolazione Residente (ANPR), the national population registry. What followed was an unprecedented and time-intensive negotiation process involving the CNR, the Garante, the Ministry of the Interior, and Sogei (the entity managing the ANPR system). Over the course of 12 months, a new administrative pathway was established, culminating in the first-ever extraction of a probabilistic sample from ANPR for research purposes. While ultimately successful, this process significantly delayed the project timeline.

Beyond regulatory challenges, the operational implementation encountered additional obstacles. During the project's lifetime, Italian public procurement regulations were modified twice. Even though these changes were intended to simplify bureaucratic procedures, the overhead of adapting to regulatory changes proved substantial and delayed the procurement process.

Despite eventual substantial investment in professional survey services, fieldwork results in the startup phase fell significantly short of targets. The causes of this slow takeup include several factors: difficulty recruiting and retaining qualified interviewers due to overlapping surveys from other institutions, dramatic postal delivery problems requiring expensive tracked mail services, and lower-than-expected response rates for web surveys. Eventually, despite substantial investment, fieldwork results, in the startup phase, fell dramatically short of targets.

The causes for the slow takeup are several: difficulty recruiting and retaining qualified interviewers, who experienced an overload due to co-occurring surveys from other institutions; unexpected and dramatic postal delivery problems, requiring a shift towards expensive tracked mail services; and lower-than-expected response rates for web surveys.

Thus, the IOPP implementation reveals significant "hidden costs" of European research infrastructure integration that are rarely accounted for in policy planning. Even with the substantial funding from the EU NextGeneration programs, the project required extensive legal consultations, regulatory negotiations, and procedural innovations that consumed considerable time and institutional resources. The need to establish unprecedented data sharing agreements between institutions (in our case, CNR, ISTAT, the Ministry of Interior, and privacy authorities) represents a form of institutional overhead that European integration policies often underestimate.

This sustainability challenge is compounded by the "institutional memory" problem: the knowledge and relationships developed through the IOPP implementation process—from regulatory navigation to operational expertise—risk being lost if funding discontinuities force project termination or institutional reorganization. The European model assumes that initial investments will create self-sustaining national infrastructures, but the IOPP experience suggests that the transition from European funding to national sustainability may be more problematic than anticipated.

Rather than a deviation from the norm, such challenges should be viewed as integral to the process of institutional innovation. The IOPP practical experience reveals a fundamental tension between European integration's emphasis on standardization and harmonization versus the need for innovation in research infrastructure development.

This creates what might be termed the "innovation paradox" of European integration: the very institutional creativity and adaptability required for successful research infrastructure development may be constrained by the standardization imperatives designed to ensure European-wide compatibility and interoperability. Managing this tension requires more flexible European frameworks that can accommodate national innovation while maintaining integration goals.

References

Blom, A. G., et al. (2016). A comparison of four probability-based online and mixed-mode panels in Europe. *Social Science Computer Review, 34*(1), 8–25.

Callegaro, M., et al. (Eds.). (2014). *Online panel research: A data quality perspective*. Wiley. https://doi.org/10.1002/9781118763520

ESFRI. (2017). *Procedural guidelines and mandate*. https://www.esfri.eu/sites/default/files/ESFRI_Procedural_Guidelines_2017.pdf

ESFRI. (2018). *ESFRI Roadmap 2018: Strategy report on research infrastructures*. https://roadmap2018.esfri.eu
ESFRI. (2021). *ESFRI Roadmap 2021: Strategy report on research infrastructures in Europe*. European Strategy Forum on Research Infrastructures. https://www.esfri.eu/esfri-roadmap.
European Commission. (2019). *Research infrastructures make science happen* (Catalogue No. KI-03-19-636-EN-N). Publications Office of the European Union. https://ec.europa.eu/info/research-and-innovation/strategy/european-research-infrastructures_en
European Commission. (2024a). *European Open Science Cloud (EOSC)*. https://research-and-innovation.ec.europa.eu/strategy/strategy-research-and-innovation/our-digital-future/open-science/european-open-science-cloud-eosc_en
European Commission. (2024b). *European research infrastructures: Strategy and funding*. https://research-and-innovation.ec.europa.eu/strategy/strategy-research-and-innovation/our-digital-future/european-research-infrastructures_en
European Commission. (2024c). *Research infrastructures as instruments of science diplomacy*. Directorate-General for Research and Innovation.
European Commission. (2024d). *European Research Infrastructure Consortium (ERIC)*. https://research-and-innovation.ec.europa.eu/strategy/strategy-research-and-innovation/our-digital-future/european-research-infrastructures/eric_en
Kocar, S., & Kaczmirek, L. (2023). A meta-analysis of worldwide recruitment rates in 23 probability-based online panels. *International Journal of Social Research Methodology, 27*(5), 589–604.
Santurro, M., Biolcati Rinaldi, F., Cerbara, L., Heins, F., Paparusso, A., Pennacchiotti, C., Piacentini, F., Taddei, L., & Vezzoni, C. (2025). Designing the Italian online probability panel: Innovations and challenges to foster open science. In *Italian statistical society series on advances in statistics* (pp. 259–264). Springer Nature Switzerland. https://doi.org/10.1007/978-3-031-96736-8_43
Saris, W. (1998). Ten years of interviewing without interviewers: The Telepanel. In *Computer assisted survey information collection*.
Scherpenzeel, A. (2009). *Start of the LISS panel: Sample and recruitment of a probability-based Internet panel*. CentERdata.
Scherpenzeel, A. (2011). Data collection in a probability-based internet panel: How the LISS Panel was built and how it can be used. *Bulletin of Sociological Methodology, 109*, 56–61.

Chapter 6
SHARE-ERIC: A European Infrastructure for Research on Ageing and Retirement

Agar Brugiavini, Stefano Castaldo, Guglielmo Weber, and Nancy Zambon

6.1 Introduction

Understanding the ageing and retirement processes across Europe necessitates a coordinated and multidisciplinary approach, going beyond isolated national statistics. This complexity can be effectively addressed through collaborative, transnational research efforts. The Survey of Health, Ageing and Retirement in Europe (SHARE) was established to fulfil this requirement. Since its beginning in 2004, SHARE has developed into a significant social science research infrastructure. It collects harmonised, longitudinal micro-data from individuals aged 50 and over throughout Europe. It provides a vital resource for exploring the relationships among health, work, family dynamics, and economic well-being over time.

With contributions from 27 European countries and Israel, SHARE aims to foster an integrated European Research Area focused on ageing. Its innovative methodology includes face-to-face interviews, objective health assessments, retrospective life history data, and modules relevant to policy, resulting in a comprehensive dataset. This dataset has facilitated numerous scientific publications and informed high-level policy initiatives. Establishing SHARE as the first European Research Infrastructure Consortium (ERIC) within the social sciences represents a significant advancement, providing a solid legal and governance framework to support its scientific objectives sustainably. This chapter will examine how SHARE-ERIC operates as both a source of data and a model for transnational collaboration, highlighting the evolving function of research infrastructures in influencing European science and society.

A. Brugiavini
Department of Economics, Ca'Foscari University of Venice, Venice, Italy
e-mail: brugiavi@unive.it

S. Castaldo (✉) · G. Weber · N. Zambon
Department of Economics and Management, University of Padua, Padua, Italy
e-mail: stefano.castaldo@unipd.it; guglielmo.weber@unipd.it; nancy.zambon@unipd.it

L. Taddei, M. Paolucci (eds.), *Longitudinal Data Infrastructures in Europe*,
https://doi.org/10.1007/978-3-032-07005-0_6

6.2 ERIC: Legal Framework and Strategic Importance

The designation of SHARE as a European Research Infrastructure Consortium (ERIC) in 2011 marked a decisive step in the institutional development of the project. Introduced by the European Commission through Council Regulation (EC) No. 723/2009, the ERIC legal form was designed to provide research infrastructures of pan-European interest with a stable and flexible legal framework. By acquiring ERIC status, SHARE was granted legal personality recognised across all EU member states and associated countries. This conferred several practical benefits: exemption from VAT and excise duties, the ability to operate across national jurisdictions under a single legal entity, and simplified rules for procurement and recruitment. These features are particularly important for a large-scale, cross-national survey such as SHARE, which must coordinate activities, contracts, and funding streams in nearly 30 countries with diverse legal and administrative systems.

Beyond its legal and administrative advantages, the ERIC status has important symbolic and strategic value for the scientific community. It signals that the infrastructure is not merely a national or institutional initiative but a public good that serves the collective needs of European research. As an ERIC, SHARE benefits from enhanced legitimacy and visibility, facilitating cooperation with policymakers, national statistical offices, and international organisations. It also aligns SHARE with the broader goals of the European Research Area (ERA), particularly those related to open science, data sharing, and cross-border collaboration. Moreover, ERIC status helps ensure long-term sustainability, as member countries commit to the financial and operational support of the infrastructure. In this sense, the legal form is not simply an administrative tool—it is an enabler of scientific ambition, institutional trust, and cross-national cohesion.

6.3 Governance and Institutional Setting

The organisational structure of SHARE-ERIC is designed to support a pan-European research infrastructure, reflecting its complexity and ambition. Established as an ERIC, SHARE employs a transnational governance model that integrates scientific, administrative, and policy expertise.

Central to this governance framework is the Governing Council, which includes representatives from each member state. This council is responsible for strategic oversight and budgetary decisions, ensuring alignment with national research priorities and broader European objectives.

The Managing Director provides leadership within SHARE, currently Professor David Richter, who oversees the operations of the SHARE Berlin Institute. This institute serves as the primary operational hub following its relocation from Munich, allowing for the consolidation of scientific and administrative functions in a single location. This shift has enhanced collaboration among core partners, which include esteemed German institutions such as the WZB Berlin Social Science Centre, the German Institute for Economic Research (DIW Berlin), the German Centre of Gerontology (DZA), the Robert Koch Institute (RKI), and Charité—Berlin University of Medicine. The SHARE framework is a distributed research infrastructure incorporating various nodes in Padua, Venice, Tilburg, and Odense. These nodes address specialised aspects of general interest, operating in conjunction with the central hub.

The Scientific Monitoring Board is responsible for ensuring the project's scientific integrity. Comprising internationally recognised scholars in fields such as epidemiology, economics, and survey methodology, this independent body plays a vital role in overseeing research outputs and advising methodological standards. This vigilance helps to maintain the academic rigour of the data produced and disseminated by SHARE-ERIC.

The legal and operational advantages of being an ERIC enable the consortium to manage a complex network of contractors, fieldwork agencies, and national teams with efficiency and transparency. In essence, SHARE-ERIC's governance structure combines national commitment with centralised coordination, creating a robust and resilient infrastructure capable of adapting to both scientific needs and policy contexts.

6.4 Core Mission and Activities

The SHARE-ERIC initiative provides a sustainable micro-data infrastructure to analyse the life courses of individuals aged 50 and over within Europe. Its mission extends beyond mere data collection; it encompasses the entirety of the research cycle, including instrument design, field implementation, data curation, and dissemination.

Central to the SHARE initiative is a meticulously composed questionnaire designed with a modular approach covering a broad spectrum of life domains. These domains include, but are not limited to, demographic characteristics, physical and mental health, cognitive function, employment and income, pensions and savings, social and familial networks, housing conditions, and subjective well-being. The questionnaire is systematically translated and culturally adapted for each participating country, ensuring comparability while adhering to strict methodological harmonisation.

Data collection occurs in biannual waves, with each iteration updating information for existing panel members and incorporating newly recruited respondents to mitigate attrition rates. Over the 2004-24 period, Axel Börsch-Supan and a group of researchers based in several European countries made it possible for SHARE to complete nine face-to-face interview waves utilising the Computer-Assisted Personal Interview (CAPI) method. Additionally, in response to the COVID-19 pandemic, two special waves were conducted via telephone interviews using the

CATI technique, ensuring data continuity in this context. The tenth regular (face-to-face) wave was instead completed in 2025 under the new managing director, David Richter.

One notable aspect of SHARE is its inclusion of retrospective life history data through the SHARELIFE waves conducted in 2008 and 2017. This feature allows for reconstructing biographical trajectories over several decades, thus enriching the longitudinal panel with contextually significant variables and facilitating causal analyses that link prior events to current outcomes.

After data collection, SHARE-ERIC undertakes a thorough data cleaning, imputation, and documentation process. The finalised datasets are made available free of charge for scientific research, with access contingent upon registration and compliance with data protection regulations. This open-access model adheres to the principles of ERIC and the European General Data Protection Regulation (GDPR), underscoring SHARE's commitment to transparency and scientific integrity.

Moreover, SHARE consistently invests in the sustainability of its infrastructure. Initiatives are directed toward securing long-term funding, updating survey content to align with emerging research themes, including digitalisation and environmental exposure, and expanding sample coverage within countries to facilitate subnational analyses. Integrating methodological innovation with strategic foresight ensures that SHARE remains a premier research resource capable of addressing academic inquiries and policy requirements.

6.5 Methodological Strengths

The scientific value of SHARE is rooted in its advanced methodology, which aims to capture the complex and evolving nature of ageing. The project adheres to four principal tenets: supranationality, comparability, multidisciplinarity, and longitudinality.

SHARE functions across nearly all EU member states and associated countries as a supranational initiative. It employs a harmonised research design that facilitates direct cross-national comparisons. Data is collected within parallel timeframes, utilising a consistent core instrument subjected to rigorous linguistic harmonisation. This framework enables researchers to examine how institutional, cultural, and policy contexts influence individual outcomes in health, retirement, and social well-being across various national settings.

The aspect of comparability is further strengthened by SHARE's affiliation with a global network of related studies, including the Health and Retirement Study (HRS) in the United States, the English Longitudinal Study of Ageing (ELSA), and surveys in other countries such as Japan (JSTAR), China (CHARLS), India (LASI), South Korea (KLoSA), and Mexico (MHAS). Through harmonisation efforts coordinated by the Gateway to Global Ageing platform, SHARE enhances an international data ecosystem that supports comparative research on worldwide ageing trends.

Multidisciplinarity is a key feature of the SHARE survey design. Including various fields—economic, biomedical, psychological, and social—facilitates the investigation of ageing as a multifaceted phenomenon. For example, one can analyse the relationship between chronic illness and retirement behaviour or between cognitive decline and informal caregiving networks, leveraging data from multiple modules within the same dataset. This comprehensive perspective benefits interdisciplinary research teams and informs evidence-based policymaking.

Longitudinality is integral to the panel's structure. By tracking the same individuals over time, SHARE allows for precise analysis of the effects of life events, health shocks, and policy changes. Incorporating retrospective modules enriches the data historically, enabling connections between early-life circumstances and later-life outcomes. Such longitudinal capabilities are crucial for unravelling causal relationships and understanding the cumulative effects of social inequalities throughout the lifespan.

Collectively, these methodological attributes position SHARE as more than a mere dataset; they establish it as a strategic infrastructure for generating scientifically rigorous and socially relevant knowledge.

6.6 Survey Waves and Innovations

The longitudinal nature of SHARE is particularly significant for examining the dynamics associated with ageing. As shown in Fig. 6.1, over more than two decades, the survey has undergone multiple waves of data collection, each enhancing the previous one regarding coverage, content, and methodological sophistication. This progression reflects the continuity essential for panel data analysis and illustrates SHARE's adaptability to the evolving research demands and societal challenges.

The inaugural wave of SHARE, conducted in 2004, marked a noteworthy milestone in European social research, incorporating data from eleven countries spanning Northern, Southern, and Central Europe and Israel. This geographical diversity established a comparative and supranational perspective from the outset. The initial questionnaire was designed to gather data across various domains, including health status, work history, financial circumstances, and family structures, laying the groundwork for the institutionalisation of SHARE as a robust research infrastructure. For further information see De Luca et al. (2005), Börsch-Supan and Jürges (2005), Börsch-Supan et al. (2005), Börsch-Supan et al. (2013), and Weber (2018).

After the first wave, Wave 2 was conducted in 2006–2007, expanding the geographical scope to include the Czech Republic, Poland, and Ireland. This wave introduced a new module centred on the end-of-life experiences of deceased spouses or relatives, representing a significant advancement in European longitudinal surveys and providing insights into the final stages of life from a household-level perspective. Results from the use of the first two waves of data are reported in Börsch-Supan et al. (2008).

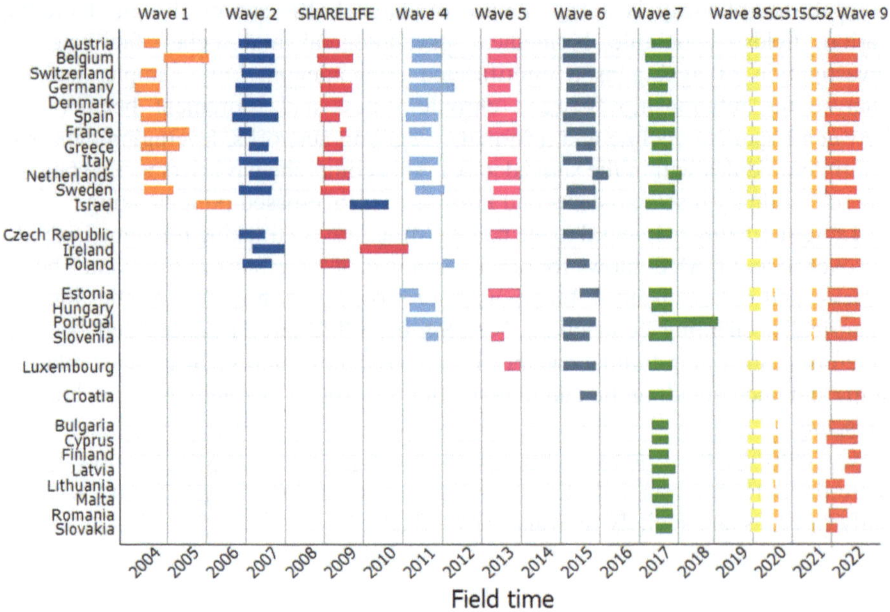

Fig. 6.1 SHARE waves overview. Image published by SHARE-ERIC at the webpage: https://share-eric.eu/data/data-documentation/waves-overview

In 2008, Wave 3, known as SHARELIFE, marked a methodological milestone by employing retrospective life-history interviews to document respondents' entire life courses, from childhood through adulthood. Collecting detailed information on early-life conditions, educational trajectories, employment histories, and family dynamics enabled researchers to adopt a life-course approach, examining how early experiences influence outcomes in later life. This retrospective design was reiterated in 2017 as part of Wave 7, further enhancing SHARE's capacity to capture the temporal layers of human development. For additional information about retrospective waves, consider Börsch-Supan et al. (2011), Börsch-Supan and Schröder (2011), and Bergmann et al. (2019).

From 2010 to 2015, the following waves encompassing Waves 4 through 6 further consolidated the panel structure while enriching the dataset with new health measurements, such as grip strength, walking speed, and cognitive testing. Notably, these waves introduced biometric innovations, including collecting dried blood spots in selected countries, which provided valuable biomarkers for studying ageing-related diseases. For further information on the survey and the first collected results, refer to Börsch-Supan et al. (2013), Abduladze et al. (2013), Börsch-Supan et al. (2015), Börsch-Supan and Malter (2015), and Malter and Börsch-Supan (2017).

Initiated in 2019, pilot studies for Wave 8 included enhanced questions regarding social participation, digital skills, and physical activity alongside the incorporation of wearable sensor technology. However, the COVID-19 pandemic necessitated an interruption in its full implementation, leading the SHARE team to adapt rapidly. In response, two telephone-based survey waves were conducted in 2020 and 2021, known as the SHARE Corona surveys, which captured critical data on how older adults in Europe navigated the pandemic—emotionally, economically, and medically. This swift transition from in-person to telephone interviews underscored the infrastructure's flexibility during a period of crisis, preserving the continuity of the panel while introducing pandemic-specific variables for real-time policy insights. Further information is provided in Bergmann and Börsch-Supan (2021).

Wave 9 occurred between 2021 and 2022 and resumed face-to-face interviews. This wave included follow-up questions related to the COVID-19 experience. It continued the collection of core modules on health, economic activity, and social networks, as well as incorporating the SHARE-HCAP (Harmonized Cognitive Assessment Protocol) sub-study in five countries to facilitate comparisons in cognitive ageing with studies such as the Health and Retirement Study (HRS) and the English Longitudinal Study of Ageing (ELSA). For additional information, see Bergmann et al. (2024), Bergmann et al. (2024), Börsch-Supan et al. (2025), and Otero et al. (2023).

The most recent survey, designated as Wave 10, was conducted in 2025 and provided certain countries with the opportunity to refresh their samples with an additional component of individuals. Italy was able to implement this enhancement due to the financial support received from the CNR and FOSSR.

Throughout its various waves, SHARE has consistently demonstrated an ability to adapt its content, coverage, and methodology in response to advancements in scientific knowledge and external circumstances. Each new wave not only refreshes the data but also broadens the analytical possibilities for researchers. The regular data collection and integration of both retrospective and real-time information position SHARE uniquely among global panel studies.

In conclusion, the cumulative design of the SHARE waves illustrates a commitment to scientific rigour and societal relevance through timely and responsive data collection. This evolution has solidified SHARE's status as a foundational element of European research on ageing and a benchmark for large-scale longitudinal studies worldwide.

6.7 Scientific and Policy Impact

Over time, SHARE has become recognised as a significant social sciences and public health research infrastructure. As shown in the left panel of Fig. 6.2, it has produced over 4000 peer-reviewed publications and boasts tens of thousands of registered users from diverse academic institutions, policy agencies, and international organisations.

As shown by the increasing number of users over time reported in the right panel of Fig. 6.2, this dataset serves as a fundamental resource for evidence-based

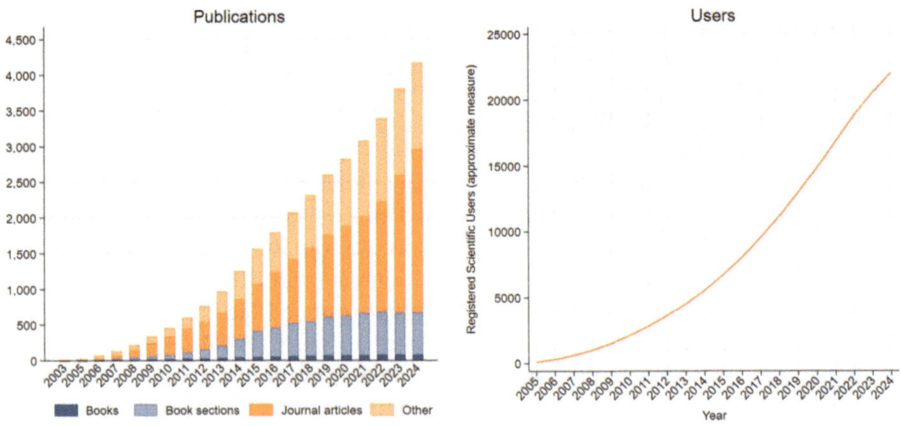

Fig. 6.2 Scientific and policy impact of SHARE. Image created by the authors using data published by SHARE-ERIC at the web page: https://share-eric.eu/publications/user-publications-statistics

research concerning ageing. The scientific contributions encompass various disciplines, including economics, epidemiology, sociology, and demography. SHARE has played a crucial role in enhancing the understanding of retirement behaviours, cognitive ageing, health inequalities, intergenerational transfers, and informal care. A range of illustrative examples showcasing the results derived from the SHARE data is systematically presented in Chap. 8, highlighting the significant insights and findings obtained from this comprehensive dataset.

From a policy perspective, SHARE has offered valuable insights to assist national governments and European institutions, particularly about pension reform, long-term care, and the resilience of health systems. The SHARE Corona Survey was rapidly implemented during the COVID-19 pandemic, allowing researchers and policymakers to promptly evaluate the vulnerabilities and adaptive capacities of older populations across Europe. This quick response and adherence to high data quality standards resulted in SHARE being designated as an ESFRI Landmark in 2016 by the European Strategy Forum on Research Infrastructures. This designation is granted to infrastructures deemed strategically important for the European Research Area. Through ongoing commitments to open access, methodological advancements, and interdisciplinary collaboration, SHARE has demonstrated its role as a vital facilitator of impactful research and policy development.

6.8 Conclusion

SHARE-ERIC is a notable example of how infrastructures with ERIC status can enhance social science research. This initiative is characterised by effective governance, legal clarity, consistent funding, and commitment to global open data access. SHARE has consistently provided significant evidence in health, economic, and social areas. Its development reflects the potential of pan-European scholarly collaboration, contributing to academic empowerment, policy formulation, and the strengthening of societal resilience.

References

Abduladze, L., Malter, F., & Börsch-Supan, A. (2013). *SHARE wave 4: Innovations & methodology*. MEA, Max Planck Institute for Social Law and Social Policy.

Bergmann, M. & Börsch-Supan, A. (2021). SHARE Wave 8 methodology: Collecting cross-national survey data in times of COVID-19. *MEA, Max Planck Institute for Social Law and Social Policy.*

Bergmann, M., Scherpenzeel, A., & Börsch-Supan, A. (2019). SHARE wave 7 methodology: Panel innovations and life histories (Vol. 4). *Munich Center for the Economics of Aging (MEA).*

Bergmann, M., Wagner, M., & Börsch-Supan, A. (2024). SHARE wave 9 methodology: From the SHARE corona survey 2 to the SHARE main wave 9 interview. *Munich: SHARE-ERIC.* https://doi.org/10.6103/mv.w09

Bergmann, M., Wagner, M., Yilmaz, Y., Axt, K., Kronschnabl, J., Pettinicchi, Y., Schmidutz, D., Schuller, K., Stuck, S., & Börsch-Supan, A. (2024). SHARE Corona Surveys: study profile. *Longitudinal and Life Course Studies*, *15*(4), 506–525. https://doi.org/10.1332/17579597Y2024D000000027

Börsch-Supan, A., Brandt, M., Hank, K., & Schröder, M. (2011). *The individual and the welfare state: Life histories in Europe*. Springer Science & Business Media. https://doi.org/10.1007/978-3-642-17472-8

Börsch-Supan, A., Brandt, M., Hunkler, C., Kneip, T., Korbmacher, J., Malter, F., Schaan, B., Stuck, S., & Zuber, S. (2013). Data resource profile: The Survey of Health, Ageing and Retirement in Europe (SHARE). *International Journal of Epidemiology*, *42*(4), 992–1001. https://doi.org/10.1093/ije/dyt088

Börsch-Supan, A., Brandt, M., Litwin, H., & Weber, G. (2013). *Active ageing and solidarity between generations in Europe*. de Gruyter. https://doi.org/10.1515/9783110295467

Börsch-Supan, A., Brugiavini, A., Jürges, H., Kapteyn, A., Mackenbach, J.P., Siegrist, J., & Weber, G. (2008). *First results from the Survey of Health, Ageing and Retirement in Europe (2004–2007): Starting the longitudinal dimension*. Mannheim Research Institute for the Economics of Aging (MEA).

Börsch-Supan, A., Brugiavini, A., Jürges, H., Mackenbach, J., Siegrist, J., & Weber, G. (2005). *Health, ageing and retirement in Europe - First results from the Survey of Health, Ageing and Retirement in Europe* (Vol. 1). Mannheim Research Institute for the Economics of Aging (MEA).

Börsch-Supan, A., Douhou, S., & Tawiah, B. B. (2025). *Cognitive impairment and the long arm of childhood education: Evidence from Europe*. Munich Center for the Economics of Aging (MEA).

Börsch-Supan, A., & Jürges, H. (2005). *The Survey of Health, Aging and Retirement in Europe - Methodology*. Mannheim Research Institute for the Economics of Aging (MEA).

Börsch-Supan, A., Kneip, T., Litwin, H., Myck, M., & Weber, G. (2015). *Ageing in Europe: Supporting policies for an inclusive society*. de Gruyter. https://doi.org/10.1515/9783110444414

Börsch-Supan, A. & Malter, F. (2015). *SHARE wave 5: Innovations & methodology*. MEA, Max Planck Institute for Social Law and Social Policy.

De Luca, G., Peracchi, F., Börsch-Supan, A., & Jürges, H. (2005). *The Survey of Health, Ageing and Retirement in Europe: Methodology* (pp. 85–100). Mannheim Research Institute for the Economics of Aging (MEA).

Malter, F. & Börsch-Supan, A. (2017). *SHARE Wave 6: Panel innovations and collecting Dried Blood Spots*. Munich: Munich Center for the Economics of Aging (MEA).

Otero, M., Douhou, S., Pettinicchi, Y., Sommer, E., Ludmark, V. P., Rieckmann, A., et al. (2023). European adaptation of the Harmonized Cognitive Assessment Protocol: Methodological lessons learned from SHARE-HCAP. *Alzheimer's & Dementia, 19*, e063042. https://doi.org/10.1002/alz.063042

Schröder, M. (2011). Retrospective Data Collection in the Survey of Health, Ageing and Retirement in Europe. *SHARELIFE Methodology*. MEA, Mannheim.

Weber, G. (2018). SHARE: A data set for ageing research. *Journal of Public Health Research, 7* (1), jphr–2018. https://doi.org/10.4081/jphr.2018.1397

Chapter 7
The Consortium of European Social Science Data Archives (CESSDA) and the Data Archive for Social Sciences in Italy (DASSI)

Filippo Accordino, Fabrizio Pecoraro, Daniela Luzi, Carlo Pisano, and Domingo Scisci

7.1 Introduction

Data sharing is a practice of considerable importance in any field of research, for multiple reasons. These include enabling the reproducibility of research and facilitating the reuse of data to answer new research questions (Borgman, 2012). Furthermore, it can be used for teaching purposes, and to inform policies and for other different and specific aims (Bishop & Kuula-Luumi, 2017; Kenfield et al., 2022; Pasquetto et al., 2019). Moreover, data sharing can have a relevant impact on return on research infrastructure investment and efficiency (Van Den Eynden & Corti, 2017). The possibility of reuse confers a significant added value to research data, that might otherwise remain in the personal archives of scholars or be lost. The practice of sharing and reusing research data raises questions related to aspects of trust, attitudes, widespread practices, social norms and incentives, issues that have been the subject of investigation in several studies (Darch & Knox, 2017; Tenopir et al., 2015; Zenk-Möltgen et al., 2018).

The objectives of this contribution are:

- Illustrating the potential of data archives in the social sciences and their main features.
- Introducing the Consortium of European Social Science Data Archives (CESSDA-ERIC) and the services offered to users.

F. Accordino (✉) · F. Pecoraro · D. Luzi
Data Archive for Social Sciences in Italy (DASSI) and Institute for Research on Population and Social Policies (CNR-IRPPS), Rome, Italy
e-mail: f.accordino@irpps.cnr.it; fabrizio.pecoraro@cnr.it; daniela.luzi@cnr.it

C. Pisano · D. Scisci
Data Archive for Social Sciences in Italy (DASSI) and University of Milano-Bicocca, Milan, Italy
e-mail: carlo.pisano@unimib.it; domingo.scisci@unimib.it

L. Taddei, M. Paolucci (eds.), *Longitudinal Data Infrastructures in Europe*,
https://doi.org/10.1007/978-3-032-07005-0_7

- Introducing the Data Archive for Social Sciences in Italy (DASSI), illustrating how data curation and preservation activities are carried out, as well as data archiving and in what terms data reuse is possible.

In general, the contribution aims to provide an overview to all those who wish to acquire the basic knowledge necessary for the practice of depositing research data, through the presentation of the CESSDA-ERIC infrastructure, the Italian archive and the services they offer.

7.2 Data Archives and Infrastructures for Social Sciences

7.2.1 Data Archives and Infrastructures: What Are We Talking About?

The purpose of data archives is twofold: to promote the sharing and findability of research data, and to ensure long-term preservation of the materials deposited and subsequently redistributed to scholars. They are pivotal intermediaries between data producers and reusers (Borgman et al., 2019).

In comparison to alternative forms of data sharing, such as websites or simpler repositories, data archives adopt specific acceptance criteria based on an appraisal process, which involves assessing the scientific relevance and quality of the research data intended for deposit, the completeness of the associated documentation, and compliance with ethical and legal standards. In particular, they pay attention and offer solutions in safeguarding the property rights of data authors. Furthermore, data archives promote the correct citation of reused data (Ball & Duke, 2015; Fenner et al., 2019). Indeed, research data constitutes a scientific product that must be correctly cited (Data Citation Synthesis Group, 2014).

Contributing to an open science and data-centric perspective of research (Recker et al., 2015), data archives aim to facilitate the reproducibility of research and encourage the reuse of data, the collection of which is a resource and time-consuming activity (Perry & Netscher, 2022). The existence of a data archive specialised in a particular field or discipline is also a motivating factor for researchers to deposit data (Mannheimer et al., 2016; Yoon & Kim, 2017), and a quality documentation affects the satisfaction of researchers practising data reuse (Faniel et al., 2016).

A data archive is characterised by numerous advantages, including:

1. An accurate activity of data curation, carried out on the deposited data before publication. This is performed by using common rules, standards and controlled vocabularies, and producing a wider set of metadata that ensures the understanding of the content, context, methodology, data management and analysis, reporting also related publications. Data are accompanied by

additional materials, such as variable description, questionnaires, interview questions, methodological notes and any other kind of useful resources.
2. The attribution of a persistent identifier (e.g., DOI) to data and a number of versions, that allow the accurate location and identification of shared material.
3. The attribution of user license to data to guarantee intellectual property.
4. The findability of data and metadata in a data catalogue, accessible through web interface or API services.
5. The interoperability of metadata exposed in the catalogue that facilitates the comparison of multiple sources and the harvesting of data from other repositories.
6. The accessibility of data according to license.
7. The reusability of data, ensured through their accurate documentation, and according to the data license.
8. The guarantee of the long-term preservation of data, dependent on the establishment of a suitable technical infrastructure, the utilisation of open formats, the implementation of procedures to avoid data obsolescence taking into account organizational issues.
9. The support to all the users as research data services: assist depositants, assisting researchers with data management plan.
10. Training activities on Data Management, deposit, reuse.

Archives are continuously engaged in the promotion of best practices regarding data management, data sharing, reuse and citation. The dissemination of knowledge and skills is facilitated by the production of materials, guidelines and training opportunities.

The archive trustworthiness (Wolski et al., 2017) is the cornerstone of the data sharing process, in the relationships between depositors, reusers and archives. It is vital that an archive has a reputation of excellence within the scientific community and is regarded as trustworthy. Adherence to criteria and best practices from a policy, organisational and technological point of view are prerequisites for achieving certification landmark, for example the CoreTrustSeal (Corrado, 2019).

The considerable possibilities offered by research reproducibility and data reuse can stimulate a paradigm shift in research data management and in the practices of sharing data. To this aim, it is crucial to stimulate the diffusion of a set of necessary skills to manage data correctly and make them adapt to be shared (Fischer et al., 2022). They should be specific and different from data analysis (Perry & Netscher, 2022), as the archives' data curation skills are highly relevant (Kouper, 2016; Tammaro et al., 2019).

7.2.2 CESSDA Infrastructure

In Europe, data archives in the field of social sciences have progressively spread in every country, gaining importance. The oldest experiences are those of Germany, where the GESIS Data Archive for the Social Sciences has been active since 1960 (Schumann & Mauer, 2013) and United Kingdom, where the first data archive was established in the 60s (Van Den Eynden & Corti, 2017).

Due to their purpose and impact on research practices, organisations hosting archives (such as universities or research centres) face the challenge of ensuring their long-term sustainability from an organisational and financial point of view. This involves guaranteeing appropriate human and material resources and adopting a flexible approach to changes in circumstances and funding mechanisms (Eschenfelder et al., 2022; Eschenfelder & Shankar, 2017). Furthermore, collaboration between archives and their cooperation through associative forms and partnership is important to enhance their effectiveness in achieving their goals (Recker et al., 2015). It was precisely these aspects that led to the idea of setting up a consortium of data archives.

CESSDA was established in 1976 by several countries, including Italy (CESSDA, 2025b; Gaspani et al., 2019a), to bring together the experiences in data archive of different countries. Now regarded as one of the most significant research infrastructures in the domain of social sciences, CESSDA addresses a plurality of actors involved in the data sharing process who share their aims and principles. Member archives, called Service Providers (SPs), have the possibility to share their expertise, receive training dedicated to their experts, and increase the value of their data. CESSDA is inspired by the FAIR data management paradigm: Findable, Accessible, Interoperable, and Reusable (Wilkinson et al., 2016).

Data producers and users have a designated place to find data for research and deposit their own (through SPs). They can make use of a unified catalogue of data (generally organised into studies) and other tools, and opportunities for training. In a broader sense, the objective is to enhance collaboration among nations with regard to data repositories in the field of social sciences. This endeavour is intended to contribute to the development of a shared infrastructure and the implementation of initiatives aimed at raising the awareness of the scientific community regarding the significance of data sharing and reuse.

To date, 23 members participate in the infrastructure through their own data repository (CESSDA, 2025c). In 2016, CESSDA was awarded ESFRI (European Strategy Forum on Research Infrastructures) Landmark status (ESFRI, 2024), and in 2017 it was officially recognized as a European Research Infrastructure Consortium (ERIC) by the European Commission (European Commission, 2017). Additionally, CESSDA is a participant in the European Open Science Cloud (EOSC) (Budroni et al., 2019).

CESSDA provides a range of tools and resources. The most significant is the CESSDA Data Catalogue (CDC), a unified catalogue where the users can retrieve the metadata of all studies deposited in over 20 CESSDA's SPs (Accordino et al., 2025b). This is made possible by the SPs' adoption of a metadata model compatible with the CESSDA Metadata Model (Bradić-Martinović & Banović, 2021). This means that data can be described in the same way, regardless of the country in which it was collected or created. This allows users to search for it in a cross-sectional and comparative manner. To date, the CDC contains more than 40,000 studies, of which approximately 75% are described in English.

Metadata descriptions are created using standards and controlled vocabularies. To this end, the CESSDA Vocabulary Service tool (CESSDA, 2025a) brings together all the common vocabularies used for describing metadata. The vocabularies created by the DDI (Data Documentation Initiative) Alliance (Vardigan et al., 2008) play a primary role among these: they are used to describe important contextual and methodological information about studies, including how data was collected, the unit of analysis, time dimension and sampling type. To describe study topics, CESSDA has created a specific controlled vocabulary called "CESSDA Topic Classification" (CESSDA, 2022). Keywords are described using the European Language Social Science Thesaurus (ELSST), a thesaurus containing over 3300 concepts and covering numerous disciplines within the social sciences, which is available in 15 languages (CESSDA and Service Providers, 2024).

CESSDA also provides comprehensive guidelines for participating communities as a valuable resource.:

- The Data Management Expert Guide (DMEG) (CESSDA Training Team, 2022) assists researchers in adopting a set of practices and procedures for describing and managing the collected data so that it is compliant with the FAIR principles and ready for sharing through a data repository.
- The CESSDA Data Archiving Guide (DAG) (CESSDA Training Team, 2025), addressed to all professionals engaged in the domain of data archives. The guide elucidates the components, practices and all aspects involved in organising an archive and depositing data.
- The Data Citation Guide, based on CESSDA Recommendations on Data Citation (Bornatici et al., 2025) aims to encourage the adoption of best practice in data citation to ensure the traceability and transparency of data (Accordino et al., 2025a; Fenner et al., 2019), while also ensuring due recognition of the authors of the data.

7.2.3 Data Archive for Social Sciences in Italy

In Italy, the first steps in creating a data archive for the social sciences were taken in the 70s with the establishment of the Data Archive for Social Sciences, (ADPSS) at the Istituto Superiore di Sociologia in Milan. In 1999, the archive expanded through collaboration with the Department of Sociology of the University of Milan, becoming ADPSS-Sociodata (Gaspani et al., 2019a). This infrastructure was followed by the establishment of the UniData—Bicocca Data Archive in 2015. The latter is incorporated into DASSI, which was established in 2021 through a joint research unit between the University of Milano-Bicocca and the National Research Council. It was subsequently recognized by the Italian Ministry of University and Research as the national SP of CESSDA.

The primary objective of DASSI is to establish itself as a main archive for all research data produced by Italian researchers or pertaining to Italy.

In recent years, the constitutive work of DASSI has been carried out by a team of experts from the two institutions involved. This team has been responsible for building the technical infrastructure, drafting the necessary policies and establishing the protocols for the functioning of the archive and the data appraisal activities. The Italian archive is currently engaged in the process of obtaining CoreTrustSeal certification. Participation in the CESSDA infrastructure enhances the activity of DASSI and the value of stored data, allowing them to be easily retrievable. The development of the archive, in terms of both size and relevance of the collections held, is pursued through an outreach activity and the creation of collaboration agreements with the Italian scientific community, institutions and universities. The collaboration with FOSSR (*Fostering Open Science in Social Science Research (FOSSR)*, n.d.) will facilitate the feeding of the archive with data from the panels and surveys that will be produced by the project. DASSI is committed to the objective of aligning itself with internationally recognised standards and best practices. It is founded on the principles of Open Science and the management of data according to the FAIR criteria. DASSI facilitates the dissemination of anonymised, meticulously documented data in open format through the attribution of a persistent identifier (i.e., DOI).

DASSI can be accessed through the website www.dassi-archive.it, where a comprehensive collection of information and introductory guides, designed to facilitate the management of research data, is published. The data archived by DASSI are searchable in an online catalogue through different search keys related to the metadata. The studies will also be searchable in the CDC, which is capable of harvesting metadata from DASSI due to the compatibility of metadata models.

In addition to archiving researchers' data, DASSI supports its users and community in several ways, such as providing advice on issues related to open science and data sharing and suggesting models of Data Management Plans shared at a European level. DASSI is therefore a national reference point within the landscape of research infrastructure in the social sciences.

7.3 The DASSI Model for Research Data Management

DASSI has developed its own Data Acquisition Policy, which outlines the principles guiding the deposit and the data evaluation process, with the aim of determining whether the submitted data are sufficiently well documented, ethically managed, and technically suitable for long-term preservation and dissemination to the relevant research community. The key elements considered during the appraisal phase will be discussed separately in the following sections.

7.3.1 Documenting Research Data

Data documentation plays a crucial role in the management and preservation of information collected in the social sciences, as it enables researchers to reconstruct the epistemological, methodological, and operational context in which the data were collected or generated. Without accurate documentation, the meaning of data can easily be misunderstood, undermining their potential for reuse, sharing, and integration into new analytical frameworks. Documenting data means providing a detailed account of the entire research data lifecycle—making explicit the processes of data collection, transformation, and organization—while offering information on the research design, sampling strategies, data collection instruments, and all subsequent modifications, such as coding or anonymization choices (CESSDA Training Team, 2022; Corti et al., 2020). In the broader context of Open Science and the FAIR principles (Wilkinson et al., 2016), data documentation becomes even more essential, as it ensures that data are not only available, but also properly understood and reusable over time.

Researchers may document their data in different ways, either by reusing documents already produced during the project—such as research proposals submitted to funding bodies or ethics committees—or by creating new materials during the research process, such as methodological notes, fieldwork diaries, or instruction guides for collaborators involved in data collection. When preparing data for deposit, it is necessary to provide consistent and structured descriptions that follow specific international standards. This harmonized approach allows for better alignment across different data archives, improving the findability and accessibility of data for the research community.

To deposit a study in DASSI, a scholar must follow some rules, and a specific process in which archive's staff provide support. Indeed, depositors have to provide information and materials in order to allow the documentation of data and have to sign a deposit agreement that, among other things, defines the end-user licence under which access and reuse will be permitted.

DASSI has developed a dedicated deposit form, an online tool researchers can use to describe the context in which the data were produced and the key characteristics of the datasets intended for deposit. The deposit form collects information such as:

- title, abstract, a list of keywords and topics covered in order to describe the content of data.
- names, roles, affiliations and persistent identifiers of the researchers involved.
- funding institutions.
- geographic and temporal coverage.
- unit of analysis.
- mode of data collection.
- sampling or selection procedures.
- file formats used.
- the intended usage license.

- related publications.

Based on this information, DASSI curates the data description using the DaMM (DASSI Metadata Model), which is built on the international DDI Codebook 2.5 standard. The Data Documentation Initiative (DDI) is the most widely adopted standard for documenting quantitative and qualitative research data in the social, behavioral, economic, and health sciences. DDI enables the documentation and management of the various stages of the research data lifecycle—from conceptualization through collection, processing, dissemination, discovery, and archiving. The use of standards like DDI not only enhances data identification, searchability, and interpretability, but also supports interoperability—the ability to integrate and use data in combination with other datasets and software tools, in line with FAIR principles. In this context, DASSI also adopts controlled vocabularies and thesauri—predefined lists of terms and concepts—that ensure semantic consistency and reduce ambiguity in data descriptions. These vocabularies, such as the ELSST and others promoted by CESSDA, facilitate connections across datasets and enhance both findability and information sharing, allowing metadata interoperability.

Ultimately, documentation emerges as an epistemologically rich practice—a foundational requirement for scientific transparency, research reproducibility, and the cumulative construction of knowledge (Bornat, 2014; Feldman & Shaw, 2019). These are all critical components in a research environment increasingly characterized by collective, distributed, and open processes.

7.3.2 Preparing Data for Archiving

For a data archive, preparing research data is a critical phase in the deposit and archiving process, as it ensures data quality, reusability, and compliance with ethical and legal standards. Without delving into the various models proposed in the literature (see, for example, Harvey, 2006; Niu, 2014), five core elements are generally emphasized when preparing data for deposit: completeness, integrity, documentation, file format, and data protection. This section focuses in particular on the latter two.

Choosing the appropriate file format is essential for technical sustainability and long-term accessibility. Data preservation is closely tied to file format, particularly in relation to software dependency. Compliant with the common best practices, DASSI favors open, non-proprietary, or well-documented formats that support long-term usability and interoperability with major analytical software. File formats are also subject to the risk of obsolescence, driven by the constant evolution of hardware and software. For this reason, DASSI maintains a list of accepted file formats based on best practices shared among international data archives. The list may vary depending on the type of data—quantitative, qualitative, numerical, textual, audiovisual, etc.

For quantitative data, accepted formats include Comma-Separated Values (.csv), SPSS (.sav, .por), STATA (.dta), SAS (.sas7bdat), R (.RData), and Microsoft Excel (.xls, .xlsx). For qualitative data, preferred formats include structured text files such as PDF/A or PDF, Microsoft Word (.doc, .docx), Rich Text Format (.rtf), Plain Text (.txt), OpenDocument (.odt), or markup formats such as HTML, XML, and JSON. When needed, DASSI converts files that are at risk of obsolescence or unsuitable for long-term preservation into more sustainable formats to ensure future reusability. For this reason, all quantitative data are converted in csv format.

Another essential aspect of data preparation concerns data protection, and more specifically, anonymization, which is necessary to ensure compliance with privacy regulations, such as the General Data Protection Regulation (GDPR, Regulation EU 2016/679) and applicable national laws. Since DASSI only accepts anonymized data, researchers are responsible for carrying out anonymization before deposit, with support from the archive if needed. Researchers must ensure that every reasonable effort has been made to prevent identification of research participants. This includes removing all direct identifiers (e.g., names, addresses, tax codes) as well as potential indirect identifiers (e.g., workplace, income, or other attributes that, when combined with external data, could lead to identification). As part of the appraisal process, DASSI performs a disclosure risk analysis on submitted data. If any risk is detected, the archive works with the researcher to determine appropriate anonymization measures.

For quantitative data, common anonymization techniques include suppressing variables or cases with high disclosure risk, generalization (e.g., of geographic data, educational attainment, or occupations), top-coding or aggregating values into broader categories (e.g., age or income groups), recoding of textual variables into numeric values, and, if necessary, the introduction of statistical noise to obscure sensitive information (Kleiner & Heers, 2024). For qualitative data—such as interview or focus group transcripts—anonymization requires careful linguistic and contextual review. Names, places, organizations, and specific events must be removed or replaced with pseudonyms, acronyms, or neutral descriptors (Corti et al., 2020; Gaspani et al., 2019b; Stam & Diaz, 2023). This process is often time-consuming, especially for qualitative data, and should ideally be planned as part of the research workflow, integrated into the data collection or analysis phases. Regardless of the strategy or techniques adopted, anonymization must strike a careful balance between protecting individual privacy and preserving the analytical value of the data—enabling meaningful secondary analysis and long-term reuse.

In conclusion, preparing data for archiving requires a careful assessment of scientific quality, technological sustainability, and confidentiality protection. In this respect, DASSI offers continuous and hands-on support to researchers throughout the process, helping ensure that deposited data are both ethically valid and scientifically reusable.

7.3.3 Preserving Research Data

Preserving research data is a crucial and complex task, distinct from merely storing files in a digital repository. The goal is not just to save data, but to ensure that they remain interpretable, understandable, and reusable over the long term by other researchers. This process requires not only robust technical infrastructure, but also a coordinated set of documentation, management, legal practices, and domain-specific expertise—elements that a basic repository alone cannot provide. In this regard, the European infrastructure CESSDA and its network of SPs represent an authoritative international benchmark for addressing these challenges.

One of the most widely adopted frameworks for supporting this type of comprehensive preservation strategy is the Open Archival Information System (OAIS) model (Consultative Committee for Space Data Systems, 2024), which offers a conceptual and operational foundation for managing data over time. The OAIS model introduces a three-tier structure of information packages: SIP (Submission Information Package), AIP (Archival Information Package), and DIP (Dissemination Information Package). The SIP is the initial package provided by the data producer to the archive; the AIP is the version adapted for long-term preservation, including all necessary contextual and preservation-related information; and the DIP is the user-facing package, designed for dissemination and reuse, containing the data and supporting documentation in an accessible form. This structure is not merely technical—it implies a thoughtful approach to data curation from the very outset of the research process. Data must be accompanied by structured metadata documenting not only the content but also the data collection context, processing methods, any legal or ethical restrictions, and the conditions for future use. Central to this model is the concept of the *designated community*—a defined audience of potential future users, whose characteristics determine what must be made explicit for the data to remain comprehensible even years after collection. This also entails the use of data formats that are widely adopted and supported within the target community, ensuring long-term readability and usability (Donaldson et al., 2020).

As Italian National SP for CESSDA, DASSI fully aligns with the OAIS model. Long-term preservation is ensured through a distributed system involving redundant physical storage, periodic integrity checks, and format migration strategies to counter technological obsolescence. In this context, the use of open formats is not a mere technical detail—it is a critical guarantee of future readability. As already discussed, DASSI also provides active support to researchers in preparing SIP packages, offering practical guidelines, validation tools (e.g., consistency checks between data files and documentation), and assistance in selecting the most appropriate license. Particular attention is given to curating the methodological documentation—as highlighted earlier—that is essential for generating metadata that comply with the DDI standard, ensuring compatibility with European discovery and interoperability systems.

This approach enables DASSI to fully implement the FAIR principles, especially with regard to long-term preservation. Data are documented in ways that ensure not only today's accessibility, but also future interpretability and technical usability across the broader scientific community. Curation and preservation are not the final steps of a project—they are integral to the entire lifecycle of data, as emphasized by numerous authors over time (Dekker, 2020; Kowalczyk, 2018; Mohler & Uher, 2003; Pennock, 2007).

7.3.4 Reusing Research Data

Data reuse is a core component of Open Science and a strategic objective for data curation infrastructures. As emphasized by Kush et al. (2020), reusability—one of the FAIR principles—cannot be ensured by mere technical availability; it also requires rich metadata, consistent structuring, and the use of standardized, clearly defined licenses. For data to be truly reusable, they must be accompanied by comprehensive documentation and made available through platforms that facilitate discovery, citation, and long-term intelligibility (Wang & Savard, 2023). Reuse can take many forms—from replicating analyses to integrating data into new research or using it for educational purposes—but all of these rely on data being accessible, interpretable, and lawfully usable under pre-defined terms. To foster such reusability, all metadata curated and published through DASSI are released under an open license (Creative Commons Attribution), ensuring unrestricted access and downstream use.

This is precisely where the Dataverse platform, adopted by DASSI for study publication and distribution, plays a crucial role. As described by Crosas (2011; see also King, 2007), Dataverse is a widely adopted, open-source infrastructure designed to provide a secure, transparent, and interoperable environment for research data. Each study is assigned a persistent identifier (i.e., DOI) to enable formal citation and is versioned to track changes over time. DASSI leverages Dataverse to ensure compliance with the DDI 2.5 metadata standard, which is critical for interoperability with infrastructures such as the CDC (Huber et al., 2021).

Access to deposited data is managed through a flexible licensing system, defined in collaboration with the researcher and clearly stated on each study's landing page. Preference is given to open licenses such as Creative Commons Attribution (CC-BY), which allow reuse in both academic and commercial contexts. However, when sensitive data or ethical restrictions are involved, DASSI allows the use of conditional access licenses, requiring user registration or prior approval. As Chapoy et al. (2020) point out, this balanced approach between openness and control provides a robust model for protecting research participants while still enabling secondary analysis.

In addition, Dataverse supports the use of embargo periods, a feature also adopted by DASSI. During an embargo, the dataset remains discoverable and citable through its DOI and metadata, while the data files themselves are temporarily inaccessible. This mechanism helps safeguard researchers' publication priorities while promoting transparency and structured planning of data release. Embargoes are especially useful in competitive research environments or when required by journal policies.

Finally, the DASSI public catalogue serves as the central access point for study exploration and retrieval. Users can search using keywords, topics, data collection methods, authors, or funding institutions. Data are Findable thanks to standardized metadata and international indexing (Doorn, 2020); Accessible through intuitive interfaces that clarify licensing and access conditions; Interoperable through the use of common standards such as DDI, enabling automatic integration with other platforms (i.e. CESSDA Data Catalogue); and Reusable thanks to extensive technical and methodological documentation. Dataverse also supports the inclusion of syntax files and analytical scripts as part of dataset publication, thereby promoting reproducibility and scientific transparency (Huber et al., 2021; Kush et al., 2020).

7.4 Conclusions

The dissemination of research data is of paramount importance for the advancement of science. In order to facilitate this process, it is essential to propose suitable tools, services and infrastructures, as well as the dissemination of appropriate data management skills. This necessitates a shift in the scientific community, which must be cognisant of these practices.

The CESSDA infrastructure and the Italian DASSI archive are intended to pursue these aims, operating in accordance with the principles and procedures outlined in this contribution. In the near future, DASSI is on track to obtain the requisite quality certifications, thereby establishing itself as a prominent entity within the Italian social science research landscape.

References

Accordino, F., Luzi, D., & Pecoraro, F. (2025a). Challenges in tracking archive's data reuse in social sciences. *Digital Library Perspectives, 41*(2), 189–206. https://doi.org/10.1108/DLP-07-2024-0112

Accordino, F., Pecoraro, F., & Luzi, D. (2025b). CESSDA data catalogue: An opportunity to enhance data in social sciences. *International Journal on Digital Libraries, 26*(1), 8. https://doi.org/10.1007/s00799-025-00416-w

Ball, A., & Duke, M. (2015). *'How to Cite Datasets and Link to Publications'. DCC How-to Guides*. Digital Curation Centre. http://www.dcc.ac.uk/resources/how-guides

Bishop, L., & Kuula-Luumi, A. (2017). Revisiting qualitative data reuse: A decade on. *SAGE Open, 7*(1), 215824401668513. https://doi.org/10.1177/2158244016685136

Borgman, C. L. (2012). The conundrum of sharing research data. *Journal of the American Society for Information Science and Technology, 63*(6), 1059–1078. https://doi.org/10.1002/asi.22634

Borgman, C. L., Scharnhorst, A., & Golshan, M. S. (2019). Digital data archives as knowledge infrastructures: Mediating data sharing and reuse. *Journal of the Association for Information Science and Technology, 70*(8), 888–904. https://doi.org/10.1002/asi.24172

Bornat, J. (2014). Epistemology and ethics in data sharing and analysis: A critical overview. In L. Camfield (Ed.), *Methodological challenges and new approaches to research in international development* (pp. 217–237). Palgrave Macmillan UK. https://doi.org/10.1057/9781137293626_10

Bornatici, C., Jernung, A., Alaterä, T. J., Tveit Sandberg, L., Strand, K., Štebe, J., & Trtíková, I. (2025). *CESSDA recommendations on data citation: Practical recommendations for key stakeholders*. https://doi.org/10.5281/ZENODO.15043854

Bradić-Martinović, A., & Banović, J. (2021). Meta-data specification for the description of social science data resources – Cessda metadata model. *Proceedings of the International Scientific Conference - Sinteza, 2021*, 193–199. https://doi.org/10.15308/Sinteza-2021-193-199

Budroni, P., Claude-Burgelman, J., & Schouppe, M. (2019). Architectures of knowledge: The European open science cloud. *ABI Technik, 39*(2), 130–141. https://doi.org/10.1515/abitech-2019-2006

CESSDA. (2022). *CESSDA topic classification (Version 4.2.2)*. [Controlled vocabulary] https://vocabularies.cessda.eu/urn/urn:ddi:int.cessda.cv:TopicClassification:4.2.2

CESSDA. (2025a). *CESSDA Vocabulary Service*. https://vocabularies.cessda.eu/

CESSDA. (2025b). *History*. https://www.cessda.eu/About/History

CESSDA. (2025c). *The CESSDA Consortium*. https://www.cessda.eu/About/Consortium

CESSDA and Service Providers. (2024). *The European Language Social Science Thesaurus (ELSST) (Version 5)* [Dataset]. Zenodo. https://doi.org/10.5281/ZENODO.4063933

CESSDA Training Team. (2022). *CESSDA Data Management Expert Guide*. https://doi.org/10.5281/ZENODO.3820473

CESSDA Training Team. (2025). *CESSDA Data Archiving Guide version 4.0*. CESSDA ERIC. https://dag.cessda.eu/

Chapoy, E., Lesnard, L., Gaultier-Voituriez, O., Groshens, E., Pedroja, C., & Beldiman-Moore, A. (2020). *Sciences Po. Une histoire de données*. Sciences Po. https://sciencespo.hal.science/hal-03612928

Consultative Committee for Space Data Systems. (2024). *Reference Model for an Open Archival Information System (OAIS)—Recommended Practice CCSDS 650.0-M-3*. CCSDS Secretariat National Aeronautics and Space Administration Washington, DC. https://ccsds.org/Pubs/650x0m3.pdf

Corrado, E. M. (2019). Repositories, Trust, and the CoreTrustSeal. *Technical Services Quarterly, 36*(1), 61–72. https://doi.org/10.1080/07317131.2018.1532055

Corti, L., Van den Eynden, V., Bishop, L., Woollard, M., Haaker, M., & Summers, S. (2020). *Managing and sharing research data: A guide to good practice* (2nd ed.). SAGE.

Crosas, M. (2011). The Dataverse Network®: An open-source application for sharing, discovering and preserving data. *D-Lib Magazine, 17*(1/2). https://doi.org/10.1045/january2011-crosas

Darch, P. T., & Knox, E. J. M. (2017). Ethical perspectives on data and software sharing in the sciences: A research agenda. *Library & Information Science Research, 39*(4), 295–302. https://doi.org/10.1016/j.lisr.2017.11.008

Data Citation Synthesis Group. (2014). Joint Declaration of Data Citation Principles. *Force11*. https://doi.org/10.25490/A97F-EGYK

Dekker, R. (2020). Social data: CESSDA best practices. *Data Intelligence, 2*(1–2), 220–229. https://doi.org/10.1162/dint_a_00044

Donaldson, D. R., Zegler-Poleska, E., & Yarmey, L. (2020). Data managers' perspectives on OAIS designated communities and the FAIR principles: Mediation, tools and conceptual models. *Journal of Documentation, 76*(6), 1261–1277. https://doi.org/10.1108/JD-10-2019-0204

Doorn, P. K. (2020). *EOSC-SYNERGY Landscaping Country Report The Netherlands* [Application/pdf]. https://doi.org/10.17026/DANS-2BY-EREU

Eschenfelder, K. R., & Shankar, K. (2017). Organizational resilience in data archives: Three case studies in social science data archives. *Data Science Journal, 16*, 12. https://doi.org/10.5334/dsj-2017-012

Eschenfelder, K. R., Shankar, K., & Downey, G. (2022). The financial maintenance of social science data archives: Four case studies of long-term infrastructure work. *Journal of the Association for Information Science and Technology, 73*(12), 1723–1740. https://doi.org/10.1002/asi.24691

ESFRI. (2024). *ESFRI Objectives & Vision*. https://www.esfri.eu/objectives-vision

European Commission. (2017) *Commission Implementing Decision (EU) 2017/995 (Decision 2017/995)*. https://eur-lex.europa.eu/eli/dec_impl/2017/995.

Faniel, I. M., Kriesberg, A., & Yakel, E. (2016). Social scientists' satisfaction with data reuse. *Journal of the Association for Information Science and Technology, 67*(6), 1404–1416. https://doi.org/10.1002/asi.23480

Feldman, S., & Shaw, L. (2019). The epistemological and ethical challenges of archiving and sharing qualitative data. *American Behavioral Scientist, 63*(6), 699–721. https://doi.org/10.1177/0002764218796084

Fenner, M., Crosas, M., Grethe, J. S., Kennedy, D., Hermjakob, H., Rocca-Serra, P., Durand, G., Berjon, R., Karcher, S., Martone, M., & Clark, T. (2019). A data citation roadmap for scholarly data repositories. *Scientific Data, 6*(1), 28. https://doi.org/10.1038/s41597-019-0031-8

Fischer, C., Hirsbrunner, S. D., & Teckentrup, V. (2022). Producing open data. *Research Ideas and Outcomes, 8*, e86384. https://doi.org/10.3897/rio.8.e86384

Fostering Open Science in Social Science Research (FOSSR). (n.d.). Retrieved June 6, 2025, from https://www.fossr.eu/en/what-we-do/

Gaspani, F., Pisano, C., & Scisci, D. (2019a). I DATI OLTRE LA RICERCA: L'ARCHIVIAZIONE NELLE SCIENZE SOCIALI. *SOCIOLOGIA ITALIANA, 14*, 71–88. https://doi.org/10.1485/AIS_2019/14_3443545

Gaspani, F., Pisano, C., & Scisci, D. (2019b). Il riutilizzo dei dati qualitativi: Opportunità e sfide. *SOCIOLOGIA E RICERCA SOCIALE, 119*, 101–117. https://doi.org/10.3280/SR2019-119005

Harvey, R. (2006). Appraisal and selection. In *DCC Digital Curation Manual (Digital Curation Centre)*. http://www.dcc.ac.uk/resource/curation-manual/chapters/appraisal-and-selection

Huber, R., Cepinskas, L., Davidson, J., Herterich, P., L'Hours, H., Mokrane, M., von Stein, I., & Verburg, M. (2021). *D4.5 Report on FAIR Data Assessment Toolset and Badging Scheme*. https://doi.org/10.5281/ZENODO.5336159

Kenfield, A. S., Woolcott, L., Thompson, S., Kelly, E. J., Shiri, A., Muglia, C., Masood, K., Chapman, J., Jefferson, D., & Morales, M. E. (2022). Toward a definition of digital object reuse. *Digital Library Perspectives, 38*(3), 378–394. https://doi.org/10.1108/DLP-06-2021-0044

King, G. (2007). An introduction to the dataverse network as an infrastructure for data sharing. *Sociological Methods & Research, 36*(2), 173–199. https://doi.org/10.1177/0049124107306660

Kleiner, B., & Heers, M. (2024). *Quantitative data anonymisation: Practical guidance for anonymising sensitive social science data*. FORS Guides. https://doi.org/10.24449/FG-2024-00023

Kouper, I. (2016). Professional participation in digital curation. *Library & Information Science Research, 38*(3), 212–223. https://doi.org/10.1016/j.lisr.2016.08.009

Kowalczyk, S. T. (2018). Modelling the research data lifecycle. *International Journal of Digital Curation, 12*(2), 331–361. https://doi.org/10.2218/ijdc.v12i2.429

Kush, R. D., Warzel, D., Kush, M. A., Sherman, A., Navarro, E. A., Fitzmartin, R., Pétavy, F., Galvez, J., Becnel, L. B., Zhou, F. L., Harmon, N., Jauregui, B., Jackson, T., & Hudson, L. (2020). FAIR data sharing: The roles of common data elements and harmonization. *Journal of Biomedical Informatics, 107*, 103421. https://doi.org/10.1016/j.jbi.2020.103421

Mannheimer, S., Sterman, L., Borda, S., & Montana State University-Bozeman. (2016). Discovery and reuse of open datasets: An exploratory study. *Journal of eScience Librarianship, 5*(1), e1091. https://doi.org/10.7191/jeslib.2016.1091

Mohler, P. P., & Uher, R. (2003). Documenting comparative surveys for secondary analysis. In *Cross-cultural survey methods*. Wiley.

Niu, J. (2014). Appraisal and selection for digital curation. *International Journal of Digital Curation, 9*(2), 65–82. https://doi.org/10.2218/ijdc.v9i2.272

Pasquetto, I. V., Borgman, C. L., & Wofford, M. F. (2019). Uses and reuses of scientific data: The data creators' advantage. *Harvard Data Science Review, 1*(2). https://doi.org/10.1162/99608f92.fc14bf2d

Pennock, M. (2007). *Digital curation: A life-cycle approach to managing and preserving usable digital information*. UKOLN, University of Bath.

Perry, A., & Netscher, S. (2022). Measuring the time spent on data curation. *Journal of Documentation, 78*(7), 282–304. https://doi.org/10.1108/JD-08-2021-0167

Recker, A., Müller, S., Trixa, J., & Schumann, N. (2015). Paving the way for data-centric, open science: An example from the social sciences. *Journal of Librarianship and Scholarly Communication, 3*(2), 1227. https://doi.org/10.7710/2162-3309.1227

Schumann, N., & Mauer, R. (2013). The GESIS data archive for the social sciences: A widely recognised data archive on its way. *International Journal of Digital Curation, 8*(2), 215–222. https://doi.org/10.2218/ijdc.v8i2.285

Stam, A., & Diaz, P. (2023). *Qualitative data anonymisation: Theoretical and practical considerations for anonymising interview transcripts*. https://doi.org/10.24449/FG-2023-00020

Tammaro, A. M., Matusiak, K. K., Sposito, F. A., & Casarosa, V. (2019). Data curator's roles and responsibilities: An international perspective. *Libri, 69*(2), 89–104. https://doi.org/10.1515/libri-2018-0090

Tenopir, C., Dalton, E. D., Allard, S., Frame, M., Pjesivac, I., Birch, B., Pollock, D., & Dorsett, K. (2015). Changes in data sharing and data reuse practices and perceptions among scientists worldwide. *PLoS One, 10*(8), e0134826. https://doi.org/10.1371/journal.pone.0134826

Van Den Eynden, V., & Corti, L. (2017). Advancing research data publishing practices for the social sciences: From archive activity to empowering researchers. *International Journal on Digital Libraries, 18*(2), 113–121. https://doi.org/10.1007/s00799-016-0177-3

Vardigan, M., Heus, P., & Thomas, W. (2008). Data documentation initiative: Toward a standard for the social sciences. *International Journal of Digital Curation, 3*(1), 107–113. https://doi.org/10.2218/ijdc.v3i1.45

Wang, M., & Savard, D. (2023). The FAIR principles and research data management. In K. Thompson, E. Hill, E. Carlisle-Johnston, D. Dennie, & É. Fortin (Eds.), *Research data management in the Canadian context: A guide for practitioners and learners (English)*. Western University, Western Libraries. https://doi.org/10.5206/EXFO3999

Wilkinson, M. D., Dumontier, M., Aalbersberg, I. J., Appleton, G., Axton, M., Baak, A., Blomberg, N., Boiten, J.-W., Da Silva Santos, L. B., Bourne, P. E., Bouwman, J., Brookes, A. J., Clark, T., Crosas, M., Dillo, I., Dumon, O., Edmunds, S., Evelo, C. T., Finkers, R., et al. (2016). The FAIR Guiding Principles for scientific data management and stewardship. *Scientific Data, 3*(1), 160018. https://doi.org/10.1038/sdata.2016.18

Wolski, M., Howard, L., & Richardson, J. (2017). A trust framework for online research data services. *Publications, 5*(2), 14. https://doi.org/10.3390/publications5020014

Yoon, A., & Kim, Y. (2017). Social scientists' data reuse behaviors: Exploring the roles of attitudinal beliefs, attitudes, norms, and data repositories. *Library & Information Science Research, 39*(3), 224–233. https://doi.org/10.1016/j.lisr.2017.07.008

Zenk-Möltgen, W., Akdeniz, E., Katsanidou, A., Naßhoven, V., & Balaban, E. (2018). Factors influencing the data sharing behavior of researchers in sociology and political science. *Journal of Documentation, 74*(5), 1053–1073. https://doi.org/10.1108/JD-09-2017-0126

Chapter 8
Retirement, Health, and Digital Gaps: Studying European Ageing with SHARE

Chiara Dal Bianco , Guglielmo Weber , and Nancy Zambon

8.1 Introduction

The Survey of Health, Ageing and Retirement in Europe (SHARE) is an interdisciplinary and cross-national panel survey that collects microdata on health, socio-economic status, and social and family networks of individuals aged 50 or older across Europe and Israel. Initiated in 2004, SHARE has become a cornerstone for research on population ageing in Europe. As of 2025, SHARE includes more than 160,000 individuals from 28 countries.

Regular waves of SHARE are conducted every two years. In addition to the standard questionnaire, Waves 3 (2008–2009) and 7 (2017) gathered retrospective life-history data. Moreover, in response to the outbreak of the COVID-19 pandemic, SHARE Wave 8 face-to-face data collection was suspended in March 2020, and two telephone-administered surveys were conducted: the first (summer 2020) and second (summer 2021) SHARE-Corona surveys. These surveys allowed the project to maintain data continuity during the pandemic, and to capture in real-time its health and economic effects.

The project's longitudinal design enables the tracking of individuals over time, capturing the dynamic nature of the ageing process. This, combined with its multi-disciplinary scope—ranging from health and cognition to income and social networks—allows for a rich understanding of how different life domains interact over the life course. In addition, the international dimension of SHARE makes it possible to study the effects of policies that vary across time and countries, such as those related to pension systems, healthcare access, education reforms, or family policy. In this sense, SHARE functions as a quasi-laboratory for the analysis of how older individuals respond to differing institutional environments.

C. Dal Bianco · G. Weber · N. Zambon (✉)
Department of Economics and Management, University of Padua, Padua, Italy
e-mail: chiara.dalbianco@unipd.it; guglielmo.weber@unipd.it; nancy.zambon@unipd.it

L. Taddei, M. Paolucci (eds.), *Longitudinal Data Infrastructures in Europe*,
https://doi.org/10.1007/978-3-032-07005-0_8

SHARE follows strict standards of comparability and harmonisation across countries, through ex-ante coordination of survey instruments and translations. It is part of a global family of ageing surveys, including the U.S. Health and Retirement Study (HRS) and the English Longitudinal Study of Ageing (ELSA), supporting international research on ageing.

Its recognition as a European Research Infrastructure Consortium (ERIC) reflects its scientific value. With open access for the research community, SHARE has supported over 4000 academic publications in diverse fields, including economics, sociology, public health, and demography.

This chapter summarises selected SHARE-based findings on economic conditions, labour market participation, health, cognitive function, and digital inclusion among older Europeans. Section 8.2 presents studies focused on financial wellbeing and employment decisions. Section 8.3 turns to issues of health, cognition, and digital skills. Section 8.4 offers concluding remarks.

8.2 Economic Conditions and Labour Market Engagement in Later Life

Understanding the drivers of financial wellbeing and labour market choices requires a multidimensional, life-course approach. This chapter leverages findings from several SHARE-based empirical studies to explore how retirement decisions, education, parental leave policies, and the COVID-19 pandemic shaped the lives of Europeans aged 50 and over.

8.2.1 Retirement Choices and Financial Hardship

Over the last decades, many European countries have introduced pension reforms that raised the minimum retirement age to address population ageing and preserve the financial sustainability of pension systems. While these reforms are primarily designed to contain public expenditure, they also significantly influence individual retirement decisions. The literature on early retirement has shown that many workers choose to retire as soon as they become eligible, largely due to the financial incentives embedded in pension rules. As a result, in many developed countries, there is a substantial unused labour capacity among the young old—individuals who are no longer working but still capable of doing so.

At the same time, there is also evidence of unused financial capacity among older individuals. Many people approaching or past retirement age do not make optimal use of financial and debt markets. They may lack diversification in their asset holdings or fail to access home equity, thus limiting their ability to cushion economic shocks. A key question is whether such individuals—who retire as early

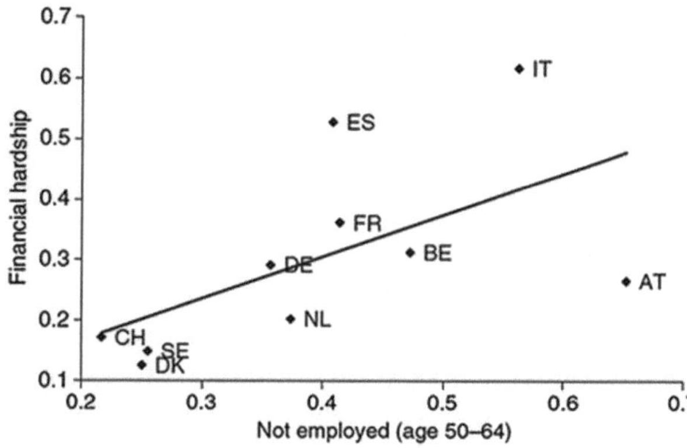

Fig. 8.1 Fraction of households reporting financial hardship plotted against the fraction of not-working individuals aged 50–64. Source: Angelini et al. (2009)

as possible and do not actively manage their financial assets—can avoid financial distress, or whether this combination increases their vulnerability.

Angelini et al. (2009) use SHARE Wave 2 data to study the relationship between early retirement, limited financial market participation, and financial hardship later in life, when some risks (such as long-term care needs) are not insured. They construct indicators capturing financial hardship (difficulty making ends meet), unused financial capacity (limited diversification and lack of home equity extraction), and unused labour capacity (years until or since retirement). They observe a strong positive association between financial hardship and unused labour capacity, represented by the fraction of households who report difficulties making ends meet, aged 50–64 who are not employed (Fig. 8.1).

The authors develop a life-cycle model in which retirement is treated as an absorbing state—retirees are not allowed to re-enter the labour market—and post-retirement income is subject to uninsurable health shocks. Within this framework, generous early retirement schemes may induce individuals with a strong enough preference for leisure into leaving the workforce prematurely. This decision may later be regretted, as early retirement appears optimal ex ante but eliminates the option of increasing labour supply ex post in response to adverse shocks—an outcome referred to as the early retirement trap.

The results indicate that individuals residing in Southern and Central European countries are particularly at risk of falling into this early retirement trap. In countries with financially attractive early retirement schemes and underdeveloped financial markets, the longer a person has been retired, the greater the likelihood of experiencing financial hardship. These findings underline the importance of integrating labour and financial policies to mitigate vulnerability among early retirees.

8.2.2 Early Life Conditions and Income

There is extensive empirical evidence showing that educational attainment significantly influences long-term individual outcomes, including earnings and career trajectories. Since cognitive abilities tend to stabilize by around age 10, early interventions can have particularly strong long-term effects (Cunha & Heckman, 2007).

Brunello et al. (2017) use SHARE data from Waves 1 to 3 to investigate how early life conditions—namely education and socio-economic background—shape lifetime earnings. SHARELIFE (Wave 3) provides retrospective information on life and labour market histories, including childhood circumstances such as whether the respondent lived in a rural area and the number of books at home at age 10. These indicators serve as proxies for early life socio-economic status and cultural capital.

The authors construct a measure of lifetime earnings based on the present value of wages earned from age 10 until retirement. To address the endogeneity of education, they exploit variation in compulsory schooling laws across countries and birth cohorts. The authors also highlight a positive relation between school reforms and educational attainments across Europe (Fig. 8.2).

Their two-stage least squares analysis shows that, on average, one additional year of education increases lifetime earnings by approximately 9%. Interestingly, while individuals from rural areas gained more in terms of educational attainment due to school reforms, those with many books at home experienced much higher returns to education—four times greater. Results also suggest that the presence of books likely captures a family's educational values and may reflect early development of cognitive skills more than just the availability of economic resources. These findings underscore the long-term economic benefits of investing in children's education and early-life environments.

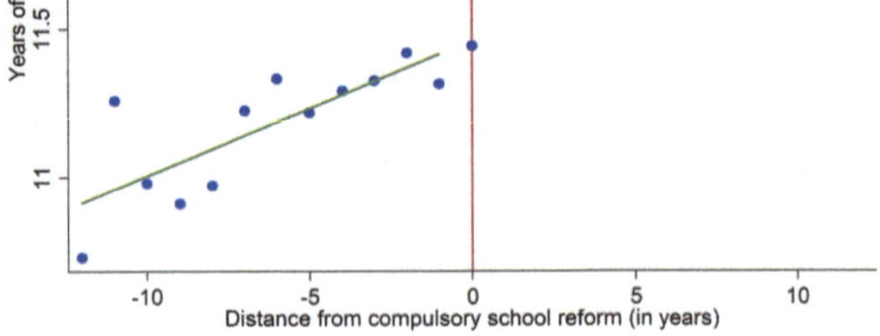

Fig. 8.2 Average years of education plotted against distance from school reforms. The figure displays average years of schooling by distance from reform. This distance results as the difference between the individual's year of birth and the year of birth of the first cohort affected by the reform. Source: Brunello et al. (2017)

8.2.3 Labour Participation and Gender Gaps

Women's labour market participation is often shaped by fertility decisions and childcare responsibilities, which can lead to career interruptions or even permanent withdrawal from the workforce. Since the mid-1960s, European countries have introduced maternity leave policies to support women around childbirth. However, the design and generosity of these policies vary greatly, influencing women's employment trajectories in different ways.

Brugiavini et al. (2013) explore how the duration and financial generosity of maternity leave schemes impact women's post-childbirth labour market participation. They use detailed fertility and employment histories from SHARELIFE (Wave 3), complemented by a comparative database of European maternity leave legislation covering the period from 1960 to 2010 (Gauthier, 2011).

The authors distinguish between time spent "in job" (employed but on leave) and "out of job" (not in the labour force) following childbirth. A triangular system of six regression equations—where the dependent variables are the number of weeks spent "in job" and "out of job" after the first, second and third childbirth—captures how maternity leave parameters affect each outcome. Results show that more generous maternity leave policies are effective in increasing women's labour force participation and reducing time spent out of work. Specifically, a longer leave increases the number of weeks spent "in job" (employed but not at work), while a higher benefit reduces the number of weeks spent "out of job" (not participating in the labour force). The analysis also shows considerable heterogeneity across countries, which likely reflects differences in cultural attitudes and institutional support for working mothers. These findings underline the importance of considering both policy design and socio-cultural context when assessing gender disparities in labour participation.

8.2.4 Economic Shocks and the COVID-19 Pandemic

The outbreak of the COVID-19 pandemic in March 2020 had significant repercussions for economic stability, health systems, and daily life across Europe. Although its medical consequences were severe—especially for older adults—its economic repercussions also revealed significant age-related and socio-economic disparities.

Bonfatti et al. (2023) use the first SHARE-Corona survey to assess the pandemic's economic impact on Europeans aged 50 and over. They develop a composite Financial Distress Indicator (FDI) based on income loss, difficulty in making ends meet, and the need to postpone payments.

Regression results show that older adults above retirement age (65+) were relatively well protected by public pension systems and welfare policies. In contrast, individuals aged 50–64 experienced more severe financial distress. For working-age households, the pandemic exacerbated pre-existing inequalities.

Bonfatti et al. (2023) also study the probability of reporting a worsening in difficulties making ends meet during the first wave of the pandemic compared to the pre-COVID-19 period. Among other findings, the authors highlight that income losses during the pandemic had a much greater impact—around five times greater—than income losses experienced in the two years prior to the pandemic. These findings highlight the protective role of welfare systems during crises, while drawing attention to persistent inequalities among working-age adults.

8.3 Health, Cognition, and Digital Inclusion in Ageing Europe

As Europe's population ages, issues related to health, cognitive functioning, and access to technology are becoming increasingly central to the policy debate. As stressed in Mazzonna and Peracchi (2017), Mazzonna and Peracchi (2024), among others, retirement marks a transition in life and influences daily routines, mental activity, and familiarity with digital tools—all of which have implications for older individuals' wellbeing. This chapter explores key evidence from SHARE-based studies on the effects of retirement on cognition and digital skills, as well as the relationship between digital literacy and preventive health behaviour during and after the COVID-19 pandemic.

8.3.1 Retirement and Cognitive Abilities

Cognitive health in later life is a growing concern across ageing societies. Cognitive functioning typically follows a life-cycle pattern, with a general decline in older age. However, the pace and extent of this decline vary significantly among individuals and appear to be influenced by lifestyle choices and major life events, such as retirement. According to the "Mental Retirement" hypothesis (Rohwedder & Willis, 2010), retirement may reduce mental stimulation, thereby accelerating cognitive decline.

Celidoni et al. (2017) investigate the relationship between (time in) retirement and cognitive functioning using longitudinal data from SHARE Waves 1 to 4. They assess cognitive decline using performance on memory tests—specifically, a 20% reduction in the number of words recalled, both immediately and after a delay, across waves. The authors address retirement decision endogeneity by instrumenting retirement with pension eligibility rules, following the methodology proposed by Angelini et al. (2009).

Regression results support the "Mental Retirement" hypothesis. The findings show that retirement affects cognition differently depending on the type of retiree. For early retirees—those who leave the labour market as soon as they become eligible—retirement has a short-term beneficial effect and no long-term detrimental impact. For statutory-age retirees—those who postpone retirement—retirement has a negative effect, which intensifies over time. The analysis also highlights compositional differences between the two groups: early retirees are more often men in low-skilled jobs, whereas statutory-age retirees are more likely to report higher job autonomy and greater satisfaction with their earnings. These findings highlight the importance of supporting cognitive engagement across all retirement pathways to mitigate mental decline in later life.

8.3.2 *Retirement and Digital Skills*

The growing importance of digital technologies in work and daily life has brought attention to the digital divide among older adults. Differences in ICT (Information and Communication Technology) usage may reinforce social exclusion and negatively affect wellbeing. As retirement changes the context in which older people engage with technology, it is crucial to understand whether it accelerates digital disengagement. While employment environments typically facilitate exposure to ICTs, retirement may increase discretionary time to engage with digital tools. Cavapozzi and Dal Bianco (2022) use SHARE Waves 5 and 6 to analyse the effect of retirement on familiarity with ICT. They focus on two indicators: self-assessed computer skills and use of the internet in the past seven days. To account for the endogeneity of retirement, the authors—following Angelini et al. (2009)—use instrumental variables based on early and statutory retirement age rules.

Regression results show that retirement significantly reduces both computer skills and the frequency of internet use. These findings remain robust even after controlling for other retirement-related factors such as health, cognitive function, and social network size. The authors also identify a dynamic component: the negative impact of retirement on ICT familiarity increases over time. These findings underscore the importance of promoting lifelong digital learning, especially at the transition to retirement.

8.3.3 *Digital Literacy and Preventive Health Behaviour*

ICT familiarity is also closely linked to health behaviour, particularly in the context of preventive healthcare. Vaccines are a key tool in reducing disease burden and mortality in a cost-effective way. However, the decision to get vaccinated is shaped by several factors—including misinformation and lack of information—which may lead to vaccine hesitancy, defined as the delay or refusal to vaccinate despite availability. The COVID-19 pandemic introduced new challenges to vaccine uptake, partly because it moved much of the relevant information and services online. The literature has documented a beneficial role for digital literacy in reducing COVID-19 vaccine hesitancy among older individuals—see, for example, Principe and Weber

(2023). However, the pandemic may also have had lasting effects on the relationship between digital literacy and uptake of other vaccines, such as the seasonal flu vaccine.

Celidoni et al. (2025) examine whether digital literacy influenced the uptake of seasonal flu vaccination among older Europeans during, and after the pandemic. They use SHARE data from, mainly, the second SHARE-Corona Survey and Wave 9, and construct two pre-pandemic indicators of digital skills—self-assessed computer skills and computer use at work—alongside indicators of increased internet use during the pandemic.

Their regression results show that individuals with better pre-pandemic digital skills, and those who increased their internet use during the pandemic, were more likely to get vaccinated, both during and after the pandemic. Moreover, those who improved their digital engagement during the pandemic were already more digitally literate prior to the crisis. This suggests that the pandemic widened existing inequalities in vaccine uptake, as individuals with lower digital literacy were less likely to benefit from the shift to online information and services during the pandemic. These findings underscore the importance of addressing the digital divide not only for social inclusion but also for equitable access to preventive healthcare.

8.4 Conclusion

The empirical evidence presented in this chapter illustrates the potential of SHARE data to inform research and policy across multiple domains of ageing. By leveraging its longitudinal and multidisciplinary design, SHARE enables the analysis of how retirement shapes not only financial wellbeing but also cognitive functioning and digital engagement, highlighting the need for integrated, life-course-oriented policy responses.

Findings on early-life conditions and educational reforms underscore the persistent influence of childhood environments on long-term economic outcomes. Similarly, the examination of maternity leave policies demonstrates their critical role in shaping women's labour market participation and reducing gender disparities over the life course. The economic consequences of the COVID-19 pandemic, particularly for individuals aged 50–64, reveal structural vulnerabilities and emphasize the need for targeted welfare interventions.

Moreover, the analysis of digital literacy—both as an outcome of retirement and as a determinant of health behaviours—highlights a new frontier in social inclusion and public health. The observed digital divide among older adults not only affects access to information and services, but may also reinforce existing health inequalities, especially in times of crisis.

Given its harmonised, cross-national data collection and public availability, SHARE stands as a prime example of a longitudinal data infrastructure aligned with the principles of Open Science. It supports replicable, policy-relevant, and comparative research across countries and over time. In this way, SHARE provides not only an empirical foundation for studying population ageing in Europe, but also a methodological benchmark for future data infrastructures aiming to inform social science research and public policy in an inclusive, evidence-based manner.

References

Angelini, V., Brugiavini, A., & Weber, G. (2009). Ageing and unused capacity in Europe: Is there an early retirement trap? *Economic Policy, 24*(59), 463–508.

Bonfatti, A., Pesaresi, G., Weber, G., & Zambon, N. (2023). The economic impact of the first wave of the pandemic on 50+ Europeans. *Empirical Economics, 65*(2), 607–659.

Brugiavini, A., Pasini, G., & Trevisan, E. (2013). The direct impact of maternity benefits on leave taking: Evidence from complete fertility histories. *Advances in Life Course Research, 18*(1), 46–67.

Brunello, G., Weber, G., & Weiss, C. T. (2017). Books are forever: Early life conditions, education and lifetime earnings in Europe. *The Economic Journal, 127*(600), 271–296.

Cavapozzi, D., & Dal Bianco, C. (2022). Does retirement reduce familiarity with Information and Communication Technology? *Review of Economics of the Household, 20*(2), 553–577.

Celidoni, M., Dal Bianco, C., & Weber, G. (2017). Retirement and cognitive decline. A longitudinal analysis using SHARE data. *Journal of Health Economics, 56*, 113–125.

Celidoni, M., Handastya, N., Weber, G., & Zambon, N. (2025). *Seasonal influenza vaccination hesitancy and digital literacy: Evidence from the European countries*. Preprint. arXiv:2501.17005.

Cunha, F., & Heckman, J. (2007). The technology of skill formation. *American Economic Review, 97*(2), 31–47.

Gauthier, A. H. (2011). *Comparative Family Policy Database* [version 3.0 release]. Netherlands Interdisciplinary Demographic Institute. Retrieved from http://www.demogr.mpg.de/cgi-bin/databases/FamPolDB/index.plx

Mazzonna, F., & Peracchi, F. (2017). Unhealthy retirement? *Journal of Human Resources, 52*(1), 128–151.

Mazzonna, F., & Peracchi, F. (2024). Are older people aware of their cognitive decline? Misperception and financial decision-making. *Journal of Political Economy, 132*(6), 1793–1830.

Principe, F., & Weber, G. (2023). Online health information seeking and Covid-19 vaccine hesitancy: Evidence from 50+ Europeans. *Health Policy, 138*, 104942.

Rohwedder, S. & Willis, R. J. (2010). Mental retirement. *Journal of Economic Perspectives, 24*(1), 119–138.

Chapter 9
GUIDE: Innovations and Challenges to Survey Child Well-Being in Italy

Emilio Maria Colella, Giulio Ecchia, Dario Germani, Ilaria Primerano, Michele Santurro, Francesca Tosi, Massimo Ventrucci, and Matthew John Wakefield

9.1 Introduction

Children's well-being is recognised as central for individuals' sustainable development: secure relationships, good health, and stimulating environments in early life lay the foundations for educational attainment, labour-market success, and intergenerational mobility (Rees et al., 2012; Goswami et al., 2016; Statham & Chase, 2010). Because children's own assessments of their lives often diverge from the judgments of adults, contemporary scholarship increasingly insists on child-centred measurement that blends subjective experience with objective conditions (Pollock et al., 2021). Understanding the factors that foster or hinder well-being is a prerequisite for effective policy—yet the childhood conditions across Europe and the world are evolving at speed.

Public debate is currently concerned about children's well-being and the implications of their attitude towards digital devices. Recently, the OECD released a report entitled "How's life for children in the digital age?" (OECD, 2025), as today's young

E. M. Colella · G. Ecchia · M. J. Wakefield
Department of Economics, University of Bologna, Bologna, Italy
e-mail: emiliomaria.colella2@unibo.it; giulio.ecchia@unibo.it; matthew.wakefield@unibo.it

D. Germani · M. Santurro
Institute for Research on Population and Social Policies (CNR-IRPPS), Rome, Italy
e-mail: dario.germani@cnr.it; michele.santurro@cnr.it

I. Primerano
Institute for Research on Population and Social Policies (CNR-IRPPS), Fisciano, SA, Italy
e-mail: ilaria.primerano@cnr.it

F. Tosi (✉) · M. Ventrucci
Department of Statistical Sciences "Paolo Fortunati", University of Bologna, Bologna, Italy
e-mail: francesca.tosi12@unibo.it; massimo.ventrucci@unibo.it

L. Taddei, M. Paolucci (eds.), *Longitudinal Data Infrastructures in Europe*,
https://doi.org/10.1007/978-3-032-07005-0_9

people are growing up in a rapidly evolving digital world, where digital media plays an increasing important role in their daily lives. Across the OECD, 70% of 10-year-olds already possess a smartphone, and by age 15 at least half devote 30 hours or more each week to connected devices (OECD, 2025). Early and intensive exposure can enrich learning, creativity, and social connection, but it also risks crowding out sleep and physical activity, deepening social comparison, and exposing children to cyberbullying or harmful content. As the diffusion of digital media and devices is becoming more and more widespread across the world, there is a need for solid data-based knowledge in order to understand how digitalisation affects child well-being and to characterise childhood conditions with a holistic and comprehensive approach.

Progress has been made, yet critical data gaps remain. Cross-national surveys such as Children's Worlds, Health Behaviour in School-Aged Children (HBSC) and OECD's Programme for International Student Assessment (PISA) provide information about certain stages and domains of children's lives, while EU-level instruments derived from EU Statistics on Income and Living Conditions (EU-SILC) underpin indicators like material and social deprivation and the at-risk-of-poverty-or-social-exclusion rate (AROPE). These tools, however, offer only fragments of a larger picture and often reflect adult perspectives. EU policy initiatives such as the 2021 European Child Guarantee underscore the need for richer evidence that can detect emerging vulnerabilities early and evaluate multidimensional interventions spanning income support, schooling, health care, and social participation.

Several countries have launched national surveys of children, but many European countries still lack coherent monitoring systems, Italy among them. The National Institute of Statistics' (Istat) occasional studies—including the 2018 survey on second-generation integration (Istat, 2020), the 2024 survey on minors' living conditions (Istat, 2025), and the 2023 survey on children's behaviours and aspirations (Istat, 2024)—provide valuable snapshots, while academic endeavours such as the DORA (Data Integration for Acknowledging Risks and Protecting Children from Violence) project catalogue administrative data on violence against minors.[1] Yet Italy, like many peers, has no longitudinal, internationally comparable source that captures children's perceptions, evaluations, and aspirations over time and provides evidence on their digital behaviour.

The Growing Up In Digital Europe (GUIDE) study has its focus on child-centred well-being measurement, observation of family and school environments, and of digital habits. With the ex-ante harmonisation of questionnaires—which ensures cross-country comparisons—GUIDE offers a strategic response to the evidence gap in longitudinal data on children and young people in Europe and—especially—in Italy.

The chapter is structured as follows. In Sect. 9.2 we provide an overview of data on children that is available in Italy. Section 9.3 describes the details of the GUIDE project in the European framework. In Sect. 9.4 we explain how the GUIDE pilot survey has been designed in Italy, focusing on sampling design and operational

[1] https://ares20.it/dora/.

issues around privacy and data flow, and on innovations with regard to interview modes. A final section concludes.

9.2 Child Well-Being in Italy: A Brief Review

Theoretical studies have long highlighted that child well-being is shaped by a combination of individual and contextual factors, including family resources, social policies, the level of community cohesion, and access to public services such as healthcare and education (Reynolds et al., 2017; Hertzman & Wiens, 1996). These factors interact throughout the life course, laying the foundation for future health, educational attainment, and social inclusion (Currie & Rossin-Slater, 2015; Joshi, 2020).

Among individual-level determinants, parental involvement in cognitively stimulating activities is especially important for children's intellectual development (Del Boca et al., 2017), while proper nutrition in early life stages strongly influences both cognitive and physical outcomes (Tosi & Rettaroli, 2022). Disability, on the other hand, represents a significant risk factor: children with disabilities often encounter barriers to healthcare, education, and social integration, which exacerbate inequalities in both health and educational outcomes (Balbo & Bolano, 2024). At the community level, access to services such as quality childcare and early education programs has proven effective in supporting cognitive and social development, particularly in disadvantaged contexts. Early childhood education, in particular, fosters both academic achievements and social cohesion, helping reduce long-term disparities (Brilli et al., 2016).

Social stratification also plays a role in determining child well-being. Children with a migration background or those who belong to ethnic minorities face additional structural disadvantages, including limited access to quality education and reduced opportunities for social mobility (Giovinazzi & Cocchi, 2021). These vulnerabilities were exacerbated during the COVID-19 pandemic, which disrupted schooling, healthcare, and other support systems, leading to increased developmental delays and psychological distress (Cusinato et al., 2020).

Recent data (Eurostat, 2025) underscore the extent of child poverty and inequality in Europe: in 2024, 24.2% of children under 18 are at risk of poverty or social exclusion—four percentage points higher than the adult rate (20.3%). Regional disparities are also marked: countries such as Bulgaria, Spain, and Romania report child poverty rates above 30%, whereas Slovenia, Cyprus, Czechia, and the Netherlands show significantly lower rates (below 16%). With 27.1% of minors affected in 2024 and an average of 29.6% over the past decade, Italy consistently ranks among the countries with the highest levels of child deprivation in the European Union. In fact, the well-being of children living in Italy is characterized by clear regional disparities and specific vulnerability factors. According to the latest Istat survey on the living conditions of minors (Istat, 2025), 26.7% of children under 16 are at risk of poverty or social exclusion, compared to 23.1% of the general population. The burden is especially severe in the South, where 43.6% of children experience deprivation, compared to 26.2% in the Centre and 14.3% in the North. Additionally, children with migratory background face heightened vulnerability: the risk of poverty and social exclusion reaches 43.6% for foreign minors living in Italy, with peaks in the South (78.2%), compared to a national average of 40.9% for their Italian peers. In the North, the gap is less pronounced but still significant, with 33.9% of foreign children at risk compared to 9.3% of their Italian peers.

Family structure also plays a significant role. Children living in single-parent households face higher deprivation rates (38.3%), particularly when the head of household is a single mother (48.4%). Large families are also more exposed to economic vulnerability, as are those facing housing costs: 22.7% live in homes with mortgages and 23.6% in rented accommodations, with even higher burdens among single-mother families (31.8%). In terms of material deprivation, data specifically collected to assess critical situations among minors under 16 indicate that, in 2024, 11.7% of children experienced at least three indicators of deprivation from a list of 17 (Guio et al., 2012). The most common forms include living in households unable to replace damaged furniture (88.6%), not being able to go on vacation (85.4%), and lacking access to recreational activities (67.5%). Food deprivation remains a concern: 4.9% of minors lacked access to necessary food, with the figure rising to 8.9% in the South. Additionally, 2.3% were unable to consume a protein-rich meal daily due to economic constraints.

Further insights on the Italian context come from the 2024 Istat study "Children and young people: behaviour, attitudes, and future projects", which surveyed over 39,000 youths aged 11–19. The study highlighted demographic decline and increasing cultural diversity among the youngsters in Italy (9.7% with a migration background). In this target group, digital habits are widespread: 79% completed the survey via smartphones or tablets, and 85% have a social media profile (97% among 17–19-year-olds). Gender differences also emerged: girls are more active in online communication; boys more in face-to-face interactions.

Educational aspirations vary strongly by socioeconomic status and migration background. While 60.3% of students from affluent families plan to attend an academic-stream high school, only 34.8% of those from less secure backgrounds do the same. Disadvantaged youth more frequently choose vocational tracks (15.6%) or remain undecided (34.5%). A gender gap is evident in university aspirations (67.4% of girls vs. 46.4% of boys), as is a migration gap (44.5% of foreign-born vs. 57.8% of Italian-born students). Notably, 32.3% of youth report anxiety about the future, with girls more affected (42%) than boys (23.1%).

Additional data from Istat and other national institutions underscore the challenges faced by second-generation youth in education. The 2018 Istat study on migrant integration found that students with a migration background are more likely to experience late school enrolment and underperformance. Complementary contributions from academic centres (e.g., CHILD at the University of Turin, UNICEF Innocenti) and NGOs (e.g., Save the Children, Fondazione Con i Bambini) have enriched the understanding of child well-being, especially for marginalized groups.

Despite the availability of multiple data sources on children's well-being in Italy, significant limitations remain, particularly the lack of longitudinal studies. Most existing surveys (such as EU-SILC and the Istat multipurpose family survey "Family, Social Subjects, and Childhood Condition") are cross-sectional and fail to capture the long-term dynamics of child development. In contrast, countries like the UK, France, Norway, and Germany conduct cohort studies that follow children from early childhood through adulthood, providing invaluable insights into the trajectories of education, health, and social integration (Pollock et al., 2021).

Finally, in Italy, surveys often focus on fragmented age groups (e.g., under-16 or over-25), neglecting key life transitions such as adolescence or early adulthood. This hampers a comprehensive understanding of how individual experiences and contexts evolve and interact over time. To fill this gap, experts recommend the development of a nationally coordinated longitudinal monitoring system that integrates multiple dimensions of child and youth well-being. Such an initiative would enable evidence-based policymaking and align Italy with European best practices and would be even more valuable if data collection were coordinated with other (European) countries.

9.3 GUIDE: European Framework

The GUIDE project[2] seeks to create the first harmonised, continent-wide birth-cohort study able to track children's lives from infancy to early adulthood and, in doing so, to supply robust longitudinal evidence for social-policy debates. By collecting comparable data across European societies—including Italy, where no national cohort study of this breadth yet exists—GUIDE promises both to close a gap in child-well-being statistics and to enable meaningful cross-national comparisons.

The study is designed with an "accelerated" longitudinal structure built around two overlapping samples. A child cohort will start with roughly 8-year-olds and their caregivers, while an infant cohort will begin with 1-year-olds. Data collection is envisaged every three years, alternating between cohorts and leaving a gap year for preparation. Children are followed into their early twenties, hence the fieldwork calendar will extend into the mid-2050s. Each first-wave sample is planned at no fewer than 10,000 families for the infants and 8000 for the 8-year-olds (smaller states can halve these targets), giving the scale needed for reliable national and cross-national inference.

Pilot studies already completed in Croatia, Finland, France, Ireland and Slovenia have demonstrated the feasibility of the design. Using convenience samples, national teams tested both instruments and field procedures with three respondent groups: caregivers of 8-year-olds, the 8-year-olds themselves, and caregivers of

[2] GUIDE was added to the ESFRI (European Strategy Forum on Research Infrastructures) roadmap in 2021.

newborns. The pilots not only evaluated questionnaire clarity but also offered laboratories for experimenting with sampling frames, incentive schemes and interview modes—from classic face-to-face CAPI (Computer Assisted Personal Interview) to video-based CAVI in Finland. Their collective experience now guides the remaining national teams as they prepare for full-scale launch.

The experience will bring both operational and conceptual insights. The questionnaires deliberately measure well-being from multiple angles. Hedonic well-being is tapped through indicators of happiness and affect balance (the balance between positive and negative emotions), whereas eudaimonic well-being is captured via items on purpose, personal growth and goal attainment. Modules on health, education, material resources and neighbourhood context provide the socioeconomic backdrop against which these subjective outcomes can be interpreted. The result is a multidimensional portrait that links children's experiences, resources and aspirations over time.

Cross-national comparability is safeguarded through rigorous translation and adaptation protocols. GUIDE adopts the TRAPD approach—translation, review, adjudication, pre-testing and documentation—so that each language version aligns conceptually while remaining culturally intelligible. Youth advisory boards have been involved from the outset, ensuring that question wording resonates with children rather than merely reflecting adult perspectives. Such participatory design should enhance both data quality and respondent engagement across diverse settings.

Italy's forthcoming pilot illustrates how national teams adapt the common blueprint to local realities. Drawing on earlier pilots, the Italian committee is fine-tuning recruitment strategies, interviewer training and incentive structures within budgetary constraints. Its feedback will feed into the transnational scientific panel, where representatives from all participant countries weigh cumulative evidence and decide on any final revisions to instruments or procedures before Wave 1. By doing so, the Italian case will enrich the shared methodological knowledge base while simultaneously building domestic capacity for large-scale panel research.

Beyond methodological dividends, the consortium's collaborative process offers a model for efficiently allocating resources in ambitious social surveys. Early, low-cost pilots surface translation glitches, logistical bottlenecks and cost drivers, allowing corrective action long before full implementation. The strategic alternation of cohorts spreads fieldwork costs, while the large starting samples future-proof the study against attrition. Together, these design features position GUIDE to deliver high-quality, policy-relevant insights for decades.

In sum, GUIDE represents an unprecedented European investment in understanding childhood and youth trajectories. By uniting rigorous longitudinal methodology, child-centred measurement and cross-national collaboration, it stands to generate evidence capable of informing policies on education, health, inequality and well-being—and, crucially, to fill the evidence gap that has long hampered Italian research on younger generations.

9.4 GUIDE: Italian Pilot Fieldwork

Fieldwork for the GUIDE pilot survey in Italy began in the central months of 2025. Families with children aged around 1-year (the "infant" cohort) and of 8-year-old children (the "child" cohort) are to be surveyed. The survey aims to collect high-quality data through a well-structured sampling design and participant recruitment process, in full compliance with current data protection regulations, and also to provide new evidence regarding the mode of data collection. We comment on each of these elements in turn.

9.4.1 Sampling Design

The aim for the pilot survey is to sample slightly more than 600 families with children in each cohort. These families will be distributed across four regions: Lombardy, Emilia-Romagna, Campania, and Apulia. In order to find the families and to ensure some diversity in their demographic characteristics, a non-probability two-stage sampling design has been chosen. Specifically, the primary sampling units, which are the same for both cohorts, are Italian municipalities divided into two categories: (1) regional capital municipalities (one for each region, i.e. Milan, Bologna, Naples, Bari); and, (2) provincial municipalities, defined as those municipalities with more than 30,000 inhabitants that are located in the province of the regional capital. Regarding the second category, a total of 10 municipalities from each province have been selected. For Bologna and Bari, ten municipalities are not available and so neighboring areas have been considered: specifically, these are all municipalities with a resident population greater than 30,000 and belonging to provinces neighboring the province of the regional capital (for Bologna: Modena, Ferrara, and Ravenna; and, for Bari: Taranto, Brindisi, and Barletta-Andria-Trani). In this way, a total of 44 municipalities have been sampled across the four regions, as shown in Fig. 9.1.

Regarding the child cohort, a key part of the second-stage sampling is based on primary schools. In Italy, the majority of children turn eight during the calendar year in which they begin the third year of primary school. This part of the sampling is therefore based on the geographic spread of primary school "comprehensive institutes" ("istituti comprensivi", hereafter "institutes", each of which may include more than one school). More specifically, the second step is to map the institutes located in the selected municipalities, from which the schools to be included in the sample can subsequently be drawn. The selection is based on the total number of students enrolled in the 2022/2023 academic year. Starting from the 44 selected municipalities, a sampling list of 862 institutes has been created. From this list, the top institutes have been selected based on the number of students in the cohort. The purposive sampling strategy adopted for selecting schools has two advantages. First, the spatial distribution of the sampled schools broadly reflects the density of

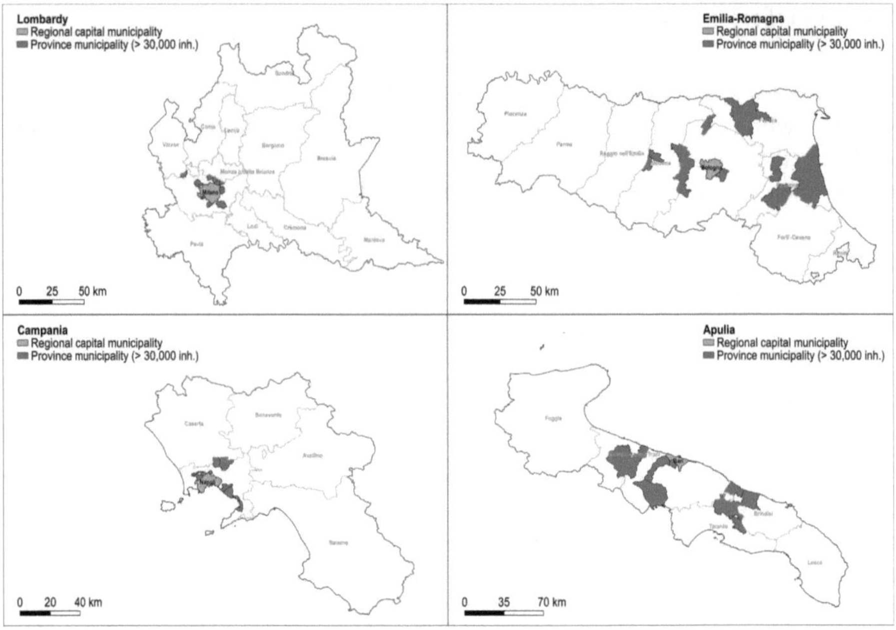

Fig. 9.1 Italian municipalities sampled for GUIDE. Source: own work

Table 9.1 Joint distribution of the sampled schools, by region and municipality type

Region\Municipality type	Regional capital municipalities	Province municipalities	Total
Lombardy	103	45	148
Emilia-Romagna	42	60	102
Apulia	24	38	62
Campania	25	21	46
Total	**194**	**164**	**358**

the population underlying the selected municipalities, as desired. At the same time, this strategy helps minimize the effort required in contacting a sufficient number of comprehensive institutes to cover the desired number of interviews. This is because it uses the cohort population size within institutes as the main eligibility criterion, thereby ensuring a higher coverage of the target population.

The selection of institutes results in the following distribution: 86 institutes in the regional capital municipalities, encompassing 194 schools; and 75 institutes in the provincial municipalities, encompassing 164 schools. Finally, considering the 358 schools belonging to the 161 selected institutes, the joint distribution by region and municipality type is reported in Table 9.1.

Designing a similar second-stage strategy for the infant cohort is more challenging as it would require finding institutions that the vast majority of families with infant children are attached to. Vaccination centres or other medical services could be a possibility in some contexts, although contacts with individuals accessing health-care must be handled with great delicacy and attention to issues around privacy.

Instead, for the infant cohort and to top up numbers in the child cohort, within the selected municipalities, the survey agency will implement a snowball sampling strategy. This strategy will start from key community spaces where families with young children typically gather—such as nurseries, early childhood education services, and summer camps. These settings have been identified as particularly effective for initiating participant recruitment, as they offer access to the social networks of parents and caregivers. The sampling strategy also includes outreach via targeted online platforms commonly used by parents of eligible children, with the dual aim of raising awareness of the survey and encouraging participation. This entire phase has been outsourced to an external agency, which is responsible for both the design and implementation of the recruitment process.

9.4.2 Fieldwork Implementation, Privacy and Data Flows

The operational procedures designed to manage fieldwork and data-flow for each cohort (D'Ambrosio et al., 2025), have been designed within the broader "Fostering Open Science in Social Science Research" (FOSSR—https://www.fossr.eu/) project funded by the National Recovery and Resilience Plan (NRRP).[3]

The process defined for the child cohort involves the participation of the primary schools sampled. Principals of the selected schools are to be contacted through a formal certified email ("Posta Elettronica Certificata"—PEC) sent by the survey agency. This email includes an invitation letter to participate in the survey, detailing the participation procedures and providing a link to the enrollment form, which also contains the privacy notice and the request for informed consent for data processing. Additionally, a follow-up telephone plan has been scheduled to reach those schools that do not complete the online form.

Participating schools will collaborate with the institutions that have been involved in implementing the important GUIDE pilot survey within FOSSR.[4] The role of the participating schools will be limited to sending the initial (electronic) communication to the families of the children in the target population, to enable these families to participate in the GUIDE pilot survey. The content of this communication will be agreed by the FOSSR research team and provided by CNR-IRPPS. The families of the target students will thus receive an email communication sent directly by their child's school, in which they will find the link to join the survey.

[3] Both the GUIDE and FOSSR projects are committed to providing data according to the FAIR (Findable, Accessible, Interoperable, Reusable) principles.

[4] These are CNR-IRPPS, and the Department of Statistical Sciences "Paolo Fortunati" and the Department of Economics at the University of Bologna.

For families that are not contacted via schools—including families of children in the infant cohort—the process of managing recruitment will be implemented by the above mentioned external agency. For families in both cohorts, the materials related to recruitment have been developed in compliance with the ethical and legal obligations established by the GDPR (EU Regulation 2016/679), with the aim of fostering informed, transparent, and accountable communication with participants. These materials include:

- Privacy notice, developed in compliance with Article 13 of the GDPR, which clearly outlines the purpose and legal basis of data processing, data retention periods, contact points, participants' rights, as well as information on the data controller and the entities responsible for the implementation of the survey. This material also includes a comprehensive overview of the questionnaire's main sections to ensure that respondents are fully informed about the nature of the questions posed in each part of the survey;
- Invitation letters, written in accessible language to ensure comprehensibility across the general population, explaining the objectives of the survey, the voluntary nature of participation, and the safeguards in place to ensure data confidentiality;
- Informed consent forms, through which participants confirm that they have read the privacy notice and provide their consent to the processing of their personal data, thereby formally agreeing to take part in the survey.

Only those families who complete the recruitment participation form, provide contact information, and authorize data processing, can be contacted for interviews.

9.4.3 Interviews and Interview Modes

The questionnaires for the GUIDE pilot in Italy are ex-ante harmonized with those used in the national pilots that have already been completed, and have already been adapted to the Italian setting and pre-tested by researchers at the University of Bologna. The questionnaires for the parents/carers of both cohorts are expected to take approximately 60 minutes and aim to collect the following information: socio-demographic data; employment and socio-economic conditions; housing, neighborhood, and community; pregnancy and birth; child health and well-being; and parental health. Eight-year-old children will also be interviewed and the questionnaire for them is expected to take approximately 30 minutes and covers the following areas: well-being; physical development; emotional development; social development; school environment; family environment; friendships; bullying; leisure time; level of digital engagement; family financial situation; neighborhood and community. In the pilot, there will also be space for questionnaire feedback and interviewer observations.

For all families in the child cohort (where children and adults are interviewed), and half of those in the infant cohort (only adult interviews), interviews will be completed face-to-face using the Computer Assisted Personal Interview (CAPI) mode. For the remaining families in the infant cohort, the Italian GUIDE pilot will trial Computer Assisted Web Interviews (CAWI). CAWI interviews are largely self-completed by the interviewee. The software that will facilitate the interviews has been developed in conjunction with Centerdata.

Families recruited to the Italian GUIDE pilot will provide contact details and initial consent in the recruitment phase. Those families interviewed using the CAPI mode will then be contacted by an interviewer to establish an appointment for the interviews. Safeguards in the software used by interviewers will ensure that interviews can be realized only after the reading of the privacy notice on personal data processing and the collection of informed consent (duplicated as necessary for cases in which both parents/tutors must provide consent for data to be collected from children) for participation in the survey. Families from the infant cohort surveyed using the CAWI mode, will instead receive an email containing the link to the online questionnaire. This questionnaire will only be accessible once the adult interviewee has read the privacy notice and provided appropriate informed consent.

The innovation of using the CAWI interview mode will be invaluable for the future development of GUIDE—and potentially other surveys—as researchers think about a "push to web" as a potentially cost-effective way of conducting survey-based research. The Italian GUIDE pilot (and the FOSSR project more broadly) is also already providing insights on how best to find a sample of families, and about best practice with regard to data-flows and privacy, when conducting survey-based research with families with children.

9.5 Conclusion

Italy's capacity to craft and evaluate child-centred policies is hampered by a conspicuous lack of longitudinal, survey-based evidence on children and young people. Whereas several European neighbours benefit from long-running cohort studies, Italy still leans on a fragmented set of cross-sectional datasets that cannot robustly prove how social, educational, digital and economic contexts shape outcomes over time. Given that well-being spans intertwined physical, emotional, material and social dimensions, only a longitudinal design can trace these dynamics accurately.

The GUIDE project offers a decisive step forward. Conceived as a harmonised, Europe-wide panel, GUIDE combines objective markers—income, health, schooling and digital use—with children's own hedonic and eudaimonic assessments, thereby capturing both circumstances and lived experience. Its child-centric approach matches today's policy emphasis on including young voices and, crucially, enables life-course analyses that current Italian data cannot support.

Participation in a synchronised European framework will allow Italy to benchmark its performance, learn from countries with more established support systems and adapt best practices to domestic conditions. GUIDE's commitment to common instruments—tested and refined across cultures—will upgrade Italian survey practice, supplying validated metrics that work nationally and regionally. The first Italian pilot, scheduled for 2025, is testing questionnaire content, mixed-mode interviewing (including CAWI) and large-scale sampling, laying the groundwork for a full national panel. Furthermore, Italian experience in piloting GUIDE will produce valuable insights on survey implementation, giving feedback to European scientific groups.

In sum, as Italy strives to harmonise its child-well-being agenda with broader European standards and to bridge persistent territorial disparities, GUIDE provides the essential framework for ensuring that children's and adolescents' perspectives inform policy—consistently, rigorously and over the long term.

References

Balbo, N., & Bolano, D. (2024). Child disability as a family issue: A study on mothers' and fathers' health in Italy. *European Journal of Public Health*, *34*(1), 79–84. https://doi.org/10.1093/eurpub/ckad168

Brilli, Y., Del Boca, D., & Pronzato, C. D. (2016). Does child care availability play a role in maternal employment and children's development? Evidence from Italy. *Review of Economics of the Household*, *14*, 27–51. https://doi.org/10.1007/s11150-013-9227-4

Currie, J., & Rossin-Slater, M. (2015). Early-life origins of life-cycle well-being: Research and policy implications. *Journal of Policy Analysis and Management*, *34*(1), 208–242. https://doi.org/10.1002/pam.21805

Cusinato, M., Iannattone, S., Spoto, A., Poli, M., Moretti, C., Gatta, M., Miscioscia, M. (2020). Stress, resilience, and well-being in Italian children and their parents during the COVID-19 pandemic. *International Journal of Environmental Research and Public Health*, *17*(22), 8297. https://doi.org/10.3390/ijerph17228297

D'Ambrosio, G., Marchesini, N., Pennacchiotti, C., & Primerano, I. (2025). Creazione e sviluppo di un'infrastruttura di ricerca nelle scienze sociali in italia: il progetto FOSSR. *IRPPS Working Papers*, *1*(1), 1–39. http://epub.irpps.cnr.it/index.php/wp/article/view/321

Del Boca, D., Monfardini, C., & Nicoletti, C. (2017). Parental and child time investments and the cognitive development of adolescents. *Journal of Labor Economics*, *35*(2), 565–608. https://doi.org/10.1086/689479

Eurostat. (2025). *Persons at risk of poverty or social exclusion by age and sex* (Online data code: ilc_peps01n). Publications Office of the European Union. https://doi.org/10.2908/ILC_PEPS01N

Giovinazzi, F., & Cocchi, D. (2021). Social integration of second generation students in the Italian school system. *Social Indicators Research*, *160*, 287–307. https://doi.org/10.1007/s11205-021-02801-9

Goswami, H., Fox, C., & Pollock, G. (2016). The current evidence base and future needs in improving children's well-being across Europe: Is there a case for a comparative longitudinal survey? *Child Indicators Research*, *9*, 371–388.

Guio, A. C., Gordon, D., & Marlier, E. (2012). *Measuring material deprivation in the EU: Indicators for the whole population and child-specific indicators* (Eurostat methodologies and working papers). Publications Office of the European Union. https://doi.org/doi:10.2785/33598

Hertzman, C., & Wiens, M. (1996). Child development and long-term outcomes: A population health perspective and summary of successful interventions. *Social Science & Medicine*, *43*(7), 1083–1095. https://doi.org/10.1016/0277-9536(96)00028-7

Istat. (2020). *Identità e percorsi di integrazione delle seconde generazioni in Italia*. Istituto Nazionale di Statistica. https://www.istat.it/produzione-editoriale/identita-e-percorsi-di-integrazione-delle-seconde-generazioni-in-italia/

Istat. (2024). *Indagine bambini e ragazzi. anno 2023. nuove generazioni sempre più digitali e multiculturali. Statistiche Report*. Istituto Nazionale di Statistica. https://www.istat.it/it/files/2024/05/Bambini-e-ragazzi-2023.pdf

Istat. (2025). *Le condizioni di vita dei minori di 16 anni. Statistiche Focus*. Istituto Nazionale di Statistica. https://www.istat.it/wp-content/uploads/2025/07/Focus_La-condizione-di-vita-dei-minori-di-16-anni.pdf

Joshi, H. (2020). Pathways towards well-being. *Longitudinal and Life Course Studies, 11*, 153–155. https://doi.org/10.1332/175795920X15809786476059

OECD. (2025). *How's life for children in the digital age?* OECD Publishing. https://doi.org/10.1787/0854b900-en

Pollock, G., Goswami, H., & Szymczyk, A. (2021). Child well-being across the life course: What do we know, what should we know? In *Sustainable human development across the life course* (pp. 165–192). Bristol University Press.

Rees, G., Goswami, H., Pople, L., Bradshaw, J., Keung, A., & Main, G. (2012). *The good childhood report 2012: A review of our children's well-being*. Springer.

Reynolds, A. J., Mondi, C. F., Ou, S. R., & Hayakawa, M. (2017). Generative mechanisms of early childhood interventions to well-being. *Child Development, 88*(2), 378. https://doi.org/10.1111/cdev.12733

Statham, J., & Chase, E. (2010). *Childhood wellbeing: A brief overview*. Childhood Wellbeing Research Centre.

Tosi, F., & Rettaroli, R. (2022). Intergenerational transmission of dietary habits among Italian children and adolescents. *Economics & Human Biology, 44*, 101073. https://doi.org/10.1016/j.ehb.2021.101073

[illegible]

Chapter 10
GGS: Generations and Gender Survey

Letizia Mencarini, Nicolò Cavalli, Elena Marseglia, Matilde Perotti, Ilaria Primerano, Michele Santurro, and Nicolò Marchesini

10.1 Introduction

This chapter presents the Italian implementation of the Generations and Gender Survey (GGP, 2025b), second wave (GGS-II), beginning with the broader framework of the Generations and Gender Programme (GGP) (GGP, 2025a) and highlighting the specific features of the survey's preparation and implementation in Italy. GGS-II is a key component of Europe's demographic data infrastructure, providing new and harmonized longitudinal data to examine individual and family transitions over time. Italy's participation in GGS-II represents a significant investment in social science research and innovation, supported by EU funding and grounded in rigorous international methodological standards.

The chapter offers an overview of the GGP as an international research infrastructure, outlining its objectives and relevance to current demographic and social

The original version of the chapter has been revised. A correction to this chapter can be found at https://doi.org/10.1007/978-3-032-07005-0_13

L. Mencarini (✉) · N. Cavalli · E. Marseglia · M. Perotti
Bocconi University, Milan, Italy
e-mail: letizia.mencarini@unibocconi.it; nicolo.cavalli@unibocconi.it; elena.marseglia@phd.unibocconi.it; matilde.perotti@phd.unibocconi.it

I. Primerano
Institute for Research on Population and Social Policies (CNR-IRPPS), Fisciano, SA, Italy
e-mail: ilaria.primerano@cnr.it

M. Santurro
Institute for Research on Population and Social Policies (CNR-IRPPS), Rome, Italy
e-mail: michele.santurro@cnr.it

N. Marchesini
Italian National Institute of Statistics (Istat), Rome, Italy
e-mail: nicolo.marchesini@istat.it

L. Taddei, M. Paolucci (eds.), *Longitudinal Data Infrastructures in Europe*,
https://doi.org/10.1007/978-3-032-07005-0_10

challenges. It then introduces the preparation of the Italian GGS-II fieldwork, the actors involved, and the data collection strategy, with particular attention to the roles of the FOSSR (FOSSR, 2025) and Age-It (Age-It, 2025) projects, funded by the National Recovery and Resilience Plan (PNRR). The chapter also describes the institutional architecture of the Joint Research Unit established to support the Italian GGS-II. Finally, it outlines the distinctive features of the Italian questionnaire and its expanded thematic modules, which address issues especially relevant to the Italian context, such as the transition to adulthood and elderly care.

Through this overview, the chapter aims to illustrate how the Italian GGS-II contributes to both national and international understandings of life course dynamics, offering valuable tools to researchers and policymakers to better comprehend and respond to the demographic and social transformations shaping contemporary societies.

10.2 Generations and Gender Programme

The Generations and Gender Programme (GGP) is a research infrastructure recognized within the ESFRI Roadmap 2021 (European Strategy Forum on Research Infrastructures) as a leading initiative in the social sciences. GGP provides scientists and policy makers with high quality and timely data about families and life course trajectories of individuals to enable researchers to contribute insights and answers to current societal and public policy challenges (GGP, 2025a). It constitutes an integrated and sustainable distributed platform, offering a range of services to the scientific community. The mission of the GGP is to generate high-quality, longitudinal, and internationally comparable data on population dynamics, family structures, intergenerational relationships, and the evolving social roles of men and women, situated within their broader economic, social, and cultural environments. The GGP has established itself as a reference point for research on fertility behaviour, work-life reconciliation, transitions to adulthood, and intergenerational solidarity.

Initiated in 2000 by the Population Unit of the United Nations Economic Commission for Europe (UNECE), the GGP has been coordinated by the Netherlands Interdisciplinary Demographic Institute (NIDI) since 2009, although UNECE continues to provide critical services to the infrastructure. The NIDI provides harmonized panel data across countries, documenting individual life courses and family trajectories. The programme offers open-access survey data and contextual datasets, thereby equipping researchers and policymakers with empirical evidence to inform analyses of demographic behaviour and the design of social policies at a cross-nationally comparative level. By following individuals longitudinally, the GGP captures key demographic events—such as partnership formation and dissolution, parenthood, and bereavement—and investigates their determinants and consequences at both the micro and macro levels. The GGP survey focuses on intergenerational and gender relations between people, expressed in care arrangements and the organization of paid and unpaid work. These features significantly improve the knowledge base for social science and policy-making in Europe and other developed countries.

10.3 Generations and Gender Survey

In the early 1990s, the United Nations Economic Commission for Europe (UNECE) launched the Family and Fertility Survey (FFS), using a standardized questionnaire administered across Europe (GGP, 2025a). The FFS aimed to generate harmonized data on marriage, cohabitation, divorce, and childbearing, addressing the growing need for demographic information considering declining fertility rates and shifting away from the so-called traditional family dynamics. The survey collected data from over 100,000 women and 50,000 men in 23 countries, enabling extensive cross-national analyses (GGP, 2025b).

Building on the success of the FFS, the UNECE, expanded its scope by establishing the Generations and Gender Programme (GGP), with the Generations and Gender Survey (GGS) as its core instrument. The GGS encompasses a broader age range (18–79) and adopts a panel design, conducting follow-up interviews every three years. The GGS questionnaire addresses a wide array of relevant topics, including life course transitions (e.g., marriage, divorce, childbirth), demographic behaviour (e.g., fertility intentions, family planning), intergenerational relationships, economic conditions and employment, and gender roles and equality (GGP, 2025b).

GGS data are freely accessible and represent a critical resource for researchers, policymakers, and other stakeholders engaged in demographic and family studies. Its high-quality and comprehensive data support a broad range of research and policy analyses, contributing to a deeper understanding of demographic trends and informing efforts to promote societal well-being (GGP, 2025b).

The GGP has conducted two major rounds of data collection through the GGS. The first round (GGS-I) has started in 2004 as a three-wave panel study with three-year time intervals. It has collected information from over 200,000 individuals aged 18 to 79 from 19 countries and contributed to the social sciences as a unique longitudinal data resource on families and life course trajectories (GGP, 2025b). Italy participated to the first round in 2003 and 2007 under the coordination of the Italian National Institute of Statistics (ISTAT). The second round of data collection (GGS-II) started officially in 2020 with an updated and renewed methodology as well as refreshed samples to ensure that social scientists and policymakers have access to the highest quality data possible. GGS-II seeks to update and extend the analytical potential of the GGS by addressing emerging demographic phenomena such as persistently low fertility, increasingly complex young adult life courses, and evolving family arrangements.

10.4 GGS-II Italy

Italy's participation in the second round of GGS (GGS-II) reflects a strategic investment in high-quality, policy-relevant social science infrastructure. The Italian implementation builds on international standards while incorporating specific innovations to address national research priorities.

The implementation of Wave 1 of the GGS-II in Italy is financed by two EU-funded initiatives under the National Recovery and Resilience Plan (PNRR). Adults aged 18–59 are surveyed through FOSSR (Fostering Open Science in Social Science Research), whereas those aged 60–79 are reached through Age-It (Ageing Well in an Ageing Society).

FOSSR equips social science researchers with platforms for data collection, analysis and archiving, fully aligned with the FAIR principles—Findable, Accessible, Interoperable and Reusable (D'Ambrosio et al., 2025; Wilkinson et al., 2016). By enhancing comparability across studies, it lays the groundwork for a national "life-course observatory" that will generate high-quality, policy-relevant data. Age-It, a national research infrastructure on ageing, advances knowledge on health trajectories, welfare systems and quality of life in later life. Its longitudinal, interdisciplinary design informs both scholarship and public policy. Within GGS-II, Age-It ensures robust coverage of older adults, enriching analyses of late-life transitions, a crucial component in the Italian society. Together, FOSSR and Age-It provide a coherent framework for collecting high-quality longitudinal data across the Italian life course, guaranteeing methodological consistency and strengthening the country's capacity to analyse demographic, family and life-course change.

Moreover, a Joint Research Unit—GGP.IT—was established in April 2024 through a collaboration between the National Research Council (CNR) and Bocconi University, with the objective of creating the Italian node of the GGP research infrastructure. Its mission is to coordinate national resources and expertise to support GGP activities in Italy and to strengthen the country's contribution to the European research infrastructure. The GGP.IT was officially recognized as scientifically worthy by the Ministry of University and Research on September 2024.

At the European level, Italy participates in the GGP-5D project, launched in late 2022 and funded by the European Union to facilitate the transition of GGP into the European Research Infrastructure Consortium (ERIC).

10.5 The Italian Questionnaire

The first wave of the GGS-II questionnaire in Italy significantly expands upon the baseline questions by introducing several supplementary modules and items. These additions have been designed to capture key facets of Italy's distinct socio-demographic setting, with the aim of offering a comprehensive understanding of the country's demographic and social dynamics. The topics introduced therefore reflect areas of growing relevance for research within the Italian context.

One of the most significant updates concerns gender self-identification. Traditionally, the GGP has used sex as a proxy for gender, a practice that can lead to misleading survey findings and reinforce a dichotomous framework. Recognizing that survey design both reflects and reinforces prevailing social beliefs (Westbrook & Saperstein, 2015; Bowker & Star, 1999), the Italian GGS-II adopted a more inclusive approach. The response options for gender were thus updated to include an "other/non-binary" category alongside the male/female options.

The fertility section of the Italian GGS-II baseline questionnaire has also been expanded to be more inclusive. Previously targeting single and partnered women under 50 (the reproductive age range of 18–49), along with women of all ages with a female partner under 50, men with a female partner under 50, and men in same-sex relationships, the Italian survey additionally collects fertility intentions from single Italian men. This decision stems from the understanding of the importance of studying men's reproductive dynamics alongside women's for a more comprehensive understanding of fertility trends (Beaujouan, 2020; Bratsberg et al., 2021; Schoumaker, 2019). In the section related to fertility, we further adopt a question on the desired gender of the child, in acknowledgment of the recent scholarship interest on the reproductive decisions based on the gender composition rather than the sole offspring size (Toulemon & Testa, 2005; Fuse, 2013; Tian & Morgan, 2015; Jones et al., 2023). In a later section, the survey explores additional traditional gender values asking the respondents' perception on the idea that daughters may have a more natural inclination towards caring for ill or aging parents. While recent European studies confirm a well-established preference for mixed-sex offspring (Cukrowska-Torzewska & Grabowska, 2023), an unexpected preference for daughters has also lately been found in some contexts, which is reflected in the lower likelihood of having a second child if the firstborn is a girl (Miranda et al., 2018).

Another objective of the survey is to collect more granular information on non-cohabiting family arrangements and Living Apart Together (LAT) relationships. This decision stems from the observation of the increasing diversity of intimate relationships, especially among younger or elderly couples, including greater prevalence of LAT couples across Europe, which are now more often the product of a deliberate choice of partners (Levin, 2004; Liefbroer et al., 2015). The questionnaire aims to provide a comprehensive framework of the phenomenon by exploring both the motivations and circumstances surrounding the decision to live apart. Along with the residential information on non-cohabiting family members, which allows for a precise detection of geographical distance, LAT couples are asked specifically about the overall travel time to reach the partner as well as the frequency of meetings and contacts, enabling a greater understanding of how the bond is maintained despite a less traditional living arrangement.

Moreover, the transition to adulthood module is particularly relevant given that Italy is still characterized by the most delayed home-leaving trends across the European countries (European Commission, 2023). Several factors contribute to this record, including high youth unemployment, economic dependence, and strong family ties which often substitute for a limited welfare state (Billari, 2004; Schwanitz et al., 2021; Reyneri, 2017). We added questions that address the multitude of reasons behind young adults' choices to remain in or leave the parental home, as they allow to distinguish between financial necessity, cultural norms, and personal preference in the choice of a prolonged cohabitation with parents. The baseline questionnaire already includes a specific question on young adults' decisions to leave home within the next three years, offering a predictive perspective on the achievement of an adult's life milestone like the exit from the family of origin.

Further on, given Italy's rapid population aging, second only to Japan and South Korea, the expansion of the target sample to 79 years old was seen as an essential adjustment for the representativeness of the older cohorts within the population. With a considerable number of individuals over 65 for every 100 working-age adults (Eurostat, 2025), Italy's pension and healthcare systems face non-negligible strain. To address these challenges, the Italian GGS includes an entire section targeted at the individuals aged 50–79, which focuses mostly on topics of health and self-sufficiency of the respondents as well as on their expectations regarding long-term care. To better understand the kind of vulnerabilities within this age group and the public system's degree of responsiveness, the survey incorporates nine experimental questions. These identify whether respondents receive welfare benefits for severe disabilities (such as "indennità di accompagnamento" from INPS) or other forms of economic support from external providers. One question covers specifically the access to health assistance including medical devices, home care and physiotherapy, or transportation. A new set of questions examines how respondents view their future needs: when they anticipate requiring assistance and their concerns about losing self-sufficiency. In fact, both preferences and predictions for future care arrangements among the options of receiving home care, living with family members or moving to a dedicated facility are further examined. The module also assesses digital literacy—familiarity and comfort with the use of smartphones and computers—given their pervasive use even for daily operations despite a persistent large digital divide in the country. One final question about advance care planning asks to indicate the preferred option, inside or outside the family network, for taking critical health decisions in the event of becoming unable to provide for oneself. Overall, the module may inform researchers on a variety of topics on challenges and decision-making in later life, which span from the receipt of disability-related benefits and access to health services, the degree of autonomy in daily life, to expectations and preferences for future care.

In its last part, the questionnaire engages respondents on relevant societal trends, asking their level of concern on issues such as armed conflicts, climate change, economic crises, and increased refugee flows. This inclusion, inherited by the Nordic countries, can provide valuable insight into how individuals perceive and prioritize risks and for the analysis of attitudinal differences across specific demographic groups or between generations. This section relies also on the concept of resilience, measured on the individuals' capacity to cope with and adapt to changes in their lives (Windle, 2011; Van Kessel, 2013). The questions assess both adaptive capacity and recovery, focusing on the respondents' ability to respond to health-related setbacks or significant challenges. By linking these indicators of resilience with earlier questions on personal concerns and optimism, the Italian questionnaire enables the capture of a broad spectrum of the psychological resources within the Italian population at different stages of adult life (Fig. 10.1).

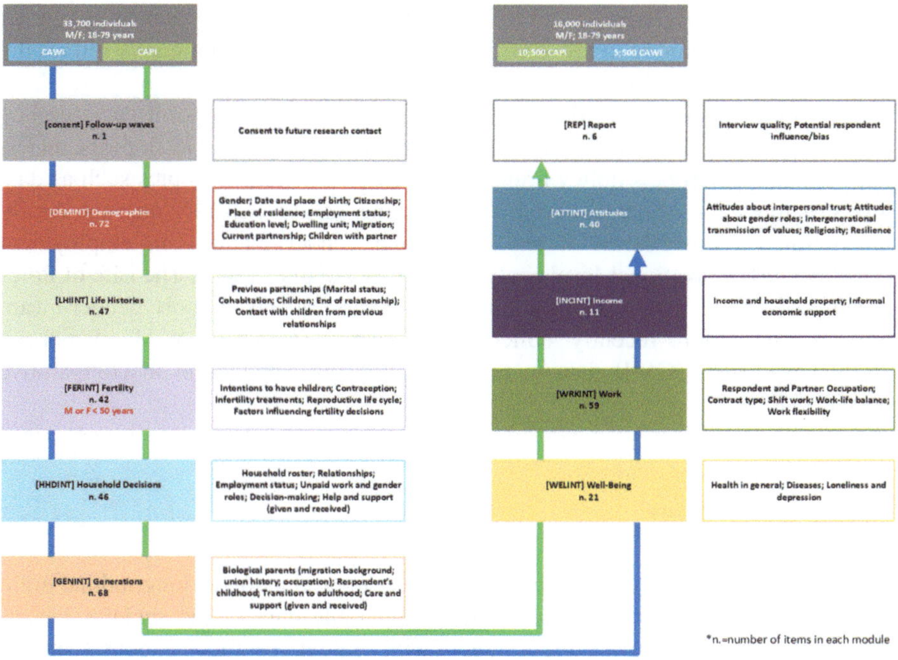

Fig. 10.1 Information collected in the Italian GGS-II. *Source*: Authors' elaboration

10.6 Impact and Use of GGS Data

Over the past 25 years since the institutionalization of the of GGP research infrastructure, GGS data has become an important resource for social science research. Its harmonised, panel design enables cross-national comparisons and has been used for a wide range of peer-reviewed publications. Researchers have used GGS data to explore, among other topics, fertility intentions and behaviour, gender ideology and the division of household labour, partnership formation and dissolution, intergenerational exchanges, transitions to adulthood, subjective well-being, and work–family reconciliation (Aassve et al., 2014, 2015; Mencarini et al., 2015; Fanelli & Profeta, 2021; Schwanitz et al., 2021; Kalmijn & Leopold, 2021). In addition, the survey's large and diverse samples allow scholars to examine heterogeneous effects within specific population sub-groups—most notably ethnic minorities and descendants of migrants—thereby advancing understanding of integration processes (Ezdi & Bas, 2020; Impicciatore & Pailhé, 2019; ten Kate et al., 2021).

A substantial methodological literature has also emerged, using the GGS as a testing ground for survey innovations and data-quality assessments. Foundational contributions such as Vikat et al. (2007) helped establish the conceptual and methodological basis of the GGP. More recent studies include evaluations of interviewer manipulation in the new GGS round, assessments of sampling and fieldwork methods, weighting procedures, and representativeness (Fokkema et al.,

2016), as well as novel approaches to estimating contraceptive prevalence and unmet need for family planning in low-fertility contexts—work that continually refines the dataset and questionnaire design.

Beyond academia, GGS data have been actively used to inform social-policy debates, public understanding, and programme development. GGS findings underpin Population Europe's policy briefs and discussion papers on topics such as data infrastructures for evidence-based policymaking (Emery, 2014), migrant family integration (Castro Martin et al., 2019), and gender equality in employment (Gauthier, 2012). National-level analyses, such as Poland's report The Life of Poles (Kotowska et al., 2016), highlight family transitions and support gender-aware policymaking. More recently, bulletins like Demos (Hendriks & Mandemakers, 2024) have used GGS-II data to report on housing satisfaction in comparative perspective.

10.7 Conclusion

The Italian GGS-II represents a major effort in the production of longitudinal high-quality, harmonized, and internationally comparable data in the social sciences. Complementing the baseline questionnaire with context-specific questions—such as the expansion of gender identity measures, non-cohabiting relationships, transitions to adulthood, and elderly care—the Italian GGS-II aims to provide a comprehensive view of Italian family and life-course dynamics. Supported by two PNRR-funded projects, FOSSR and Age-It, and coordinated by the newly established Joint Research Unit, the Italian GGS-II contributes to the global GGP research infrastructure and enhances internal capacity and availability for longitudinal, cross-national data comparison. These innovations are expected to improve inclusivity, analytical depth, and responsiveness to emerging socio-demographic trends.

The data collected through the Italian GGS-II aim to inform public policy and academic research. They will offer fresh insight into key societal challenges intrinsic to Italian society, such as persistently low fertility, delayed transitions to adulthood, and the pressing issues related to an increasingly aging population. The coordinated effort to implement the Italian GGS-II underscores the importance of sustained investment in social science infrastructures to address emerging demographic and cultural shifts.

Disclaimer The opinions expressed in this article by Nicolò Marchesini are his own and do not reflect the view of ISTAT.

References

Aassve, A., Fuochi, G., & Mencarini, L. (2014). Desperate housework: Relative resources, time availability, economic dependency, and gender ideology across Europe. *Journal of Family Issues*, *35*(8), 1000–1022.

Aassve, A., Fuochi, G., Mencarini, L., & Mendola, D. (2015). What is your couple type? Gender ideology, housework-sharing, and babies. *Demographic Research, 32*, 835–858.

Age-It. (2025). *Home*. https://ageit.eu/wp/

Beaujouan, E. (2020). Latest-late fertility? Decline and resurgence of late parenthood across the low-fertility countries. *Population and Development Review, 46*(2), 219–247.

Billari, F. C. (2004). Becoming an adult in Europe: A macro(/micro)-demographic perspective. *Demographic Research, Special Collection 3*(2), 15–44.

Bowker, G. C., & Star, S. L. (1999). *Sorting things out: Classification and its consequences*. MIT Press.

Bratsberg, B., Kotsadam, A., & Walther, S. (2021). *Male fertility: Facts, distribution and drivers of inequality* (Discussion Paper No. 14506). IZA.

Castro Martin, T., Koops, J., & Vono de Vilhena, D. (Eds.). (2019). *Migrant families in Europe: Evidence from the generations & gender programme* (Vol. 11). Max Planck Society for the Advancement of Science. https://www.ggp-i.org/wp-content/uploads/2020/01/dp_11_migrant_familes_web.pdf

Cukrowska-Torzewska, E., & Grabowska, M. (2023). The sex preference for children in Europe: Children's sex and the probability and timing of births. *Demographic Research, 48*(8), 203–232. https://www.demographic-research.org/volumes/vol48/8/

D'Ambrosio, G., Marchesini, N., Pennacchiotti, C., & Primerano, I. (2025). *L'esperienza fossr: la pianificazione integrata dell'infrastruttura di ricerca "fostering open science in social science research"* (Working Paper). CNR-IRPPS.

Emery, T. (2014). *How do generations support each other in an ageing society?* (Tech. Rep. No. 06). Netherlands Interdisciplinary Demographic Institute. https://www.ggp-i.org/wp-content/uploads/2017/08/ggp_research_note_006.pdf

European Commission. (2023). *Estimated average age of young people leaving the parental household by sex*. https://ec.europa.eu/eurostat/databrowser/explore/all/all_themes

Eurostat. (2025). *Population structure and ageing*. Statistics Explained. Retrieved from https://ec.europa.eu/eurostat/statistics-explained/index.php?title=Population_structure_and_ageing

Ezdi, S., & Bas, A. M. (2020). Gender preferences and fertility: Investigating the case of Turkish immigrants in Germany. *Demographic Research, 43*, 59–96.

Fanelli, E., & Profeta, P. (2021). Fathers' involvement in the family, fertility, and maternal employment: Evidence from Central and Eastern Europe. *Demography, 58*(5), 1931–1954.

Fokkema, T., Kveder, A., Hiekel, N., Emery, T., & Liefbroer, A. C. (2016). Generations and gender programme wave 1 data collection: An overview and assessment of sampling and fieldwork methods, weighting procedures, and cross-sectional representativeness. *Demographic Research, 34*, 499–524.

FOSSR. (2025). *Home*. https://www.fossr.eu/

Fuse, K. (2013). Daughter preference in Japan: A reflection of gender role attitudes? *Demographic Research, 28*, 1021–1052.

Gauthier, A. H. (2012). *Home vs. paid work: The labour market intention of mothers in Europe* (Tech. Rep. No. 01). Netherlands Interdisciplinary Demographic Institute. https://www.ggp-i.org/wp-content/uploads/2011/09/ggp_research_note_001.pdf

GGP. (2025a). *About the GGP*. https://www.ggp-i.org/

GGP. (2025b). *About the GGS*. https://www.ggp-i.org/generations-and-gender-survey/

Hendriks, I., & Mandemakers, J. (2024). Housing satisfaction in a European perspective. *Demos: Bulletin on Population and Society, 40*(10), 6–7. https://nidi.nl/demos/woontevredenheid-in-europees-perspectief/

Impicciatore, R., & Pailhé, A. (2019). *Do the descendants of immigrants become adults sooner or later than native-born? Evidence from the French generations and gender survey* (Tech. Rep.). INED. https://hal.science/hal-02160479v1

Jones, T. R., Millington, M. J., & Price, J. (2023). Changes in parental gender preference in the USA: Evidence from 1850 to 2019. *Journal of Population Economics, 36*(4), 3057–3070.

Kalmijn, M., & Leopold, T. (2021). A new look at the separation surge in Europe: Contrasting adult and child perspectives. *American Sociological Review, 86*(1), 1–34.

Kotowska, I. E., Matysiak, A., & Mynarska, M. (Eds.). (2016). *The life of poles: From leaving the parental home to retirement.* Warsaw School of Economics, Collegium of Economic Analysis, Institute of Statistics and Demography. https://www.ggp-i.org/wp-content/uploads/2017/10/ggp_Life_of_Poles_eng_fin.pdf

Levin, I. (2004). Living apart together: A new family form. *Current Sociology, 52*(2), 223–240.

Liefbroer, A. C., Poortman, A.-R., & Seltzer, J. A. (2015). Why do intimate partners live apart? Evidence on LAT relationships across Europe. *Demographic Research, 32*(8), 251–286.

Mencarini, L., Vignoli, D., & Gottard, A. (2015). Fertility intentions and outcomes: Implementing the theory of planned behavior with graphical models. *Advances in Life Course Research, 23*, 14–28.

Miranda, V., Dahlberg, J., & Andersson, G. (2018). Parents' preferences for sex of children in Sweden: Attitudes and outcomes. *Population Research and Policy Review, 37*(3), 443–459.

Reyneri, E. (2017). *Introduzione alla sociologia del mercato del lavoro.* Il Mulino.

Schoumaker, B. (2019). Male fertility around the world and over time: How different is it from female fertility? *Population and Development Review, 45*(3), 459–487.

Schwanitz, K., Rampazzo, F., & Vitali, A. (2021). Unpacking intentions to leave the parental home in Europe using the generations and gender survey. *Demographic Research, 45*(2), 17–54.

ten Kate, R. L. F., Bilecen, B., & Steverink, N. (2021). The role of parent–child relationships and filial expectations in loneliness among older Turkish migrants. *Social Inclusion, 9*(4), 291–303.

Tian, F. F., & Morgan, S. P. (2015). Gender composition of children and the third birth in the United States. *Journal of Marriage and Family, 77*(5), 1157–1165.

Toulemon, L., & Testa, M. R. (2005). Fertility intentions and actual fertility: A complex relationship. *Population & Societies, 415*(8), 1–4.

Van Kessel, G. (2013). The ability of older people to overcome adversity: A review of the resilience concept. *Geriatric Nursing, 34*(2), 122–127.

Vikat, A., Spéder, Z., Beets, G., Billari, F. C., Bühler, C., Désesquelles, A., et al. (2007). Generations and gender survey (GGS): Towards a better understanding of relationships and processes in the life course. *Demographic Research, 17*, 389–440.

Westbrook, L., & Saperstein, A. (2015). New categories are not enough: Rethinking the measurement of sex and gender in social surveys. *Gender & Society, 29*(4), 534–560.

Wilkinson, M. D., Dumontier, M., Aalbersberg, I. J., Appleton, G., Axton, M., Baak, A., et al. (2016). The FAIR guiding principles for scientific data management and stewardship. *Scientific Data, 3*, 160018.

Windle, G. (2011). What is resilience? A review and concept analysis. *Reviews in Clinical Gerontology, 21*(2), 152–169.

Chapter 11
The Italian Way to an Online Probability Panel

Luciana Taddei, Ferruccio Biolcati Rinaldi, Frank Heins, Nicolò Marchesini, Angela Paparusso, Claudia Pennacchiotti, Francesco Piacentini, Ilaria Primerano, Cristiano Vezzoni, and Michele Santurro

11.1 Challenges and Opportunities of an OPP

Online Probability Panels (OPP) have emerged as pivotal tools in the field of social sciences, particularly suited for longitudinal analysis. Unlike online surveys based on convenience samples—often affected by self-selection bias (Cornesse & Blom, 2023)—OPPs employ rigorous probability-based sampling procedures that reflect the demographic composition of the target population, offering a more robust and representative foundation for digital data collection. The resulting data are not only cost-effective and timely but also maintain high standards of quality and representativeness (Callegaro et al., 2014; Blom et al., 2016).

L. Taddei (✉)
Institute for Research on Population and Social Policies, National Research Council, Fisciano (SA), Italy
e-mail: luciana.taddei@cnr.it

F. Biolcati Rinaldi · F. Piacentini · C. Vezzoni
University of Milan Statale, Milan, Italy
e-mail: ferruccio.biolcati@unimi.it; francesco.piacentini@unimi.it; cristiano.vezzoni@unimi.it

F. Heins · A. Paparusso · C. Pennacchiotti · M. Santurro
Institute for Research on Population and Social Policies (CNR-IRPPS), Rome, Italy
e-mail: frank.heins@cnr.it; angela.paparusso@cnr.it; claudia.pennacchiotti@cnr.it; michele.santurro@cnr.it

N. Marchesini
Italian National Institute of Statistics (Istat), Rome, Italy
e-mail: nicolo.marchesini@istat.it

I. Primerano
Institute for Research on Population and Social Policies (CNR-IRPPS), Fisciano, SA, Italy
e-mail: ilaria.primerano@cnr.it

L. Taddei, M. Paolucci (eds.), *Longitudinal Data Infrastructures in Europe*,
https://doi.org/10.1007/978-3-032-07005-0_11

The main characteristics that distinguish OPPs as a robust methodological infrastructure for longitudinal research can be summarized across three core dimensions:

1. Survey Technique: Web-based and self-administered questionnaires (CAWI) are the primary mode of data collection in OPPs. They support complex routing and multimedia integration while minimizing interviewer bias and logistical costs. Challenges such as digital literacy gaps and device access are often addressed through mixed-mode strategies or the provision of technological support to participants (Scherpenzeel, 2009; Yeager et al., 2011).
2. Sampling Strategy: Unlike convenience-based online surveys, OPPs employ rigorous probability sampling, typically derived from population registries, ensuring representativeness and external validity (Cornesse & Blom, 2023). This approach mitigates self-selection bias and enables generalizability, a critical feature for national-level analyses.
3. Longitudinal Design: A defining feature of OPPs is their longitudinal architecture. Participants are surveyed repeatedly over time, allowing researchers to trace individual and group-level changes. Such a design enables the study of dynamic processes such as attitude shifts, behavioural changes, and the influence of contextual variables (Menard, 2002; Biolcati-Rinaldi & Vezzoni, 2012). However, issues such as attrition and panel conditioning remain relevant and are addressed through refreshment samples and conditional incentives (Maslovskaya & Lugtig, 2022).

From a methodological point of view, OPPs support rich advancements: they can *link data* with administrative records, integrate embedded experiments, and capture metadata (e.g., response times, device usage, etc.), incorporating AI tools, wearables, and data donation mechanisms (Das, 2025). Importantly, OPPs are aligned with current trends in digital innovation and *Open Science* (Scherpenzeel, 2011), following FAIR principles (Findable, Accessible, Interoperable, Reusable) and building a potentially collaborative environment. They support *modular designs*, promote *interdisciplinarity*, and offer scalable infrastructures that can adapt to *emerging research needs* (e.g., the COVID-19 pandemic). Modular panel structures enable both standardized data collection and researcher-proposed thematic modules, thereby enhancing flexibility and analytical scope (see Sect. 11.2).

On the other hand, it is crucial to mitigate the risk of *panel attrition*—participants dropping out over time—which can threaten the representativeness of longitudinal data. However, the use of incentives and periodic refreshments of samples has proven effective in maintaining engagement over multiple waves remains a methodological and logistical challenge (see Sect. 11.4). *Panel conditioning* also deserves careful attention. The repeated measurement of the same individuals may influence their responses, leading to artificial stability or change that does not reflect actual societal dynamics. This effect, although difficult to eliminate, can be monitored through methodological adjustments and experiment-based validations. Another major concern is the *digital divide*. Despite increasing internet penetration, digital exclusion still affects certain sociodemographic groups, such as older adults or individuals with lower socioeconomic status. This can introduce coverage bias and hinder the generalizability of findings. To mitigate this, many European OPPs adopt hybrid recruitment strategies and mixed modes of survey administration, providing sometimes also technological tools to ensure participation (Scherpenzeel, 2009). Financial and institutional *sustainability* is another key challenge. Establishing and maintaining an OPP requires considerable investment in infrastructure, personnel, and data quality assurance. Ensuring long-term funding and operational continuity is essential for the reliability and usefulness of these panels.

Nevertheless, the opportunities associated with OPPs are significant. They enable the collection of high-frequency, high-quality data at relatively low costs compared to traditional techniques, promote data-driven research in social sciences and interdisciplinary collaboration, data integration, methodological innovations, and offer scalable infrastructures that can adapt to emerging research needs. In doing so, they can contribute not only to scientific advancement but also to social monitoring and evidence-based policy making.

The following paragraphs illustrate the choices made in building the first Italian OPP.

11.2 Architecture of the Italian Online Probability Panel

The Italian Online Probability Panel (IOPP) is designed in line with other European probability-based panels, following a methodologically structured architecture. The goal is not only to achieve initial representativeness but also to ensure long-term consistency, quality, and epistemological value of the collected data. Every aspect—ranging from recruitment to questionnaire modules—is oriented toward producing robust, methodologically sound, and socially valuable data. The combination of rigor and flexibility enables the panel to adapt to social changes while maintaining scientific solidity.

IOPP hybrid recruitment relies on a push-to-web strategy (CAWI self-completion)—individuals who do not complete the questionnaire online are subsequently recruited through a Computer-Assisted Personal Interviewing (CAPI)—departing from a two-stage sample extracted from the Italian National Register (see Sect. 11.3).

IOPP is characterized by a structure of five annual waves administered via CAWI (Computer-Assisted Web Interviewing) but also includes postal deliveries for self-administration via PAPI (Paper and Pencil Interviewing), to include individuals with limited digital skills or access (Couper, 2000; De Leeuw, 2005). In fact, Italy is still marked by a significant digital divide, linked to both geographic and sociodemographic factors (Plan International & University Bocconi, 2021; European Commission, 2024; Italian Government, 2021). The surveys, spaced 2–3 months apart, are designed to continuously detect social changes (Haas et al., 2021; Blom et al., 2020), and are scheduled to avoid high-mobility periods (e.g., summer or Christmas holidays) to maximize participation (Dillman et al., 2014;

Callegaro et al., 2015). To this end, various support tools are also implemented, such as a help desk, follow-up reminders, and in-app notifications alongside a web app, which facilitates user access and interaction.

During the first year of calibration, three consecutive waves will allow for testing the sample quality and optimizing instruments and procedures. These surveys will serve as benchmarks for correcting nonresponse bias through weighting and post-stratification (Groves et al., 2009), and for calibrating the design in preparation for the regular data collection phase scheduled for 2026.

At full implementation, the five IOPP waves will be structured so that the same parts of the Core Questionnaire are administered during the same periods each year distributed across the first three waves (70% of each wave). These waves will also include Additional Questionnaires (30% of the entire wave) proposed by the scientific community and evaluated by the IOPP Scientific Committee based on criteria such as coherence, methodological rigor, operational sustainability, and scientific and social relevance. The remaining two waves will be allocated to external researchers or institutions (100%), whose proposals will likewise be assessed through an open call process.

The panel design also includes a periodic sample refreshment to maintain longitudinal representativeness (Lynn, 2009), by integrating new cohorts (e.g., newly turned 18-year-olds) and compensating for panel attrition (participants voluntary or involuntary dropping out).

IOPP is therefore based on three main data collection instruments:

1. Recruitment questionnaire, administered via CAWI/CAPI using a push-to-web approach: it collects sociodemographic, behavioural, attitudinal information, and respondents' perceptions of the study. This information can also be used to define subsamples, to which different questionnaires may be administered, depending on specific research objectives and the evolving needs of social research over time (see Sect. 11.4).
2. Core Questionnaire (CQ), the backbone of longitudinal data collection, administered via CAWI and supported by postal PAPI: it covers key areas such as family, health, work, values, behaviours, etc., and is distributed over the first three waves of the year (70% of each wave), for approximately 120 min of survey time (see Sect. 11.5).
3. Additional Questionnaires (AQ), administered to the entire panel or selected subsamples, via CAWI (app or web) integrated by postal PAPI. They can be rotating modules (administered regularly) or non-rotating modules (one-time). These modules can become diachronic instruments if repeated over time.

The integration of CQ and AQ enables the joint analysis of different thematic areas, thus increasing the depth and interpretative potential of the research. The modular architecture of IOPP is designed to be flexible, collaborative, and aligned with Open Science principles, in accordance with leading European models.

11.3 Sampling Strategy

In line with the standards of probability-based social research, the sampling strategy designed for the IOPP ensures that the resulting dataset is statistically representative and able to support detailed analysis across national and subnational domains. The overarching aim is to create a reliable infrastructure capable of capturing the socio-demographic heterogeneity of the population resident in Italy aged 18–74 while maintaining feasibility in terms of implementation and long-term sustainability.

At the core of the IOPP sampling design lies a two-stage probabilistic approach, drawing directly from practices developed by the Italian National Statistical Institute (Istat). The primary sampling units are represented by the Italian municipalities, with respondents serving as the secondary sampling units. Both stages were constructed to preserve proportionality to the target population and to ensure stratification across key variables such as geographic area, demographic size of the municipalities, urban status (regional capitals vs. non-capitals), sex, and age groups.

The reference population was defined based on official Istat data as of January 1, 2023, encompassing all residents in Italy within the defined age range. To reflect the diversity of the population and to support estimates across various domains, the sample was stratified by region (including separate treatment of the autonomous provinces of Bolzano and Trento) and municipal typology, including metropolitan cores and peripheries, small municipalities (up to 10,000 inhabitants), medium-large municipalities (over 10,000 inhabitants) and regional/provincial capitals.

The net effective sample size was set at 10,000 completed interviews extracted from an initial list of approximately 30,000 individuals and distributed across 550 municipalities. This numerical target was determined through successive approximations, balancing the need for estimation accuracy with practical constraints related to cost and fieldwork management. The sampling strategy followed a compromise allocation model—neither fully proportional nor purely equal across strata—aimed at ensuring both national-level efficiency and sufficient statistical power in smaller territories.

In detail, in the first stage, a systematic random sampling method was used to select municipalities within each stratum. The design guarantees self-weighting within strata, meaning that all individuals within a given stratum share the same probability of selection. Over-sampling was applied particularly in regional capitals to counteract risks of under-representation and to ensure more accurate estimation in these strategic areas.

In the second stage, individuals were drawn randomly while preserving the proportional distribution of the population by sex and 5-year age classes. The selection process at the individual level involved a stratified sampling plan combining gender with age brackets (18–29, 30–39, 40–49, 50–59, and 60–74), resulting in ten mutually exclusive groups. Within each sampled municipality, the allocation of interviews was proportional to the local demographic distribution to ensure internal coherence and national comparability.

Importantly, the design allows for post-stratification weighting, based on known population margins, to correct any residual disproportionality and to enhance the generalizability of findings (Groves et al., 2009). The interplay between rigorous statistical planning and context-sensitive adjustments renders IOPP not only a technically sound survey infrastructure but also one that is methodologically transparent and adaptable to expected and unexpected complexities.

11.4 Recruitment and Maintenance of the Panel

Within the Italian context, the IOPP stands out as the first structured OPP employing a mixed-mode approach (CAWI/postal), inspired by leading European initiatives such as LISS, GESIS, and ELIPSS. The project integrates both digital and traditional data collection techniques to overcome the digital divide and to maximize response rates and the timeliness of data collection (Dillman et al., 2014).

During the recruitment phase, it was essential to rely on contact lists extracted from the National Population Register, alongside the adoption of effective outreach and motivational strategies to encourage initial participation (Groves et al., 2009). Recruitment ensures sample representativeness through personalized invitations and a push-to-web strategy, initially involving the postal delivery of a letter containing a QR code, a detailed informational brochure, and a personal ID (PID) for accessing the web-based enrollment questionnaire.

The overall sample is released in three batches: an initial pilot batch of 4,000 cases—used as a test phase for procedures, tools, and platform usability—followed by two main batches of 13,000 cases each. This staggered release allows for progressive calibration and quality control before full-scale implementation.

In the recruitment phase, while the primary goal is to maximize participation via CAWI (Computer-Assisted Web Interviewing), non-respondents are systematically followed up through CAPI (Computer-Assisted Personal Interviewing), according to an adaptive sequential design (Dillman et al., 2014). Up to six contact attempts are made on different days and times. In case of success, interviewers conduct a brief recruitment interview, after which individuals may choose to join the panel and receive credentials to access future surveys via web or mobile app or decide to participate through postal contact.

Economic incentives are essential for fostering participation and long-term engagement (Singer & Ye, 2013). IOPP adopts a mixed incentive scheme: €15 unconditional upon registration and €10 conditional upon the completion of each wave (Göritz, 2006; Scherpenzeel & Toepoel, 2012). These are disbursed as gift vouchers at the end of the calendar year in compliance with Italian legal regulations.

As previously emphasized, panel attrition can jeopardize long-term representativeness, particularly among vulnerable or initially underrepresented groups (Lynn, 2009). Addressing attrition requires personalized communications, reminders, symbolic engagement strategies, and reactivation mechanisms, in addition to planned sample refreshment procedures.

Participation and its maintenance also entail a relationship built on trust and transparency. IOPP guarantees full compliance with GDPR principles, including anonymity, voluntary participation, and regular feedback on how data are used.

Finally, long-term sustainability should be supported not only through government and stakeholder engagement but also via open calls to the academic community. These calls can contribute financially by funding additional modules, while promoting collaborative and multidisciplinary use of the infrastructure.

11.5 Core Questionnaire

The core questionnaire serves as the central tool for collecting data that is comparable over time on key aspects of individual and social life—such as values, opinions, attitudes and behaviours. Designed to ensure longitudinal consistency, it also functions as the foundational layer upon which additional thematic modules can be added. While maintaining stability in content, it can be adapted in response to exceptional events, as demonstrated by adjustments made during the COVID-19 pandemic by various panels (Davern et al., 2021). Its structure reflects analytical needs typical of panel surveys, drawing on established models such as the European Social Survey (ESS) and the GESIS Panel (GESIS, 2025; ESS, 2025).

The development of IOPP's core questionnaire was guided by an empirical and comparative approach, informed by evidence from sociological, demographic, and psychological literature (e.g., Aassve et al., 2013; Ajzen, 2001). The working group analysed the content of major European social science panels—such as LISS (Netherlands), GESIS panel (Germany), UKHLS (UK), and ELIPSS (France)—to ensure broad coverage of key life domains and support international comparability.

Additionally, the questionnaire integrates selected items from European and national surveys, including GGS, SHARE, ESS, EVS, and national studies by Istat, chosen for thematic coherence and analytical utility, while avoiding redundancy in the possible integration between databases. Some questions were specifically developed for the Italian context, in order to capture local nuances and sociocultural specificities.

The outcome is a robust instrument, suitable for both longitudinal and cross-sectional analysis, designed to be flexible and adaptable to future thematic extensions.

The IOPP core questionnaire is structured into ten thematic modules, comprising around 300 items, grouped into three macro-areas: sociographic characteristics, attitudes, and behaviours. Topics include sociodemographics, health, economic conditions, family, education, social integration, media usage, religion, politics, and science and technology, distributed as shown in Table 11.1.

The questionnaire design carefully balanced depth of content with the burden on respondents, estimating an average of five items per minute for a total of approximately 60 min, to be distributed across multiple waves during the year. This

Table 11.1 Modules and corresponding number of questions in the IOPP core questionnaire

Module	N. of items
Sociodemographics	33
Health	18
Economic situation	24
Family and household	65
Education and training	14
Social integration and neighborhood	28
Media usage and leisure	30
Religion	6
Personal attitudes and politics	63
Science and technology	19
Total	300

balance aimed to mitigate fatigue and ensure high data quality, in line with findings from online survey research (Gummer & Daikeler, 2018; Revilla & Höhne, 2020).

To monitor social change, the questionnaire includes both time-invariant variables (e.g., structural characteristics that remain stable) and time-varying measures (e.g., opinions or behaviours subject to change). These are administered at different intervals depending on expected variability—annually, biennially, or on a one-time or conditional basis (Callegaro et al., 2014). It is also possible through IOPP app to update structural variables most subject to change (e.g., employment).

The entire process addressed several challenges, such as managing sensitive items, adapting questions to the Italian context, ensuring correct translation of the items, and balancing international comparability with local relevance.

11.6 Archiving and Dissemination

Within social science research, archiving and dissemination have often been relegated to the end of the project lifecycle, perceived more as formalities than as integral components of the research process. However, a contemporary and more comprehensive perspective treats data stewardship as an ongoing, cyclical activity beginning at the planning stage and continuing through collection, processing, documentation, secure storage, open sharing, and eventual reuse (Ball, 2012). In this brief paragraph, we present part of what Scisci et al. (forthcoming, 2026) clarify and explore in greater depth in the chapter on archiving and dissemination dedicated specifically to IOPP.

A cornerstone of modern data management is the application of FAIR principles—ensuring data is easy to locate, accessible for legitimate use, interoperable with other systems, and reusable in new research contexts (Wilkinson et al., 2016). Rather than being linear, the data lifecycle is inherently dynamic. IOPP data management fits into this protocol where datasets are often revisited for validation or new analysis; they are constantly updated and refined, necessitating continuous documentation and oversight (CESSDA, 2022).

Key to this lifecycle are dedicated data repositories and archival institutions. Organisations like CESSDA (https://www.cessda.eu) and its Italian partner DASSI (https://www.dassi-archive.it) not only provide safe storage but also enable long-term accessibility and reusability of data. These infrastructures help establish best practices, such as the adoption of standardized metadata formats like DDI (https://ddialliance.org), which allow both humans and machines to interpret datasets efficiently (Marker & Fink, 2018). IOPP complies with such archival practices as such repositories do more than safeguard data; they also support data producers with methodological guidance, metadata support, and resources for ethical sharing, which is crucial, on the one hand, for IOPP's compliance with FAIR principles, and it also encourages a culture of openness and responsibility in data handling (Gaspani et al., 2019).

However, longitudinal research, where data is gathered over time, introduces additional layers of complexity. IOPP's curation efforts will ensure consistency across survey waves, the meaningful tracking of missing data, and logical inconsistencies in responses. We are also aware that documentation must evolve with the study. As survey instruments, sampling methods, or variable definitions change, so must the metadata. Semantic web technologies and controlled vocabularies now play an increasing role in ensuring that datasets remain discoverable and intelligible across platforms and over time (Van den Eynden et al., 2011).

To facilitate comparisons across time periods or countries, harmonization is also essential. International classifications such as ISCO Standard Classification of Occupations—and ISCED—International Standard Classification of Education—provide a shared framework for aligning diverse data. Successful examples include the European Social Survey (Kolsrud & Skjak, 2005) and the Cross-National Equivalent File (Frick et al., 2007), which rely on transparent and consistent harmonization processes to maintain cross-country comparability. IOPP complies with such policies for harmonization and also data preservation, adopting open formats, checking file integrity regularly, and planning long-term access. The OAIS model (Consultative Committee for Space Data Systems, 2024), long used in digital archiving, provides a robust framework for structuring this preservation work across stages—from initial submission to archival maintenance and eventual public dissemination.

Equally important is how data is disseminated and reused. Modern platforms like Dataverse (King, 2007) use persistent identifiers and detailed version tracking to maintain transparency and citation accuracy. We are aware that licensing terms must strike a balance between openness and protection, especially when sensitive data is involved (Chapoy et al., 2020). In such cases, access can be restricted while maintaining catalog visibility, allowing responsible discovery and planning for reuse.

Many archives are now investing in more accessible front-end interfaces. These allow users to visualize, filter, and conduct basic analyses without needing specialized software. Examples include Germany's SOEP (Socio-Economic Panel), the

UK's Understanding Society, and the European Social Survey. These systems aim to serve a broader audience, including educators, students, and policy stakeholders (Dekker, 2020). Building upon the principles of open data, IOPP aims to extend accessibility beyond professional researchers by enabling non-expert users to explore datasets interactively. The initiative may incorporate tools directly within the data repository platform, allowing users to examine variable distributions and perform basic statistical analyses.

Effective data governance in social science is not just about regulatory compliance or technical safeguards. It is an enabler of rigorous, transparent, and open science. Incorporating reusable documentation, modular structures, and reproducible workflows ensures that data does not simply serve its initial purpose but contributes meaningfully to broader knowledge systems. The evolving integration of software practices into data management points to a future where data curation is not merely supporting work but a defining element of scientific rigor and public accountability (Accordino et al., 2025).

Disclaimer The opinions expressed in this article by Nicolò Marchesini are his own and do not reflect the view of ISTAT.

References

Aassve, A., Sironi, M., & Bassi, V. (2013). Explaining attitudes towards demographic behaviour. *European Sociological Review, 29*(2), 316–333. https://doi.org/10.1093/esr/jcr069

Accordino, F., Pecoraro, F., & Luzi, D. (2025). CESSDA data catalogue: An opportunity to enhance data in social sciences. *International Journal on Digital Libraries, 26*(1), 8. https://doi.org/10.1007/s00799-025-00416-w

Ajzen, I. (2001). Nature and operation of attitudes. *Annual Review of Psychology, 52*, 27–58. https://doi.org/10.1146/annurev.psych.52.1.27

Ball, A. (2012). *Review of data management lifecycle models*. University of Bath.

Biolcati-Rinaldi, F., & Vezzoni, C. (2012). *L'analisi secondaria nella ricerca sociale*. Il Mulino.

Blom, A. G., Bosnjak, M., Cornilleau, A., Cousteaux, A. S., Das, M., Douhou, S., & Krieger, U. (2016). A comparison of four probability-based online and mixed-mode panels in Europe. *Social Science Computer Review, 34*(1), 8–25. https://doi.org/10.1177/0894439315574825

Blom, A. G., Cornesse, C., Friedel, S., Krieger, U., Fikel, M., Rettig, T., et al. (2020). High frequency and high quality survey data collection: The Mannheim Corona study. *Survey Research Methods, 14*(2), 171–178. https://doi.org/10.18148/srm/2020.v14i2.7735

Callegaro, M., Baker, R. P., Bethlehem, J., Göritz, A. S., Krosnick, J. A., & Lavrakas, P. J. (Eds.). (2014). *Online panel research: A data quality perspective*. Wiley.

Callegaro, M., Manfreda, K., & Vehovar, V. (2015). *Web survey methodology*. Sage.

CESSDA Training Team. (2022). *CESSDA Data Management Expert Guide*. CESSDA ERIC. https://dmeg.cessda.eu/

Chapoy, E., Lesnard, L., Gaultier-Voituriez, O., Groshens, E., Pedroja, C., & Beldiman-Moore, A. (2020). *Sciences Po. Une histoire de données* (p. 91) [Research Report]. Sciences Po. https://sciencespo.hal.science/hal-03612928

Consultative Committee for Space Data Systems. (2024). *Reference model for an Open Archival Information System (OAIS)* (Recommended Practice No. CCSDS 650. 0-M-3; Magenta Book). NASA. https://ccsds.org/Pubs/650x0m3.pdf

Cornesse, C., & Blom, A. G. (2023). Response quality in nonprobability and probability-based online panels. *Sociological Methods & Research, 52*(2), 879–908. https://doi.org/10.1177/0049124120914940

Couper, M. P. (2000). Web surveys: A review of issues and approaches. *The Public Opinion Quarterly, 64*(4), 464–494. https://doi.org/10.1086/318641

Das, M. (2025). *Building on the LISS experience: Future challenges and opportunities for online probability-based panels*. Conference "European Online Probability Panels (EOPPs): Opportunities for the social research", Milan, May 5–6.

Davern, M., Bautista, R., Freese, J., Morgan, S. L., & Smith, T. W. (2021). *General Social Survey 1972-2021*. NORC at the University of Chicago.

De Leeuw, E. (2005). To mix or not to mix data collection modes. *Surveys. Journal of Official Statistics, 21*(2), 233–255.

Dekker, R. (2020). Social data: CESSDA best practices. *Data Intelligence, 2*(1–2), 220–229. https://doi.org/10.1162/dint_a_00044

Dillman, D. A., Smyth, J. D., & Christian, L. M. (2014). *Internet, phone, mail, and mixed mode surveys: The tailored design method* (4th ed.). Wiley.

European Commission. (2024). 2030 Digital Decade. Annex 1: Competitiveness And Sovereignty, People, Smart Greening, Policy Coherence And Synergies. *Publications Office of the European Union.*https://doi.org/10.2759/635

European Social Survey. (2025). *Source questionnaire development*. Retrieved May 5, 2025, from https://www.europeansocialsurvey.org/methodology/source-question-naire/source-questionnaire-development

Frick, J. R., Jenkins, S. P., Lillard, D. R., Lipps, O., & Wooden, M. (2007). The Cross-National Equivalent File (CNEF) and its member country household panel studies. *Journal of Contextual Economics – Schmollers Jahrbuch, 127*(4), 627–654. https://doi.org/10.3790/schm.127.4.627

Gaspani, F., Pisano, C., & Scisci, D. (2019). I dati oltre la ricerca: L'archiviazione nelle scienze sociali. *AIS, 14*, 71–88. https://doi.org/10.1485/AIS_2019/14_3443545

GESIS – Leibniz Institute for the Social Sciences. (2025). *Documentation GESIS Panel*. Retrieved May 5, 2025, from https://www.gesis.org/en/gesis-panel/documentation/documentation-gesis-panelpop

Göritz, A. S. (2006). Incentives in web studies: Methodological issues and a review. *International Journal of Internet Science, 1*(1), 58–70.

Governo Italiano. (2021). Piano Nazionale di Ripresa e Resilienza (Missione 1: Digitalizzazione, innovazione, competitività, cultura e turismo).

Groves, R. M., Fowler, F. J., Couper, M. P., Lepkowski, J. M., Singer, E., & Tourangeau, R. (2009). *Survey methodology* (2nd ed.). Wiley.

Gummer, T., & Daikeler, J. (2018). A note on how prior survey experience with self-administered panel surveys affects attrition in different modes. *Social Science Computer Review, 38*(4), 490–498. https://doi.org/10.1177/0894439318816986

Haas, G. C., Müller, B., Osiander, C., Schmidtke, J., Trahms, A., Volkert, M., & Zins, S. (2021). Development of a new COVID-19 panel survey: The IAB high-frequency online personal panel (HOPP). *Journal for Labour Market Research, 55*(1), 16. https://doi.org/10.1186/s12651-021-00295-z

King, G. (2007). An introduction to the dataverse network as an infrastructure for data sharing. *Sociological Methods & Research, 36*(2), 173–199. https://doi.org/10.1177/0049124107306660

Kolsrud, K., & Skjak, K. K. (2005). Harmonising background variables in the European Social Survey. In J. H. P. Hoffmeyer-Zlotnik & J. Harkness (Eds.), *Methodological aspects in crossnational research* (Vol. 11, pp. 163–182).

Lynn, P. (2009). *Methodology of longitudinal surveys*. Wiley.

Marker, H. J., & Fink, A. S. (2018). CESSDA – A history of research data management for social science data. In J. B. Thestrup & F. Kruse (Eds.), *Research data management—A European perspective* (pp. 25–42).

Maslovskaya, O., & Lugtig, P. (2022). Representativeness in six waves of cross-national online survey (CRONOS) panel. *Journal of the Royal Statistical Society Series A: Statistics in Society, 185*(3), 851–871. https://doi.org/10.1111/rssa.12801

Menard, S. (2002). *Longitudinal research. Quantitative applications in the social sciences*. Sage.

Plan International & Università Bocconi. (2021). *Sfide attuali e future per la Parità di Genere in Italia: Il divario digitale di genere*. Università Bocconi.

Revilla, M., & Höhne, J. K. (2020). How long do respondents think online surveys should be? New evidence from two online panels in Germany. *International Journal of Market Research, 62*(5), 538–545. https://doi.org/10.1177/1470785320943049

Scherpenzeel, A. (2009). *Start of the LISS panel: Sample and recruitment of a probability-based Internet panel*. CentERdata. https://www.lissdata.nl/app/uploads/sites/4/2023/10/1.-Sample_and_Recruitment.pdf

Scherpenzeel, A. (2011). Data collection in a probability-based internet panel: How the LISS panel was built and how it can be used. *Bulletin de Méthodologie Sociologique, 109*, 56–61. https://doi.org/10.1177/0759106310387713

Scherpenzeel, A., & Toepoel, V. (2012). Recruiting a probability sample for an online panel: Effects of contact mode, incentives, and information. *Public Opinion Quarterly, 76*(3), 470–490. https://doi.org/10.1093/poq/nfs037

Scisci, D., De Santis, G., & Piacentini F. (2026, forthcoming). Archiviazione e disseminazione. In *Italian Online Probability Panel*. FrancoAngeli.

Singer, E., & Ye, C. (2013). The use and effects of incentives in surveys. *The ANNALS of the American Academy of Political and Social Science, 645*(1), 112–141.

Van den Eynden, V., Corti, L., Woollard, M., Bishop, L., & Horton, L. (2011). *Managing and sharing data*. UK Data Archive.

Wilkinson, M., Dumontier, M., Aalbersberg, I., et al. (2016). The FAIR Guiding Principles for scientific data management and stewardship. *Scientific Data, 3*, 160018. https://doi.org/10.1038/sdata.2016.18

Yeager, D. S., Krosnick, J. A., Chang, L. C., Javitz, H. S., Levendusky, M. S., Simpser, A., & Wang, R. (2011). Comparing the accuracy of RDD telephone surveys and internet surveys conducted with probability and non-probability samples. *Public Opinion Quarterly, 75*(4), 709–747. https://doi.org/10.1093/poq/nfr020

Chapter 12
Synthetic Populations in Research Infrastructures

Rocco Paolillo, Nicholas Roxburgh, Alice Sbrana, Gary Polhill, Evelina Carmen Sabatella, and Mario Paolucci

12.1 Collective Phenomena and Social Complexity

Many issues of interest to social and economic policies are complex phenomena, not derivable from the individuality of citizens. Phenomena such as opinion polarization or spatial segregation need a theoretical framework that embraces their complexity as an aggregated outcome of the collective dynamics of social actors and institutions interacting within contextualized spaces (Hedström & Bearman, 2009; Cioffi-Revilla, 2014). Following what is known as the metaphor of the society as a *common boat* by James S. Coleman (1994) (see Fig. 12.1), the methodological challenge to understand such phenomena is to address the transformative mechanisms that link the micro-level of individual actors, driven by their representations and motives, to the macro-level of the emerged observable phenomenon (Hedström & Ylikoski, 2011). Agent-based modeling is a methodology to this aim, building artificial societies in simulation scenarios used to study the emergence of collective phenomena in a dynamic and reproducible manner (Railsback & Grimm, 2019). The transformative mechanisms mentioned above are addressed through the interactive processes of virtual agents representing social actors and institutions, provided with dynamic and stable attributes to mimic their empirical counterparts (Macy & Willer, 2002; Grimm et al., 2006, 2010, 2020). Researchers can experiment how

R. Paolillo (✉) · M. Paolucci
Institute for Research on Population and Social Policies (CNR-IRPPS), Rome, Italy
e-mail: rocco.paolillo@cnr.it; mario.paolucci@cnr.it

N. Roxburgh · G. Polhill
The James Hutton Institute, Aberdeen, Scotland, UK
e-mail: nick.roxburgh@hutton.ac.uk; gary.polhill@hutton.ac.uk

A. Sbrana · E. C. Sabatella
Institute for Research on Population and Social Policies (CNR-IRPPS), Fisciano, SA, Italy
e-mail: alice.sbrana@cnr.it; evelinacarmen.sabatella@cnr.it

L. Taddei, M. Paolucci (eds.), *Longitudinal Data Infrastructures in Europe*,
https://doi.org/10.1007/978-3-032-07005-0_12

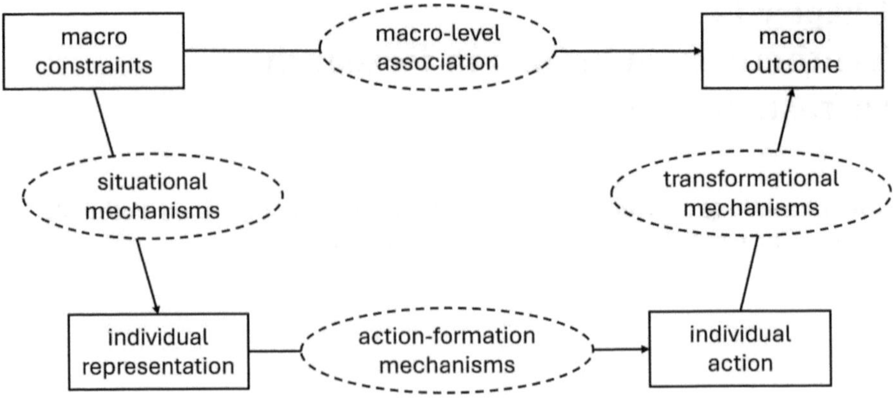

Fig. 12.1 Coleman's boat, additions by Hedström and Ylikoski (2010), adapted

the interaction between agents can lead to collective phenomena by manipulating the execution of plans, behavioral rules, desires and beliefs imbued into the virtual agents, based on the theoretical assumptions to test in *what-if* scenarios (Manzo, 2021; Epstein & Axtell, 1996; Gilbert & Troitzsch, 2005).

12.2 Agent-Based Modeling for Public Policy

Agent-based modeling has had a wide application in supporting policymakers in the management of complex issues, spanning from urban planning to natural hazards, leveraging the flexibility to apply modeling of social dynamics to a variety of topics. An example is the HUMAT model (Jager et al., 2025), an integrated model focusing on individual motivations, cognitions and exchanges within social networks used for the different cases of political referendum, social dialogue and vaccination rates. The method can support policymakers both in the ex-ante and post-ante implementation of a policy (Gilbert et al., 2018). In the ex-ante policy design, the main contribution of simulations is to show what unexpected consequences a policy might have, and how they could propagate to domains other than the policy itself (Gilbert et al., 2018; Lippe et al., 2019). The post-ante evaluation focuses on the comparison between the conditions where a policy is implemented or not in the same scenario (Gilbert et al., 2018). The comparison can occur also when the policy has been already implemented in an empirical context. In that case, counterfactual scenarios can be modeled, starting from the known outcomes of the policy, testing how different results could be achieved by modifying features of the policy (Furtado, 2023). Another contribution of agent-based modeling to policymaking is to facilitate the dialogue between stakeholders and researchers (Voinov & Bousquet, 2010). Through interactive GUIs, visualizations and co-participation in modeling design, stakeholders can grasp an intuitive understanding of system dynamics and representation of the reality to co-design policy interventions with researchers (Le Page et al., 2014).

In sum, agent-based modeling and social simulation can support both ex-ante and post-ante evaluation of policy design facilitating a co-participatory framework. However, this application of the method should take into consideration how the emerging patterns of the policy implementation, and therefore also conclusions from evaluation of policies, are bounded to the initial conditions policy dynamics are embedded in. Taking the example of health interventions, ignoring how a disease is differently distributed across geographical areas or social strata within one city or region might translate into an evaluation of the policy insensitive to the targeted society the policy aims at. The contribution of research infrastructures to agent-based modeling as a tool for policy making is to provide data for the initialization of models to be representative of the target society they want to mirror, so to provide reliable conclusions. A challenge to this aim might be the lack of micro-data either because distributed across different data sources, stored with different scales, or protected by privacy issues. Synthetic populations are a set of techniques and tools to face these challenges, so to guarantee artificial societies able to reproduce the socio-demographics and constraints of the target populations they represent.

12.3 Synthetic Populations: Algorithms and Strategies

While a synthetic population is implicitly an artificial population, an artificial population is not necessarily a synthetic population. In broader terms, an artificial population is the representation of a *stylized* (social) system, leaning towards formal models that leverage the independence from empirical constraints over the possible range of variables and features of agents modeled by the researcher. This allows the exploration and manipulation of the whole space of the theoretical model studied, to whom artificial societies are both the tool and the object of investigation, serving a deeper foundational understanding of sociological phenomena. On the other side, synthetic populations are artificial populations initialized so to reproduce individual citizens or institutions that mimic a target empirical society through techniques and tools to manipulate seed data. The initialization to the empirical constraints of a society allows to better understand what are the conditions that narrow to specific outcomes when a set of behavioral rules is applied to *that* society. This better serves an applied policy-oriented usage of the method. A main challenge of agent-based modeling to this aim is to reproduce joint and complex attributes of the individuals of the population in front of lacking or incomplete micro-data. Bigi et al. (2024) identify two steps to the process: the *synthesis* as integration of data sources to identify joint distributions, and the *generation* of the actual synthetic population. The number and typologies of algorithms for synthetic populations are many, with common underlying logic or own peculiarities. A common trait is an iterative process comparing synthetic distributions to empirical data constraints, setting a benchmark to their difference for validation. Chapuis et al. (2022) identify two main classes based on the scope of algorithms. *Synthetic reconstruction* is used when micro-data of joint distributions are not known, so that the generation of synthetic populations implies the synthesis of separate variables or data sources from the same population. *Combinatorial optimization* is used to scale up or down synthetic populations, optimizing the match between synthetic populations extracted from seed data to the constraints of the target population. The boundaries between the two classes are not set in stone and some algorithms might lay at their intersection. The archetypal algorithm for synthetic reconstruction algorithms, and in general for synthetic data, is the Iterative Proportional Fitting (IPF). The aim of the algorithm is to adjust the cell values of a matrix where columns and rows represent the marginal distributions of aggregated empirical variables, so that each cell represents a category intersection. In the fitting procedure, each cell is calibrated by a weight equivalent to the ratio of the empirical marginal of the variable over its estimated value at each step. The Multiple Iterative Proportional Fitting (MIPF) extends the IPF to multiple dimensions, first estimating the synthetic population for two variables and calibrating each resulting cell to the weights of other marginal variables. Other two extensions of IPF to include multidimensionality are the Hierarchical Iterative Proportional Fitting (HIPF) and the Iterative Proportional Update (IPU), though with different nuances and initializations. HIPF uses marginal distributions as input data and it is mainly used for multi-layered nested data, fitting firstly marginals for one layer (e.g. household attributes), and subsequently for lower nested level (e.g. individuals' attribute per household type) (Yameogo et al., 2021). The IPU instead moves from micro-data to synthesize multiple dimensions and layered data. Each input of the algorithm is an individual associated with one supra-layer, e.g. dwelling, and characteristics of both. Once weights are computed, they are compared with the distribution over different layers (e.g. individuals across dwellings) so to adjust backwards. The output of IPU are weights for each category intersection of individuals and distribution across supra-layers with their own features.

While algorithms within the IPF framework are mathematically transparent and robust, they require ad hoc adjustments when dealing with complex data and multidimensionality. Furthermore, they risk to be nullified in the computation when a category level is absent in the units of observations, what is called the zero-cell problem (Choupani & Mamdoohi, 2016). Combinatorial optimization generally fills this gap. Two main procedures in this framework are simulated annealing (SA) and Markov Chain Monte Carlo (MCMC) (Harland et al., 2012; Bigi et al., 2024), both generating randomly an estimate of the synthetic population, including multi-layers and multiple intersections simultaneously, to then *optimize* results backward comparing to empirical target constraints. SA estimates synthetic populations from micro-data, and proposes the one solution that best fits empirical data. MCMC instead computes synthetic populations from marginal data, providing a collection of samples that can be estimated from observed data. MCMC has the advantage to produce output for multiple variables and complex relations computationally efficiently, but at cost of heavy computational power (Bigi et al., 2024).

Machine Learning techniques are a third class of algorithms and the most recent in time. They aim at identifying complex pattern relations in high dimensional data with low computational power. One main technique used are the Generative Adversarial Networks (GANs), where a training set of micro data is used to identify data relations to reproduce (Ramzan et al., 2024). The training session occurs through two *competing* networks: a generator and a discriminator. The generator aims at producing synthetic data distributions that it considers realistic, by adjusting initial random distributions to real data used for training. The discriminator then assesses both real data and data from the generator, with the task to discriminate which one is real and which is not. The learning process occurs through reinforcing the output of the two competitors considered successful: for the discriminator to distinguish correctly real data from fake data, for the generator to lead the discriminator to fail, meaning that the generator has been able to reproduce data highly similar to real data. A limit of GANs for synthetic populations is that they will reproduce more robustly distributions based on their frequency in the training dataset, so to ignore, or reproduce more inaccurately sociodemographic groups that are underrepresented in the training dataset. Falck (2025) addresses specifically this issue for agent-based modeling, using Wasserstein Generative Adversarial Network (WGAN), balancing the original sample used for training so as to match empirical constraints. Alternative strategies are fitting to known marginals in the population with other techniques (WGAN-impute), or applying official statistical weights to categories numerically underrepresented (weight-imputed).

12.4 Synthetic Populations in the Era of Research Infrastructures

Research infrastructures can be a fundamental support to initialize agent-based models with synthetic data for policymaking. They first reply to the need of data to integrate and harmonize (Avazpour et al., 2016), fulfilling the 4V in Big Data: *volume* of data amount, *velocity* in collection and delivery, *variety* of their topic and *veracity* of information through data curation and maintaining. However, in the era of Open Science, the contribution of research infrastructures for agent-based modeling goes beyond the mere abundance of data for synthetic populations. Some European research infrastructures for the social sciences provide datasets of synthetic populations already extracted via national projects,[1] available for public use. Algorithms for extraction of synthetic populations are common to different suites envisaged in research infrastructures platforms, such as AI4EOSC[2] in the European Open Science Cloud (EOSC). Within the Next-Generation project FOSTERING

[1] A keywords search by the authors for the queries ("synthetic" AND "data") and ("synthetic population*") on CESSDA resulting in 58 studies in the social sciences in June 2025.

[2] https://ai4eosc.eu/.

Open Science in Social Science Research (FOSSR)[3] to establish an Italian Open Science Cloud for the social sciences, a synthetic populations generator is in construction, enabling users to autonomously extract synthetic data on the target population from data selected. As an additional service for agent-based modeling, research infrastructures can provide services such as access to High Performance Computing (HPC) for the parallel execution of experiments with complex numerical analysis on large artificial populations in short time (Polhill et al., 2023).

The main advantage of research infrastructures in relation to data is the adherence to the FAIR principles (Findable, Accessible, Interoperable and Reusable) (Wilkinson et al., 2016), which can facilitate the initialization of agent-based models and handling of data for synthetic populations extraction. In particular, semantic ontologies, as a formal and explicit representation of knowledge about a domain (Gruber, 1993) raise the interoperability of data, representing entities of a system and relations between them in the form of triples *subject-property-object* (Liu & Özsu, 2009). Ontologies have found some applications in the field of agent-based modeling for facilitating the conceptual description of the relations between agents and components of the simulated system (Gotts et al., 2019; Livet et al., 2010). Another application has been for the exportation of data from simulation experiments (Salecker et al., 2019; Polhill, 2015). However, in the framework of Open Science and FAIR principles, the main contribution of ontologies is the interoperability of data and their readability by diverse machines. This facilitates fetching original data from independent data servers to one infrastructure endpoint where they can be integrated and harmonized (Avazpour et al., 2019). Research infrastructures thus allow for a continuous integration, enriching synthetic populations with a continuous updating of real data. Recent advancements, also leveraging progress in *Information and Communication Technologies* (ICT), have extended these concepts, as the case of the Semantic Web (Berners-Lee et al., 2001), which stresses standardized practices and tools to share meaningful information attributed to data from the web to support the functioning of either, or both, physical or artificial complex systems. Two technologies associated are the Internet of Things (IoT) as a network of interconnected physical objects able to share information and data, and the Web of Things (WoT) as their web-based interoperability and distributed action. These instruments enable research infrastructures to host hybrid forms of distributed complex systems, such as digital twins as "a virtual representation of a process with parts of it in the real world" (Barachini & Stary, 2022, p. 9). Synthetic populations, and so also agent-based models, can thus not be limited to stored data to run over with algorithms described above, but also include updating information through distributed sensors, as in the case of smart cities.

In sum, research infrastructures in the era of Open Science offer opportunities to agent-based modeling as a tool for policymaking, from the abundance of data to describe the target society to the interoperability of data themselves, and computational power for large scale simulations. The rest of the chapter describes

[3] https://www.fossr.eu/.

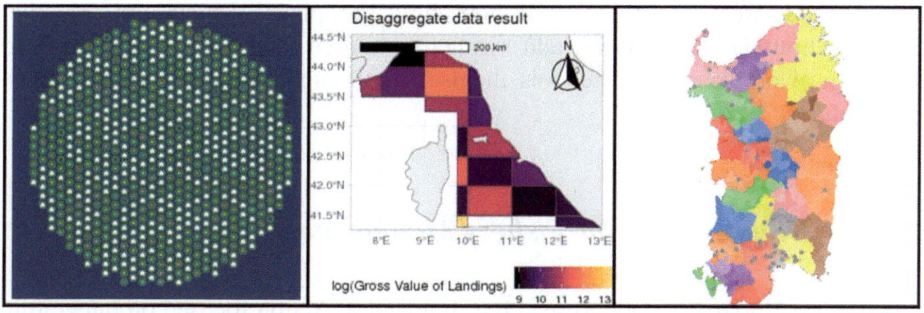

Fig. 12.2 Synthetic populations from the three cases presented. From left to right: Scotland's rural area, representing households and local service units (schools, businesses, etc.); SURIMI's disaggregated value for Gross Value Landing mapped to *ices* cells; REIS capability of charity organizations mapped to local social services areas (*PLUS*)

three case studies where agent-based models, synthetic populations and research infrastructures converge (see Fig. 12.2).

12.5 Applied Research: Case Studies

12.5.1 Scenarios of Rural Economy

As part of a project exploring the future of Scotland's rural economy,[4] two of the authors (NR and GP) are developing a scalable, sandbox-style agent-based model to simulate rural communities, capturing the complex interplay between people, housing, services, organisations, transport networks, and other critical infrastructures. A foundational framework has been established to represent a "virtual Scotland", beginning with the spatial initialisation of addresses using data from Ordnance Survey,[5] the national mapping agency of Great Britain. Using real micro-data of individuals would raise serious ethical concerns and consent issues. To populate this virtual landscape, the authors drew on a synthetic population developed by the SIPHER project,[6] a consortium whose products are accessible via the UK Data Service research infrastructure. The project delivers an artificial adult population generated at data zone level to reflect key characteristics of the real population. Synthetic data are generated using simulated annealing based on micro-data from UK Understanding Society and regional constraints (Wu et al., 2022).

[4] https://ruralfutures.hutton.ac.uk/, funded by Rural and Environment Science and Analytical Services (RESAS) Division as part of the Scottish Government's Strategic Research Portfolio (JHI-E1-1, JHI-E2-2, JHI-C4-1).

[5] https://www.ordnancesurvey.co.uk/.

[6] https://www.gla.ac.uk/research/az/sipher/.

While the dataset does not include household groupings, the authors construct plausible household structures, add synthetic children, and assign individuals to dwellings, workplaces, and schools themselves through heuristics and estimates from data.

12.5.2 Digital Twins for Fishery Management

SURIMI is a Horizon Europe Research & Innovation Action focused on integrating socio-ecological models into the European Digital Twin of the Ocean to enhance data interoperability and support sustainable ocean governance.[7] One of its key contributions lies in the coupling of simulation approaches with digital twin infrastructures to enhance interoperability of data and reproducibility of models to policy relevance. Within the SURIMI project, researchers are implementing and adapting an agent-based model called POSEIDON (Bailey et al., 2019) to simulate the behaviour of fishing agents under varying regulatory, ecological, and economic scenarios. The project will apply possible scenarios of policies including the behavior of vessels, strategy of fishermen and norms applied to the ecological empirical scenarios synthetically integrated. A training set in the SURIMI project focuses on fishing in the Northern Tyrrhenian Sea (GFCM GSA 09). Here, synthetic data are used to estimate the spatial distribution of fishing effort and reconstruct vessel tracks from fishing grids to landing ports. Some of the authors (AS, ES, RP) work on the reconstruction of individual vessels from aggregated data collected across multiple fisheries registers and datasets (e.g. logbooks, vessel monitoring systems) at different governance and spatial level. These reconstructions allow the team to explore and compare different behavioural rules and cognitive strategies for fishers in complex policy environments.

12.5.3 Regional Welfare Policies

One of the authors (RP) is involved in the REIS - V project in the Italian region of Sardinia, aimed at the monitoring and evaluation of the REIS welfare policy program, consisting of a set of social services spanning from economic support (e.g. food-purchasing) to social inclusion (e.g. training).[8] Agent-based modeling is used for the post-ante evaluation of the policy, in addition to participatory understanding

---

[7] https://www.surimi-project.eu/, funded by the European Commission (European Climate, Infrastructure and Environment Executive Agency) through the call for Research and Innovation Actions HORIZON-MISS-2023-OCEAN-01.

[8] https://www.irpps.cnr.it/reis-v/, funded by Autonomous Region of Sardinia, Department of Hygiene and Health and Social Welfare, General Directorate of Social Policies—Family and Social Inclusion Policy Service.

of the policy dynamics with stakeholders. To this aim, a spatial representation of the region has been implemented leveraging the integration of economic and socio-demographic data on the population from national registers in absence of micro-data harmonized at the municipality level. Synthetic reconstruction so provides a spatial distribution of the economic frailties of citizens grouped at different governance levels (e.g. municipalities) and civil organizations levels (e.g. Caritas association). In addition, the synthetic population includes the dislocation in space of charitable organizations collected via separate datasets. The policy evaluation measures how much the distribution of services covers the need of the synthetic population at the municipality level and what disparities occur across the region. The simulation also enables alternative what-if scenarios where the effect of different services allocations are compared, over the same synthetic population. The goal of synthetic data, and limits based on input data available, is also to demonstrate the need of harmonized data from municipalities for the construction of a research infrastructure observatory.

12.6 Conclusions

The synergy between agent-based modeling and research infrastructures can be beneficial to the application of simulation methods to policymaking. Synthetic populations are instrumental in this framework to initialize models representative of the target population. In this chapter, we illustrated some algorithms for synthetic populations extraction and the actual contribution of research infrastructures, from interoperability of data to digital twins for multidisciplinary interventions, as illustrated by the three case studies we report. Technological advances in research infrastructures and FAIR practices can support the initialization of ever richer empirical agent-based models to be used in applied research and policy design, enabling the complexity of societies in the whole to be better accounted for. However, the instruments provided by research infrastructures risk to be empty without a critical judgment by researchers and policymakers when using them. While synthetic data can provide a snapshot of reality, making up for missing information, it does not provide information on the *story* through which distribution of attributes in the population came to be. Considering the case of REIS - V project in Sardinia in the previous paragraph, this is particularly relevant since economic frailties of the population can reflect deeper vulnerabilities of the territory policymakers want to contribute to. Empirically *rich* models are valuable not as ends in themselves, but insofar as they can effectively answer *meaningful* and policy-relevant questions. The case of rural economy in Scotland is an example, needing to integrate local multi-layered demographics and networks to SIPHER available data zone synthetic population. Finally, the SURIMI case is an example of the sectoriality a research infrastructure might deal with, which requires understanding the nature of data and how they should be interpreted through an endured knowledge of the phenomenon and dynamics it describes. In front of massive investments in research infrastructures, these insights indicate that infrastructures should not only be used as a source of data, but as an environment to raise critical learning and practices of research, where agent-based models can serve as an instrument for managing the complexity of policy inquiry.

References

Avazpour, I., Grundy, J., & Zhu, L. (2016). V for variety: Lessons learned from complex smart cities data harmonization and integration. In *2016 IEEE International Conference on Pervasive Computing and Communication Workshops (PerCom Workshops)* (pp. 1–6).

Avazpour, I., Grundy, J., & Zhu, L. (2019). Engineering complex data integration, harmonization and visualization systems. *Journal of Industrial Information Integration*, *16*, 100103.

Bailey, R., Carrella, E., Axtell, R., Burgess, M., Cabral, R., Drexler, M., et al. (2019). A computational approach to managing coupled human–environmental systems: the Poseidon model of ocean fisheries. *Sustainability Science*, *14*(2), 259–275.

Barachini, F., & Stary, C. (2022). *From digital twins to digital selves and beyond: Engineering and social models for a trans-humanist world.* Springer Nature.

Berners-Lee, T., Hendler, J., & Lassila, O. (2001). The Semantic Web. *Scientific American*, *284*(5), 34–43.

Bigi, F., Rashidi, T. H., & Viti, F. (2024). Synthetic population: A reliable framework for analysis for agent-based modeling in mobility. *Transportation Research Record*, *2678*(11), 1–15.

Chapuis, K., Taillandier, P., & Drogoul, A. (2022). Generation of synthetic populations in social simulations: A review of methods and practices. *Journal of Artificial Societies and Social Simulation*, *25*(2), 6.

Choupani, A.-A., & Mamdoohi, A. R. (2016). Population synthesis using Iterative Proportional Fitting (IPF): A review and future research. *Transportation Research Procedia*, *17*, 223–233.

Cioffi-Revilla, C. (2014). *Introduction to computational social science.* Springer.

Coleman, J. S. (1994). *Foundations of social theory.* Harvard University Press.

Epstein, J. M., & Axtell, R. (1996). *Growing artificial societies: Social science from the bottom up.* Brookings Institution Press.

Falck, V. (2025). Generating spatial synthetic populations using Wasserstein generative adversarial network: A case study with EU-SILC data for Helsinki and Thessaloniki. Preprint. arXiv:2501.16080.

Furtado, B. A. (2023). Simulation modeling as a policy tool. In *The Routledge handbook of policy tools.* Taylor & Francis.

Gilbert, N., Ahrweiler, P., Barbrook-Johnson, P., Narasimhan, K. P., & Wilkinson, H. (2018). Computational modelling of public policy: Reflections on practice. *Journal of Artificial Societies and Social Simulation*, *21*(1), 14.

Gilbert, N., & Troitzsch, K. (2005). *Simulation for the social scientist.* McGraw-Hill Education (UK).

Gotts, N. M., van Voorn, G. A., Polhill, J. G., de Jong, E., Edmonds, B., Hofstede, G. J., et al. (2019). Agent-based modelling of socio-ecological systems: Models, projects and ontologies. *Ecological Complexity*, *40*, 100728.

Grimm, V., Berger, U., Bastiansen, F., Eliassen, S., Ginot, V., Giske, J., et al. (2006). A standard protocol for describing individual-based and agent-based models. *Ecological Modelling*, *198*(1–2), 115–126.

Grimm, V., Berger, U., DeAngelis, D. L., Polhill, J. G., Giske, J., & Railsback, S. F. (2010). The odd protocol: A review and first update. *Ecological Modelling*, *221*(23), 2760–2768.

Grimm, V., Railsback, S. F., Vincenot, C. E., Berger, U., Gallagher, C., DeAngelis, D. L., et al. (2020). The odd protocol for describing agent-based and other simulation models: A second update to improve clarity, replication, and structural realism. *Journal of Artificial Societies and Social Simulation*, *23*(2), 7.

Gruber, T. R. (1993). A translation approach to portable ontology specifications. *Knowledge Acquisition*, *5*(2), 199–220.

Harland, K., Heppenstall, A., Smith, D., & Birkin, M. H. (2012). Creating realistic synthetic populations at varying spatial scales: A comparative critique of population synthesis techniques. *Journal of Artificial Societies and Social Simulation*, *15*(1), 1.

Hedström, P., & Bearman, P. (2009). *The Oxford handbook of analytical sociology*. Oxford University Press.

Hedström, P., & Ylikoski, P. (2010). Causal mechanisms in the social sciences. *Annual Review of Sociology*, *36*(1), 49–67.

Hedström, P., & Ylikoski, P. (2011). Analytical Sociology. In *SAGE handbook of philosophy of social science* (pp. 386–398). SAGE.

Jager, W., Antosz, P., Li, T., Polhill, G., Szczepanska, T., & Wang, S. (2025). HUMAT: An integrated framework for modelling individual motivations, social exchange and network dynamics. *Journal of Artificial Societies and Social Simulation*, *28*(1), 4.

Le Page, C., Abrami, G., Barreteau, O., Becu, N., Bommel, P., Botta, A., et al. (2014). Models for sharing representations. In M. Étienne (Ed.), *Companion modelling: A participatory approach to support sustainable development* (pp. 69–101). Springer Netherlands.

Lippe, M., Bithell, M., Gotts, N., Natalini, D., Barbrook-Johnson, P., Giupponi, C., et al. (2019). Using agent-based modelling to simulate social-ecological systems across scales. *GeoInformatica*, *23*(2), 269–298.

Liu, L., & Özsu, M. T. (2009). *Encyclopedia of database systems* (Vol. 6). Springer New York.

Livet, P., Müller, J. P., Phan, D., Sanders, L., & Auatabu, T. (2010). Ontology, a mediator for agent-based modeling in social science. *Journal of Artificial Societies and Social Simulation*, *13*(1), 3.

Macy, M. W., & Willer, R. (2002). From factors to actors: Computational sociology and agent-based modeling. *Annual Review of Sociology*, *28*(1), 143–166.

Manzo, G. (2021). *Research handbook on analytical sociology*. Edward Elgar Publishing.

Polhill, J. G. (2015). Extracting owl ontologies from agent-based models: A NetLogo extension. *Journal of Artificial Societies and Social Simulation*, *18*(2), 15.

Polhill, J. G., Heppenstall, A., Batty, M., Salt, D., Colasanti, R., Milton, R., et al. (2023). Exascale computing and 'next generation' agent-based modelling. *Review of Artificial Societies and Social Simulation*. 9 Mar 2023. https://rofasss.org/2023/09/29/exascale-computing-and-next-gen-ABM

Railsback, S. F., & Grimm, V. (2019). *Agent-based and individual-based modeling: A practical introduction*. Princeton University Press.

Ramzan, F., Sartori, C., Consoli, S., & Reforgiato Recupero, D. (2024). Generative adversarial networks for synthetic data generation in finance: Evaluating statistical similarities and quality assessment. *AI*, *5*(2), 667–685.

Salecker, J., Sciaini, M., Meyer, K. M., & Wiegand, K. (2019). The NLRX R package: A next-generation framework for reproducible NetLogo model analyses. *Methods in Ecology and Evolution*, *10*(11), 1854–1863.

Voinov, A., & Bousquet, F. (2010). Modelling with stakeholders. *Environmental Modelling & Software*, *25*(11), 1268–1281.

Wilkinson, M. D., Dumontier, M., Aalbersberg, I. J., Appleton, G., Axton, M., Baak, A., et al. (2016). The fair guiding principles for scientific data management and stewardship. *Scientific Data*, *3*(1), 1–9.

Wu, G., Heppenstall, A., Meier, P., Purshouse, R., & Lomax, N. (2022). A synthetic population dataset for estimating small area health and socio-economic outcomes in Great Britain. *Scientific Data*, *9*(1), 19.

Yameogo, B. F., Vandanjon, P. O., Gastineau, P., & Hankach, P. (2021). Generating a two-layered synthetic population for French municipalities: Results and evaluation of four synthetic reconstruction methods. *Journal of Artificial Societies and Social Simulation*, *24*, 27.

Correction to: GGS: Generations and Gender Survey

Letizia Mencarini, Nicolò Cavalli, Elena Marseglia, Matilde Perotti, Ilaria Primerano, Michele Santurro, and Nicolò Marchesini

Correction to:
Chapter 10 in: L. Taddei, M. Paolucci (eds.), *Longitudinal Data Infrastructures in Europe*, https://doi.org/10.1007/978-3-032-07005-0_10

The last name of 'Letizia Mencarini' was unfortunately published with an error. The initially published version has now been corrected.

The updated version of this chapter can be found at
https://doi.org/10.1007/978-3-032-07005-0_10

L. Taddei, M. Paolucci (eds.), *Longitudinal Data Infrastructures in Europe*,
https://doi.org/10.1007/978-3-032-07005-0_13

Open Conclusions

Luciana Taddei and Mario Paolucci

Building longitudinal research infrastructures is not rocket science—but it is something perhaps more demanding: an act of collective foresight, political courage, and epistemic ambition. These infrastructures are not mere data pipelines; they are intricate ecosystems of governance, ethics, interoperability, and care. They are where legal frameworks meet societal expectations, and where scientific aspirations are negotiated through institutional coordination and long-term stewardship. If we take seriously the idea that infrastructures are the invisible architecture of collective intelligence, then the call is clear: we must build patiently, transparently, and with purpose. This is not just technical work—it is a political and democratic project.

Throughout this volume, we have seen what this means in practice. The SHARE ERIC infrastructure offers perhaps the most advanced model of a harmonized, pan-European panel on ageing and health, enabling comparative analyses across decades and borders, and providing data that are central to understanding demographic change and intergenerational dynamics. CESSDA, together with its Italian node DASSI, shows what happens when data archiving is treated not as an afterthought but as a public service: standardized, interoperable, and open to the scientific community. SHARE Survey builds on this legacy, pushing forward high-frequency and high-quality data collection to respond in real time to social and economic shocks. GUIDE introduces a bold and urgent proposal: a Europe-wide longitudinal study of children, designed to trace their life trajectories from birth through adolescence. It is an infrastructure of anticipation, imagining how digital environments, education systems, and family contexts shape futures not yet written. Similarly, the Generations and Gender Survey (GGS) provides a sophisticated lens on how individuals form families, navigate work and care, and pass on values and responsibilities—an infrastructure that speaks directly to population policy and social cohesion. The IOPP initiative focuses on modular, online probability panels, proposing infrastructures that are adaptable, sustainable, and methodologically robust. These platforms point to a future where responsiveness and scientific rigor can coexist. Finally, the work on synthetic populations explores a different

L. Taddei, M. Paolucci (eds.), *Longitudinal Data Infrastructures in Europe*,
https://doi.org/10.1007/978-3-032-07005-0

but complementary path: how we can simulate complex social realities without compromising individual privacy. By constructing realistic, data-driven models, synthetic populations can extend the reach of traditional panels and open new horizons for forecasting, simulation, and policy design.

These experiences, different in scope and scale, share a common thread: the belief that social knowledge must be cumulative, open, and collectively governed. They are grounded in the conviction that infrastructures are not just containers of data, but vectors of trust, continuity, and strategic capacity.

What we propose, then, is not simply to collect more data or refine methodologies. It is to enable a new relationship with the social: one that is sustained, open, inclusive, and reflexive. This is the challenge—and the promise—of longitudinal infrastructures in the social sciences. If we are to face planetary-scale transformations with dignity and precision, we must invest not only in what we know, but in how we choose to know together.

This is not a luxury. It is a foundational choice.

MIX
Papier aus verantwortungsvollen Quellen
Paper from responsible sources
FSC® C105338

If you have any concerns about our products,
you can contact us on
ProductSafety@springernature.com

In case Publisher is established outside the EU,
the EU authorized representative is:
Springer Nature Customer Service Center GmbH
Europaplatz 3, 69115 Heidelberg, Germany

Printed by Libri Plureos GmbH
in Hamburg, Germany